PRAISE FOR *THINK PRETTY*:

"*Think Pretty* is a beautifully crafted book packed with practical wisdom, uplifting stories, and life-changing insights. It's the kind of reading that inspires you long after the last page."

KIM L. SORENSEN, cofounder of Trove Brands, mother of six, and author of *EQ Explorers*

"In a very complex world, Callie has insightfully outlined key concepts to navigate life, guiding us to the opportunity to choose happiness. One of my favorite quotes from the book is: 'Happiness is not an external condition, but an internal choice.' *Think Pretty* is not just for women, but for anyone seeking a better life."

FRASER BULLOCK, Executive Chair and President, 2034 Olympic and Paralympic Winter Games

"*Think Pretty* is a gift to every woman who's ever questioned her value or compared herself to others. It's uplifting, empowering, and exactly what we need right now. Callie lives her message. Through her friendship, she's shown me the beauty of kindness, confidence, and staying true to who you are. There's no one more qualified to remind women of their inner beauty."

ROBIN TOWLE, Mrs. International 2019 and founder of Robin Towle Designs and the Wolf Pact

"Unlock your potential by mastering your mindset and listening to your heart. In *Think Pretty*, you'll discover valuable techniques like 'Spilling the TEA,' designed to help you shift from your head to your heart, fostering positivity and overcoming negative thinking with courage and love."

JOHNNY COVEY, author of *5 Habits to Lead from Your Heart*

"I am so proud of my sister Callie. The concepts and message of this book are both timely and essential for women of all ages. In a world where true self-care, self-love, and deep connection are often misunderstood or overlooked, this book provides the keys to lasting happiness. It's a guide to embracing kindness, confidence, and purpose—helping every woman leave a legacy and truly live like a Pretty Sister."

REBECCA HINTZE, PH.D.-C, author, *Healing Your Family History*

"*Think Pretty* is such a refreshing and empowering read! It's a beautiful reminder that confidence, joy, and true friendship all start from within. Callie's words inspire self-belief in a world that too often makes us doubt ourselves. This book is a must-read for any woman ready to embrace her worth and step into her best self!"

ALEXIS WARR, *So You Think You Can Dance* winner, pro dancer, and choreographer

"*Think Pretty* is such a beautiful reminder that real confidence comes from knowing who you are and choosing joy on purpose. Callie's stories are heartfelt and relatable, and her five empowering beliefs feel like a pep talk from your wisest, kindest friend. This book is a love letter to sisterhood and self-worth—and a reminder that we're all made to shine!"

VANESSA QUIGLEY, Chatbooker-in-Chief, Chatbooks, and host of the MomForce Podcast

"*Think Pretty* is a bloom-worthy guide that encourages women to shift their thought patterns, celebrate their uniqueness, and redefine beauty as substance, smarts, and inner confidence. With heartfelt stories and practical tools, this book is a heartwarming, uplifting reminder that true worth comes from within—and when we think pretty, we bloom into our best selves."

SHAUNA SMITH, CEO, *Savory*

THINK PRETTY

5 Beliefs to Cultivate Friendship, Confidence & Joy

CALLIE C. STEUER

FOREWORD BY SEAN COVEY

Steuer Management
ALPINE, UTAH

Copyright © 2025 by Callie C. Steuer

All rights reserved. No part of this publication may be reproduced, distributed, or transmitted in any form or by any means, including photocopying, recording, or other electronic or mechanical methods, without the prior written permission of the publisher, except in the case of brief quotations embodied in critical reviews and certain other noncommercial uses permitted by copyright law. For permission, contact the author via the website below.

Steuer Management / Callie C. Steuer
Alpine, Utah
Website: CallieSteuer.com
Email: info@calliesteuer.com

Cover design by Gus Yoo
Editing and book production by Stephanie Gunning

Think Pretty/Callie C. Steuer—1st edition

Library of Congress Control Number: 2025908276

ISBN 978-0-9993337-3-0 (paperback)
ISBN 978-0-9993337-4-7 (epub)

To my sisters, who nicknamed me Pretty and showed me how to live up to the name.

To my friends, who inspired me and lived "pretty" with me.

To my mom, who has always believed in me and loved me unconditionally.

To my beautiful daughters and the Pretty Sisters who surround me, lift me up, and remind me of the power of love and connection.

And to the remarkable women who came before me—my great-grandmother and namesake, Callie Catherine, and my grandmother, Francis—whose pretty lives and legacies continue to guide and inspire me.

This book is for all of you.

CONTENTS

Foreword by Sean Covey	ix
Introduction	xiii

BELIEF #1:
You Are Pretty

1. You Are Enough	3
2. You Are Unique	17
3. You Were Made for This	37
Pinky Promise #1	**55**

BELIEF #2:
You Are Not Alone

4. You Have Divine Guidance	63
5. She's Pretty, Too	73
6. Together We Rise	89
Pinky Promise #2	**105**

BELIEF #3:
You Can Do It

7. You Begin with a Dream	109
8. You Must Believe in Yourself	137
9. You Create Your Reality	157
Pinky Promise #3	**177**

BELIEF #4
You Are Meant for Joy

10. Life Is Happening *for* You, Not *to* You	181
11. You Might as Well Be Happy	199
12. It's Not the End Yet	211
Pinky Promise #4	**225**

BELIEF #5
Love Is the Answer

13. Always Love Your People	229
14. It's Okay to Love Your Things	245
15. Fall in Love with Your Life	259
Pinky Promise #5	**273**

P.S. I Love You	*275*
What's Next?	*277*
Acknowledgments	*279*
Notes	*281*
About the Author	*284*

FOREWORD
SEAN COVEY

AS SOMEONE WHO HAS SPENT MY CAREER TEACHING timeless principles of human effectiveness to youth and families across the world, and as the father to beautiful, strong daughters, I was honored when Callie Steuer asked me to write the foreword to her relevant, entertaining, and insightful book, *Think Pretty*. In today's fast-paced, popularity-centered world, it seems to be increasingly challenging for people to realize their true worth and potential, especially young women. It's why I've spent decades championing *The 7 Habits of Highly Effective Teens* and developing frameworks to help young people navigate life. It's also why I'm so passionate about the mission of Bridle Up Hope, a foundation my wife and I started to inspire hope, confidence, and resilience in girls and women through equestrian training and life skills development. (Go to BridleUpHope.org for more information).

When I first learned about the *Think Pretty* project, I immediately recognized that this is not just another feel-good book; it's a rallying cry for young women and women to reclaim the word *pretty* and anchor it in something far more lasting than outward appearance. In a culture flooded with unrealistic beauty standards, filtered photos, and comparison-driven platforms, *Think Pretty* redefines what it means to be beautiful. It teaches that being pretty isn't about how you look, but about how you think, how you connect, and how you show up for yourself and others. True beauty, as this book reveals, is found in your character and how you treat others.

There are two types of greatness in the world: primary greatness and secondary greatness. Secondary greatness is based on appearances, on outward achievements, on popularity and "likes." Primary greatness is based on your character: on who you are as a person, how you treat other people, and your integrity and honesty. This book illustrates how to devel-op primary greatness, first and foremost. Secondary greatness will often come to those who achieve primary greatness. But even if it doesn't, who cares? It doesn't really matter after all. What matters is what's within you.

Callie's voice is personal and rooted in lived experience. Drawing from her journey as a mother, mentor, and entrepreneur, she introduces us to five core beliefs that form the heart of the *Think Pretty* message, teaching us "You are pretty," "You are not alone," "You can do it," "You are meant for joy," and "Love is the answer." This is a powerful way to organize the book because beliefs are paradigms like pairs of glasses through which you see the world. Everything we see is filtered through the lenses of our belief systems, and we are usually unaware that we are even "wearing glasses."

Our paradigms drive our behavior, which in turn leads to the outcomes we get in life. Thus, the key to making big changes in our lives is first to change the way we see the world—to change our paradigms. If you want to make small changes in life, change your behavior. But if you want to make quantum changes, change the paradigms of your core beliefs.

You'll find the structure of this book is clear and the advice easy to implement. Through relatable stories and reflective exercises, readers are invited to "Spill the TEA"—a simple, memorable process that guides them through an examination of their thoughts, emotions, and actions (TEA). This process gives readers a way to explore their inner world with honesty and grace, and then course-correct when their thoughts don't serve them. It elevates their conversations into something healing and real. Friends can sit down together and spill the TEA—not gossiping or comparing, but connecting and lifting each other up.

This book offers a powerful road map for growth through Callie's "Dream–Believe–Create" methodology. I love this sequence because it taps into the essence of personal growth: having a clear vision, believing in yourself deeply, and taking action. With this mindset, any woman—

whether she's navigating hardships or rediscovering herself—can begin to live a life she loves.

Think Pretty also speaks to something we desperately need in today's world: sisterhood. Disconnection has become epidemic. In my work with Bridle Up Hope, I've seen firsthand how lonely and discouraged many girls feel. Too many girls are quietly battling low self-worth, anxiety, and depression. Social media isn't helping, as it creates a world where girls are living as if on a stage for everyone to see and compare. This book provides a remedy. It calls for us to be better friends to one another, to celebrate each other's wins, to offer encouragement instead of critique, and to believe in each other's potential even when we can't see it ourselves yet. It reminds us that there is strength in solidarity and that when one girl rises, we all rise.

More than a recurring phrase, *Pretty Sisters* is an invitation to join a new kind of community. It is a title extended with love, just like it was to Callie as a little girl. It says: "You have infinite worth and potential, not to be compared with anyone else. You are beautiful just as you are. And you have sisters—right here—who are ready to stand with you and cheer you on."

This book is a clear answer to the damaging "mean girl" culture so many young women have experienced. It offers a better way, one rooted in love and personal responsibility. Through healthy beliefs and practices, young women can cultivate genuine confidence, create safe and supportive relationships, and foster environments in which everyone can shine. When women stop competing and start encouraging each other, the atmosphere changes. Potential is unlocked and the world becomes a more beautiful place.

As you read through these pages, you'll feel like Callie is right there with you, cheering you on and gently nudging you forward. Her stories are real and practical, and she has a big heart. She affirms the truth that women can be wildly successful in whatever roles they choose to focus on. *Think Pretty* gives us permission to dream big, to believe we are enough, and to get to work creating lives we're proud of.

I believe the world is ready for this book and for a new definition of beauty based upon kindness, character, and high-trust relationships.

If you're holding this book, it's because someone believes in you. Now, it's your turn to believe in yourself. Read it. Spill the TEA. Practice the beliefs. Let yourself shine. And then go help another shine, too.

This is how we change the world.

Sean Covey
International best-selling author of *The 7 Habits of Highly Effective Teens,* founder of Bridle Up Hope: The Rachel Covey Foundation

INTRODUCTION

AFTER THREE GRUELING DAYS ON THE ROAD, OUR CAR wheezed to a halt at a service station in Ogallala, Nebraska. The heat was relentless, matching the tension inside our cramped vehicle. This unexpected pit stop was a cruel twist in my mom's carefully laid plan to start afresh in Utah, where extended family awaited with open arms. As a ten-year-old, I was caught in the whirlwind of emotions that came with leaving behind a fractured home to embark on a journey toward an uncertain future.

I was the youngest of five siblings, clinging to the hope that this move would bring my family the happiness and stability we desperately craved. But reality sometimes dampens even the brightest dreams. Two years of watching my parent's relationship unravel had taught me the harsh truth that some things cannot be fixed with prayers alone.

My brothers, Bobby and Rich, ages thirteen and fourteen, were a constant source of both protection and chaos. Their sibling rivalry often erupted into heated arguments. Yet, amid the turmoil, I found solace in their unwavering support. My sister Martha, on the cusp of adulthood at seventeen, had moved to Utah early to complete her junior year and hopefully ease her transition into high school. Her absence left a void, a reminder of the fragmented family we already were. And then there was my sister Becky, my eldest sibling, age nineteen, who had already moved to Utah the year before to attend Brigham Young University. Her absence during her freshman year in college was a bittersweet reminder of the passage of time and the distance that had grown between us.

As the mechanic delivered the news of a prolonged delay, my mom's facade of composure cracked. The strain of managing a tight budget and a car on the brink of collapse was etched on her face. But for me, the prospect of a few days in a motel felt like a reprieve, a chance to escape the suffocating confines of our car and the weight of the unknown pressing on me. It also gave a chance for Martha and Becky, who had flown back to help and were left to do the final pack-up of the house and drive a second car across country, the time to catch up to us and reunite in Ogallala for the final push to Utah. This reunion was made especially memorable because we celebrated Martha's seventeenth birthday in that little town.

When we finally hit the road again, now together, carpooling as a family, the cool breeze from the repaired air conditioning offered a fleeting sense of comfort. With Ogallala fading into the rearview mirror, optimism mingled with apprehension. Our journey was far from over, but for that moment, we were filled with a glimmer of hope that maybe, just maybe, a happy new beginning awaited us in Utah where we could all be together again.

Looking back, I admire my mother's unwavering courage as she packed up our little family and only home we knew in Vienna, Virginia, and embarked on a journey to forge a new path. Leaving behind a marriage of twenty years, her career, and her friends, she carried with her a deep faith and determination to create a better future for us. She didn't have all the answers, but she moved forward step by step, fueled by the love of her family and the hope for a brighter tomorrow. This resilience, this unwavering belief in the possibilities of a new beginning, became central to my foundational beliefs.

Now, forty years later, as a mother of five myself, I reflect on our journey with a mix of nostalgia and gratitude. The truth is, moving was never going to be easy, especially under the weight of financial strain and the challenges faced by a single mother. Growing up without a father brought its share of sadness and disappointment. Yet despite the hardships, many moments of joy and laughter ultimately would define my childhood.

My sisters played a pivotal role in shaping my perspective and resilience during my formative years. Martha, in her affectionate way, bestowed upon me the nickname Pretty, a term of endearment that carries far more meaning than I realized at the time. To her, the name Pretty wasn't just about appearance; it symbolized the love and kindness that bound us together as sisters. Naturally, I started calling her Pretty as well, and we soon became the Pretty Sisters.

Becky was a pillar of strength and support for me. Though she was away at college during our family's move, she remained connected to us as a Pretty Sister in spirit. When we finally arrived in Utah, where she was attending college, Becky's presence became more tangible, and her love and guidance were always present, reinforcing the bonds that held me, her, and Martha together as Pretty Sisters.

As the youngest child in the family, I initially felt a bit self-conscious about the nickname I'd been given. But over time, it became a badge of honor, a reminder of the love and support I received. Martha's intention was clear: to shield me from the harsh realities of our circumstances and to uplift me with her affection. Our bond as three sisters grew stronger with each passing day. Pretty Sisterhood became a code of conduct—a way we can be kind and good to ourselves and others. We found joy in simple pleasures like sharing meals, dancing, and indulging in treats together. The rituals we created became a source of comfort and strength, helping us endure difficult times.

Over the years, we extended the concept of being a Pretty Sister beyond our family to include friends and loved ones. It became a symbol of unity and positivity, a reminder to choose kindness and goodness in all our interactions. In 2003, during a heartfelt family reunion, we experienced a pivotal moment that would forever change the dynamics of our sisterhood. For this special gathering, Becky, Martha, and I decided to create Pretty Sister tee-shirts for all the women and girls. These shirts weren't just pieces of clothing to us, but emblems of our shared beliefs and spirit. As we wore these shirts proudly, they strengthened our little tribe and caught the attention of others.

The response was overwhelming. Women who saw us wearing our tee-shirts were drawn to the sense of camaraderie and positivity they represented.

They wanted to be a part of it, to share in the bonds of love and friendship that defined us as Pretty Sisters. We decided to make more and invite others into our circle of sisterhood. We invented a welcoming ritual to initiate them. Before we knew it, the demand for these tee-shirts grew, and we found ourselves committing more and more women and girls to the principles of Pretty Sisters.

Filled with a magical sense of purpose and empowerment, we felt like we were making the world a better place one Pretty Sister at a time. As the virtues of love, friendship, and goodness took root not just within our immediate family but also among our extended community of family and friends, and their daughters, the gift of a simple nickname blossomed into something truly extraordinary. The positive message it conveyed was touching hearts and minds. Illuminating lives.

In 2006, inspired by our overwhelming success in selling our Pretty Sister tee-shirts and the growing sisterhood that was wearing them, we embarked on a new adventure: a Pretty Sisters cruise. Close to a hundred women from different corners of the world gathered for a few days on board to celebrate being Pretty Sisters, revel in friendship, and create lasting memories together. This inaugural cruise marked the beginning of an annual tradition of cruising and playing, while basking in the joy of shared beliefs and values, which lasted for four years.

Immersed in laughter, love, and camaraderie, the cruise became an opportunity for my sisters and I to reaffirm our commitment to uplifting each other and spreading kindness and positivity wherever we went. We had become flourishing, empowered women.

Today, I realize with amazement how much my simple nickname has shaped my identity and outlook on life. Though it was a simple gesture to bestow it upon me as a youngster, it has guided me to honor the best qualities I possess and to be resilient when necessary, and it has inspired me to empower others to recognize their inner worth and potential.

As I share this story, I hope to inspire you to embrace your own inner "prettiness" —not just as a label, but as a reflection of your inherent goodness, strength, and ability to create a life filled with happiness and purpose.

Imagine if you knew deep down that you were pretty not just in appearance, but in your worth, your divine essence, your ability to achieve and create. How would your life change? Would you be braver? Would you dare to dream bigger and believe in your abilities more? The purpose of this book is to support you in discovering and expressing your potential.

Pretty Sisters share a mindset and spirit that make us bold. We view ourselves as beautiful and strong. We also value the beauty and strength of other women. And we see the friendship of women as a superpower. Pretty Sisters approach every challenge as an opportunity to grow and every setback as a stepping stone toward greatness because of our positivity and also because we trust that we can rely on the friendships we've forged to encourage and sustain us.

So, I invite you to join me in embracing the spirit of being a Pretty Sister: to believe in yourself, uplift those around you, and create a life that shines brightly with love, friendship, and goodness.

Together, We Can Shine Brightly

When women unite in positive and supportive friendships, magic happens. Together, we accomplish dreams that we do not necessarily believe or know we can accomplish on our own. Supportive friends amplify each other's strengths by inspiring each other in good times and uplifting each other during challenging times. Friendships between Pretty Sisters are wellsprings of positivity and happiness that make the journey of life more rewarding.

In this book, you'll be introduced to the core beliefs of Pretty Sisters and lessons I've learned from other women and girls. I'll tell you stories about the beautiful gifts of sisterhood, friendship, and love that have shaped my approach to life and contribute to my happiness in ways I never could've imagined when I was a child. You'll also see how I used these beliefs to raise my daughters to know their worth and inner beauty and help them gain the confidence they needed to go out in the world and be successful. My daughters and their friends have become exemplary Pretty Sisters.

You'll have the opportunity to understand the ways that you are a Pretty Sister, too—or could be—and the positive influence you can become in the world when you adopt these magical principles. I hope you love these beliefs and traditions as much as I and my family do.

Together, we can shine our lights brightly in the world. Let's celebrate the strength, resilience, and love that unite us as Pretty Sisters, creating a ripple effect of positivity and joy that extends far beyond ourselves.

Let's get started.

Welcome, Here's What's Coming

First of all, way to go, girl! The fact that you are reading this book means to me that you are ready to create more abundance in your life, embrace the power of sisterhood, and let your light shine brightly. I honor you for joining me in this adventure.

In *Breakfast at Tiffany's*, Holly Golightly, the character played by Audrey Hepburn, says, "I believe that happy girls are the prettiest girls."[1] I agree wholeheartedly! And in a way, that is our objective. We are on a journey to discover happiness within ourselves so that we may share our joy with the world.

It's important to realize that living small means one is taking the path of least resistance. It's easy to stay in our comfort zones. What's harder is overcoming our internal resistance to step out in faith and claim one's birthright: the blessings of a life lived with purpose and abundance. We were created with a divine essence and are meant to live happily. It's only our own inability to understand our true nature that limits us from claiming all the blessings that are rightfully ours.

A Few Things to Expect

The truth is, you *can* have everything you want, based solely on your purest desires and good intentions. Isn't that wonderful to know? Now that you are here, your life is going to change. You will begin to see that magic unfolds for those who claim their happiness. Just know:

Your life as you know it will change. It's okay because you are ready for this. A shift happens once you decide to take a leap of faith and trust in your success, happiness, and the sisterhood of like-minded women by your side. The very act of decision will begin to attract miracles into your life. You will learn the secrets to recognizing them and staying in the flow of continual peace and joy. It's a beautiful place to live, so now is the time to get excited.

People around you will notice. Be prepared for the responses you will get as you step into your power, claim your gifts, and decide to join the ranks of the Pretty Sisters. Some people you know may not be comfortable with the changes you make in the way you conduct yourself or the goals you are striving for, and that's okay. You may need to attract different people into your circle of influence, and the shift could be exponentially beneficial. As people adjust to your new light, be patient with them, and don't allow their judgments to hold you back. Just keep shining brightly! This is your right, and as Pretty Sisters, you and your friends can uplift each other.

Consistency is hard. You will have some good days and some bad days as you begin to act like a Pretty Sister. Don't allow the bad days to derail your success and diminish how happy you feel on the good days. Life is a journey, and it's how consistently you practice new beliefs that determines whether they will stick. Your consistency in practicing these beliefs will allow you to realize the happiness that can be yours. Each day will get easier as you strengthen your resolve and form habits that stick. Just remember, all the effort and practice is worth it! You are worth it, and the bonds of sisterhood will keep you moving forward.

Happiness is a choice. People spend whole lifetimes in search of happiness when, in fact, they could choose to be happy at any time, in any place. Joy is always there for the taking. Would you like to be happy right now? Then, please stop searching and start choosing to embrace your life and all the joy that is yours.

In this book I will guide you through steps that will help you raise your awareness and do what's necessary to create a happy life for yourself. Don't hesitate. Simply jump in and trust that you can create joy together with your fellow Pretty Sisters!

Get Ready

In my opinion, Pretty Sisters are as powerful in real life as the most powerful superheroes in comic books—the female ones, of course! If that comparison appeals to you, then it's time to put on your superhero suit and show up as the heroine of your own story. It's time to activate your superpowers, which will emanate from your inner prettiness.

If you're like the women who came on Pretty Sisters cruises, the moment of decision to live as a Pretty Sister and think pretty will be an incredibly meaningful moment for you. You are about to step into *being who you truly are,* possibly for the first time in your life, alongside other Pretty Sisters. You are choosing to be a victim of your circumstances no longer, and to recognize yourself as a *heroine!* Things are not going to just happen to you anymore; you are going to think differently and create your life, as a Pretty Sister. This will take some learning, practicing, and patience. In time, I will encourage you to unite with some women friends or acquaintances and work in tandem with them. Sisterhood is amplifying. Then you can rely on one another's support.

I've been using the foundational beliefs that I teach in this book—and which I sometimes refer to as my *secret formula*—for over three decades to create a beautiful life that I love with the support of my Pretty Sisters. The formula leads to a mindset shift, a new way of *thinking pretty.* These simple yet profound beliefs helped me find my soulmate, Dave, who is the love of my life, and helped me parent five beautiful, thriving children through to adulthood. They also gave me the courage to go on entrepreneurial adventures leading to the growth of million-dollar businesses, to build dream homes, to establish deep and meaningful relationships, and to travel the world. The list could go on and on.

The mindset of thinking pretty has helped me and countless others manifest dream after dream to fulfill the creation of joy and happiness. And now, you, as a Pretty Sister, can adopt these beliefs too.

As I look back on that little girl in the car with her mother and siblings, embarking on a journey to start life fresh in a new town with hopes and dreams and not much else, I realize that with the right perspective and resilience, her dreams did come true. As she grew up, that little girl was able to create a life filled with love, success, and happiness, overcoming challenges and setbacks along the way. Her belief in her own abilities, including her faith that she would receive the support of her Pretty Sisters, was key.

This book is structured around five core beliefs. Each belief is discussed in three consecutive chapters, followed by a ritual that I like to call a Pinky Promise. We will begin with the easiest belief to embody, and then watch as each new belief builds upon the previous one. Every step to adopt a new belief takes energy and practice. Some might say the journey of the Pretty Sister gets harder as you go, but that's not necessarily true—each step is equally important, and based on your perception, can be easy or hard.

In my mind, now that I deliberately choose to live this way every day, it's all very simple, and that's what I'd like you to choose to believe too. Although some things might come naturally to you, and some tasks might seem impossible, what's most important is that you open your mind to trust that I'm presenting the information in a good order and surrender to the process in this book completely. Your conscious mind may know the truth of these beliefs already, and even find the simplicity of the steps to be too easy. However, the real task here is to tap into your subconscious mind, where your deep beliefs are held and your programming is stored. This level of your thinking needs to be reprogrammed.

It will take understanding and practice to create a new vision and reality for your life, hand in hand with Pretty Sisters, but I believe in you. You've got this!

Together, We'll Create a World of Joy

What you are about to learn is based upon the precept that you are not alone; rather, you were divinely created by a loving God *to have joy!*

I realize we all use different names to recognize this higher power, and as you read this, I want you to please feel free to substitute the name that fits your personal beliefs. Then, let's embark on an incredible journey of self-discovery and dream fulfillment together, hand in hand.

This is my prayer: *May you find inspiration, guidance, and the lasting bonds of sisterhood that will illuminate your path to greatness.*

Clear your mind, be open, and be ready to receive inspiration as you create a *brand-new vision* for your life as a Pretty Sister. What will it look like, sound like, feel like? You are going to be a new woman, and able to support other women going through a similar transformation in their mindset as you. Open up to the possibilities of living larger than you've been living until now. Open up to the potential for grandeur, and to be delighted.

Pretty Sister, I will be standing hand in hand with you, as you embrace the power of our shared sisterhood and the realization of your most cherished dreams! It's time to think pretty!

THINK PRETTY

BELIEF #1
YOU ARE PRETTY

"Beauty begins the moment you decide to be yourself."

COCO CHANEL

ONE

YOU ARE ENOUGH

*God created you as you are because He knew
the world needed you to be exactly who you are.*

I REMEMBER STANDING IN FRONT OF THE MIRROR, CLAD in a swimsuit, as the summer sun teased promises of fun-filled days at Dunlooring, our community pool, just a block away. The anticipation was palpable; this summer held a special excitement because I was on the cusp of taking the swim test. Passing meant earning a coveted badge, a symbol of independence that would allow me to dive into the pool without supervision. Ah, those were the days of carefree childhood, where we roamed the neighborhood until the streetlights flickered on. The freedom awaiting me felt exhilarating!

Yet, as I scrutinized my reflection, a familiar cloud of self-doubt crept in. I noticed what I perceived as extra weight, a flaw magnified by the appearance of my short brown hair, which seemed plain in comparison to my friend Diana's long, lustrous blond locks draping over her slender frame. In hindsight, as a seasoned mother reflecting on my childhood, I recognize that I was simply carrying remnants of baby fat at nine years old. But in that moment, staring at my reflection, I felt imperfect and melancholic.

Then, like a gentle whisper cutting through the noise of my insecurity, a profound thought emerged: *God created me just like this.* The revelation washed over me, filling me with a profound sense of acceptance. If this was how God intended me to be, why question His design? Wouldn't it be ungrateful to reject the person I was meant to be? And what if by embracing my features, I could unlock hidden talents and abilities?

That insight marked a pivotal shift in my thinking. My sadness transformed into curiosity, igniting a flame of wonder about my potential. Instead of dwelling on my perceived imperfections, I chose to trust in God's plan for me. I believed that He had crafted me with intention, and this belief fueled my fascination with dreaming about what the future held. Embracing myself as God's creation was not just about appearance. It was about embracing my identity and the journey of discovering my purpose.

The moment has been a cornerstone memory for me, a touchstone I've revisited time and again to anchor my perspective on myself. Little did I know, at that tender age, how profoundly that moment would shape my life and contribute to the person I am today. It laid the foundation for my deeply rooted belief that *I am enough.*

Of course, life's trials have tested this core belief. I've faced moments of doubt and had to learn tools to guide me back to it at points. But I can personally attest that embracing a belief in our own sufficiency brings us far more joy than the alternative, sadly embraced by many: a belief in unworthiness, lack, or unlovability. Such ideas will slowly corrode the essence of our being, sowing seeds of destructive patterns of thought that can consume us.

Once you embrace the truth that a loving God with perfect wisdom and foresight intentionally created you to be exactly who you are, everything shifts. Understanding that your imperfections are part of your unique journey on Earth, and designed to help you realize your potential, allows you to surrender to the flow of life. This awareness fuels your ability to dream because you know you possess all that is needed to become who you are destined to be.

This empowering realization doesn't promise an easy path. In fact, it often leads to a new set of challenges. Embracing your true self means embarking on a journey of growth, learning, and courage that involves facing adversity and trials, and occasional failures and discouragement. Yet, the core belief in your ability to meet the moment keeps you on the path.

In building the dream life in which you're fulfilling your potential, the fundamental belief that will serve as your bedrock is your belief in your own worthiness. It's all too common for women to question our capabilities, to wonder if we're "enough" to reach for our dreams. But let me assure you, believing in your inherent worthiness is not merely a comforting thought, it's a powerfully sustaining, and motivating, truth. To truly step into the life you desire, you must understand that *you are enough*. With conviction about this, you can master your thoughts, navigate challenges, and seize opportunities from a place of self-love and self-assuredness.

You are about to embark on a journey of self-discovery. As you do, please remember that you are worthy, you are capable, and you are enough.

Remembering Who You Are

Have you ever found yourself questioning your worth? Wondering if you measure up or are strong enough to do what you want to do? We've all been there, caught in a moment of self-doubt when we're focused on our faults rather than on our inherent worthiness.

To get in touch with how much you have to offer, take a moment to envision yourself as a little child, a tiny miracle sent from heaven to this world. You arrived with an inherent sense of worth, perfectly and beautifully *you*. You were enough in every way, just as you still are now.

As you took your first tentative steps, you stumbled and fell, and it was utterly endearing. Picture your parents cheering you on as you toddled forward, occasionally falling to the floor, but always getting back up. You weren't afraid to try. You made mistakes, learned from them, and improved. And your inherent worthiness remained intact, untouched by the bumps, bruises, and tears of your learning journey.

The process of learning is the essence of life.

Any time you find yourself *feeling* unworthy and "not enough," it's because of how you are *thinking*. The reason is your mindset. There's really no mystery about it. Our minds are powerful, but our thoughts can also lead us astray. If we're not intentional, negative thoughts can overshadow our intuition—the inner wisdom that flows from both our hearts and our guts. When this happens, those thoughts can convince us of falsehoods about our abilities, potential, and intrinsic worth.

It's crucial to remember that you're not alone in the struggle to feel worthy; it's a shared human experience. A negative mindset, shaped by experiences of painful and confusing events that we didn't understand or feel in control of, can become deeply ingrained in our subconscious minds, creating patterns of thought that affect our self-perception and influence our behavior. We fall prey to negative thinking and become self-protective.

But look! There's good news: You can change, become more self-aware, forgive yourself for your vulnerability as a child or an adult who experienced a trauma, and master your thoughts! Emotions, even the most challenging ones, are your allies in turning things around. They can offer you insights and a perspective of your inner world you've never seen if you will let them guide you. Then, just like the tiny toddler you once were who learned to walk by heeding an indomitable desire to move and explore, you will learn and explore your value.

You Are Worthy

Belief in one's own worth is the cornerstone of unshakable faith in oneself. My deepest wish for you is that you will recognize your boundless worth. You deserve love, compassion, friendship, and unbridled joy—all the beautiful things life has to offer. At the end of the chapter, I will teach you the Spilling the TEA Technique, a powerful method for shifting beliefs through self-reflection. If you keep practicing it, soon your belief in your worthiness will become unwavering.

You may stumble and fall, but you should pick yourself up, brush yourself off, and aim to find forgiveness for your mistakes and missteps—self-forgiveness—and carry on. None of us is infallible. Making mistakes is a natural aspect of learning. Within you lies an extraordinary potential waiting to be awakened. Your intrinsic value endures, and you can start anew—as many times as necessary—as you pursue your passions and dreams.

Doubts may surface, but as soon as you recognize them, remind yourself that it's normal to have uncertainty especially when you're trying to accomplish something new. You have the power to silence those fears and thoughts. As you learn to think pretty, hold tight to this simple yet profound declaration: *"I am worthy."* Believe it with unwavering conviction, allowing no room for competing thoughts.

You possess more power than you realize, the power to change your thoughts. Deciding you are worthy is a decision well worth making. You'll need to make it repeatedly, but you can come to believe it down deep, where it gets established as one of your subconscious beliefs.

Embrace your worthiness, treat yourself with the utmost respect, and become your own most ardent cheerleader. You can do this, one baby step at a time.

You Can Be the Architect of Your Own Confidence

Your beliefs are the architects of your life. They originate from your thoughts. If you can change your thoughts, you can change your life. This is a simple truth that holds more power than you might realize. The ability to choose which thoughts to think is a superpower you possess, and it should fill you with hope!

Now, let's witness this superpower in action through the inspiring example of my middle daughter, Sophia, and see how a shift in perspective can unlock boundless confidence, leading to a life filled with self-assuredness and radiant positivity.

My adorable daughter Sophia truly personifies the word *confidence*. I've had the privilege of witnessing her innate self-assuredness from a young age, and it's been nothing short of a marvel. She would gleefully sing and dance to the catchy, self-celebratory lyrics from Meghan Trainor's song "Me Too," not because she believed she was superior to others, but because she genuinely cherished herself and who she was. Her infectious self-love has not only warmed my heart but has also imparted invaluable lessons.

As I watched Sophia over the years, I couldn't help but reflect on my self-perception. Did I view myself with the same level of appreciation and self-love? The question naturally extends to all of us: "How would our lives transform if we approached them with unwavering confidence, seeing only the best in ourselves?"

Sophia's experience is a remarkable testament to the power of self-belief. Several years ago, she embarked on the countdown to a momentous day: the day her braces were due to come off. To Sophia, this day was on par with Independence Day, an event anyone might eagerly anticipate. However, there was a twist in her tale, a tiny chip on her front tooth, a battle scar from a childhood incident involving her older sister, a snow fort, and a shovel.

I couldn't help but fret that her joy at having her braces removed might be overshadowed by the revelation of this chipped tooth. I steeled myself for her reaction when she gazed at her newly transformed smile in the mirror.

To my immense surprise and delight, Sophia's response was nothing short of magical. She looked at herself, her eyes sparkling with sheer joy, and exclaimed, "I look so beautiful!" She seemed to completely overlook the chipped front tooth, a detail that was hard to miss but inconsequential to her. At that moment, all Sophia could see were her radiant, newly liberated pearly whites. For her, it was the fulfillment of her teeth-related dreams, and she couldn't wait to flaunt her new smile.

So, what does Sophia's perspective have to do with all of us? How would we act differently if we were as confident as her, able to see our beauty despite any perceived flaws? It's a thought-provoking question, one that encourages us to envision lives marked by greater boldness, self-confidence, and an unwavering commitment to pursuing our dreams.

Sophia's story serves as a poignant reminder that genuine confidence is rooted in recognizing and embracing our inherent beauty and worth, even when confronted with imperfections. It's an example of resilience and choosing to focus on the positives in life. We all bear unique imperfections, but those very quirks make us *perfectly* ourselves.

Through Sophia's example, we're encouraged to navigate life with boldness, courage, and hope, embracing our true selves with unwavering confidence. Her narrative inspires us to let go of self-doubt and insecurity and, instead, to shine brightly with authenticity, knowing that when we do, we unlock a world of boundless happiness and the pursuit of our dreams.

Sophia's example beautifully illustrates the power of shifting our thoughts and beliefs, showing us that we can choose to focus on our beauty rather than our imperfections. It's a wonderful example of how altering our perspective can have a profound impact on our self-confidence.

How to Transform Your Thinking

Now, let's dive deeper into the process of rewiring your thinking, recognizing that it may require some effort as we navigate established neural pathways and thinking habits. Changing our thought patterns is key to transforming our lives, and it all begins with a willingness to embrace new, elevated ways of thinking that will ultimately shape our actions. But before we delve into this transformation, let's take it one step at a time.

Because your thoughts are the fundamental building blocks of everything happening in your life, it's essential to "rewire" your brain for new thinking. Although you are definitely *not* a machine with actual wires in your head, your brain does form physical connections between cells, aka *neurons*, that create pathways for chemical-electrical impulses. These paths are analogous to the systems of electrical wiring in a house that keep your lights on, or to the circuitry in our computers that enables them to do binary calculations.

The process of rewiring thinking can be a bit tricky because we all have established neural pathways or thinking habits that shape our daily actions and, essentially, who we are. To effect real change, you must be open to thinking in entirely new, elevated, and better ways that will inevitably influence your actions. But let's not rush ahead of ourselves.

Let's start with the simple, yet profound idea that you are "perfect." I'm telling you right now that you are, and it's true. You are perfectly you in all your imperfect ways. Just like I realized as a little girl, and then my daughter Sophia has reflected back to me time and time again, we are all beautiful in our own ways, and that includes you. How does that feel? Can you believe it? I mean truly, deeply, and all the way to your core. Do you believe it?

This is the fundamental building block to more beliefs that will transform you and help you internalize the Pretty Sister way of thinking. Adopting the belief *"I am enough"* is the foundation of a transformative mindset that could significantly impact your confidence and outlook on life. Internalizing this thought involves recognizing and accepting your inherent worth and value just as you are, without needing external validation or comparison to others. It's about embracing your strengths, acknowledging your imperfections, and understanding that you deserve love, respect, and fulfillment simply by being yourself.

I recommend that you let this powerful belief serve as your foundation for building self-confidence and resilience. When you have truly come to believe that you are enough, you will approach your challenges with a sense of inner strength and optimism. You'll be more likely to take risks, pursue your passions, and navigate obstacles with grace and determination. This mindset shift can enable you to let go of self-doubt and fear of failure, freeing you to explore new opportunities and reach for your full potential. I bet you'd like that a lot.

When we embrace the belief "I am enough," it fosters in us a deep sense of gratitude and contentment in the present moment while fueling hope for the future. It allows us to release the pressure of constantly striving for perfection and instead focus on growth, learning, and living authentically. With this empowering mindset, we can move through life with ease, confidence, and a profound sense of purpose, ready to embrace new experiences and fulfill our dreams.

Just the other day, I caught Sophie and her sister, Isabella, standing in their swimsuits, looking at themselves in the mirror. This was an after-sun freckle examination. Sophie was examining her freckles that had darkened after being in the sun. Sophie is more fair-skinned with lighter hair like me, and her sister, Bella, who's just a year younger, looks more like her father. Bella has darker skin, brown eyes, and dark brown hair, and she tans very easily and has far fewer freckles than her sister. She has to search for them to prove she has some.

Since I gathered after observing Sophie that finding freckles was desirable, I declared proudly that Sophie could thank me for her freckles and Bella could thank Dad for her dark features. Sophie then announced that her freckles were her favorite feature and that the more she had, the more beautiful she was! I smiled at her response. Sometimes I feel there are no bounds to her confidence. She has a gift for seeing certain features (which some might not want or not find attractive) as perfectly beautiful just the way they are. While some girls may not want freckles, Sophie embraces hers. They make her who she is, distinct and different and uniquely her.

Of course, I think it helps that she believes—because I told her so when she was younger—that her freckles are kisses from angels. While that helped her when she was little and asking why she had freckles and others didn't, now, as an adult, she continues to embrace the childhood fable and loves herself all the more for her angel kisses. Regardless, she loves herself and knows she's perfect just the way she was created.

Reflecting back to my nine-year-old self in my swimsuit looking at my reflection in the mirror, with my first instinct to see my flaws, I'm grateful I had the divine insight to see myself as a child of God, created perfectly in His image and for a unique purpose that only I could fulfill. I've now raised my girls to see that truth reflected back at them, and I'm so grateful they can see their beauty when they look at themselves in the mirror, freckles and all.

Do you see your beauty? Do you understand that you are enough just the way you are? Because you are!

You may stumble and make mistakes, but you can find forgiveness, including self-forgiveness, for we are not infallible. Within you lies extraordinary potential waiting to be awakened. Your intrinsic value endures, and you can start anew, as many times as necessary.

Believe that you were created with purpose, intentionality, and more strength than you can imagine. You are more than enough, and the world eagerly awaits your unique gifts and talents.

Spilling the TEA:
A Game-Changer for Girl Talk

We all know the phrase *spill the tea*. It's what we say when we're about to share the latest news, vent about our feelings, or have deep girl talk. But what if we could take that phrase and give it a whole new meaning, one that actually helps us grow, break free from negative patterns, and support each other in the best way possible?

Welcome to the Spilling the TEA Technique, your chance to cultivate awareness of your thoughts, emotions, actions (TEA). This technique is a powerful tool for self-exploration, helping you recognize the thoughts driving your emotions and actions, and to shift them to a place of love, hope, and faith. Whenever you feel stuck, overwhelmed, or unsure about a situation . . . it's TEA time!

Whether you Spill the TEA alone in your journal or in the company of a Pretty Sister, this process will help you get clarity, shift your mindset, and take control of your actions.

How to Spill the TEA

With curiosity, you will explore your TEA.

Thoughts—T: What are you thinking? Write down all the thoughts running through your head. Let them flow freely—no judgment. Thoughts can be protective, but they can also be negative or fear-based. Acknowledging them is the first step in taking control. Some common negative thoughts you may have are:

- *"I'm not good enough."*
- *"No one really cares about me."*
- *"I always mess things up."*

Emotions—E: How do these thoughts make you feel? Identify the emotions your thoughts are triggering. Are you feeling fear? Sadness? Anxiety? Understanding your emotions will help you gain clarity on how your thoughts are affecting you.

Actions—A: What do these feelings make you want to do? Our emotions drive our actions—sometimes in ways that don't serve us. Do you feel like shutting down? Lashing out? Giving up? Writing it all down helps you see the connection between your thoughts, emotions, and actions—and gives you the power to change them.

Why TEA Time Works

The goal of Spilling the TEA is to shine a light on the thought patterns that are holding you back. Once you're aware of them, you can consciously shift your mindset.

If you're struggling to figure out what you're thinking, start with emotions instead. If you feel anxious or upset, ask yourself, "What thought triggered this feeling?" Sometimes, tracking your TEA backward helps uncover hidden beliefs that need to be addressed.

Once you've spilled your TEA, take a deep breath, acknowledge yourself for doing the work, and get ready for the next step, which is flipping the script and replacing those negative thoughts with ones that empower you.

So, the next time you and your Pretty Sisters are having girl talk, take it to the next level. Instead of just venting, help each other Spill the TEA in a way that leads to real breakthroughs. Because this is what Pretty Sisters do—we lift each other up.

Flipping the Script: Moving to Your Heart

After you've explored your headspace, it's time to shift your attention to your *heart*. The point of this next exercise is to transform the fear-based ideas you identified in the previous exercise into their positive counterparts. Because the heart is more aligned with love, faith, and possibility than the head, the ideas that you come up with now will be more compassionate, tolerant, and supportive. This will motivate you to move forward with more purpose and passion.

As you look at the same situation, start fresh with the familiar Spilling the TEA questions, but this time, intentionally focus on thoughts that reflect hope, empowerment, and worthiness.

1. **T—Thoughts: What do I *think*?** Reflecting on your original fear-based thoughts, replace them with heart-centered ones. For example:
   - "I am enough."
   - "I am loved."
   - "I have everything I need to succeed."
   - "The world is waiting for me to share my gifts."

2. **E—Emotions: How do these thoughts make me *feel*?** Review what you're just written and notice how your positive new thoughts shift your emotions. You might feel lighter, more hopeful, even excited.

3. **A—Actions: What do these new feelings make me want to *do*?** Finally, consider how your empowering new feelings inspire action. You may feel ready to take bold steps, reach out for connection, or move forward with renewed confidence.

The Power of the Shift

Spilling the TEA—pouring out your thoughts, emotions, and actions—first clears space for the opposite perspective to emerge. It helps you see that you are not trapped by your negative thoughts; they are simply one part of the story. When you operate from your heart, your actions are aligned with your highest self, and they feel more purposeful and uplifting.

This process is a reminder that we always have a choice to dwell in fear or lean in to faith, love, and hope. By regularly practicing TEA Time, shifting your thoughts, emotions, and actions, you'll cultivate resilience, self-awareness, and the confidence to approach life with the grace of a Pretty Sister, someone who thinks pretty and uplifts herself and others through inspired, love-based action.

Sometimes when going through lengthier challenges in life this process may require you to sit down with a pen and paper for a longer period of time. As you become proficient you will find that you can walk yourself through Spilling the TEA in your car while sitting at a stoplight. Either way, Spilling the TEA is designed to help you get unstuck. I love how it allows you to pause and recognize patterns that might otherwise go unnoticed, giving you the power to choose a new way forward.

When practiced regularly, Spilling the TEA is a compass for navigating life's challenges. It helps you embrace setbacks as opportunities for growth, strengthens your relationships, and empowers you to move through life successfully. Whether applied to work, family, or personal struggles, this simple yet profound process equips you with the tools to create the life you truly desire—one loving and intentional choice at a time.

Always remember, your feelings of low self-esteem are nothing to be ashamed of; they're there to help you evolve. Recognize them for what they are, signs that you are bumping up against an internal barrier. Once you have awareness of a barrier, you can choose to do something about it.

Be patient with yourself. You're on a journey to fulfill a grander purpose, always rooted in the belief that you are worthy, deep inside. Trust me, You are ENOUGH! And if you're struggling to believe this just yet, borrow my belief in you for now. In time, I guarantee you'll come to believe in your own worthiness. I have faith in you!

You are enough, just as you are.

You are capable of greatness.

You possess the strength to overcome any challenge.

You are deserving of love, joy, and all the beautiful things life offers.

You are enough. Believe it. Embrace it. Live it.

TWO

YOU ARE UNIQUE

A pretty woman is a woman of substance, intelligence, and elegance whose actions speak louder than her words and whose confidence shines from within.

BEDTIME WITH FIVE YOUNG KIDS WAS ALWAYS A CHORE. I had the mindset *If I'm going to be in the trenches, I'll stay there until I'm done having kids.* I've always liked hard work, and I am willing to take on a challenge as long as there is the promise of my burdens lifting in the not too distant future. And so it was with bearing children. I intentionally had them close in age and planned to put my head down and get the work of raising them done in as similar stages as I could. My oldest son, Chase, was seven when my youngest child, my daughter Isabella, was born. That's right, five kids in almost eight years. Bella was born in August and Chase turned eight that same year in October. Regardless, because of the age similarities of my brood, our family life was chaotic for quite some time.

My husband, Dave, and I had to come up with routines for just about everything we did with the kids, and bedtime was no different. Thankfully, Dave is a great parent and would often tackle the older kids on his own while

I put the babies to sleep. The last two girls, Sophia and Bella, were only fifteen months apart in age, so their nighttime routine was challenging. For the most part, two babies, two separate cribs, two bottles, and lots of diapers were what I had to deal with.

Dave was a fantastic storyteller, and our second child and oldest daughter, Taylor, loved to create stories with him. Their imaginations would soar as they took turns weaving bedtime tales that blended bits of truth with lots of wild and vivid descriptions of fantastical lands and characters. What we didn't know at the time was the slow and steady development of Taylor's fascination with storytelling.

As she grew, she became an avid reader and writer. We noticed this love in her and made sure to tell her how imaginative she was, how creative her mind was, and how gifted she was at creating stories. This affirmation set her on a path to carve out more time to write and develop this talent. She spent hours upon hours devouring books and filling pages of journals with her stories. Long car rides turned into family sessions where everyone gave input into her stories, often without her consent, trying to help her craft the right plots. Without a doubt, she became the writer in the family, and everyone was pleased to affirm her abilities.

It was no surprise that at a young age, she set the goal to have her first book published by eighteen. To some, this might have seemed unrealistic, something to temper with caution and realism. Yet, I firmly believe that real life will do that for you, so there's rarely a need for me to dampen the wind. I'd rather be the wind beneath my children's wings and help their dreams take flight. So we continued to help her plot, imagine, and cultivate her talent.

This was especially hard when her laptop crashed in junior high and she lost the manuscript she had worked on for a few years. This was a devastating blow that set her back. For two years, she lost interest and pursued other things. That seemed fine, as she was a busy high schooler adjusting to our move from Maine to Utah the summer before her junior year in high school. Adjusting to a new school at that tender age is hard, and I admired her grit and determination to fit in, find friends, and thrive in a new atmosphere. She would admit now it was harder than she had imagined, with many ups and downs. We smile, remembering her tenacity as she ran for student body vice president her junior year, despite hardly knowing anyone. Not surprisingly, given this, she lost. But she won in other ways.

The biggest win was that, in her downtime, instead of being sad, she returned to her writing. She remembered her childhood dream of publishing a novel by eighteen and set out to do it. She found that rewriting her book came easier than she had expected, and I'm sure it was much better with age, experience, and education on her side. Once again, she came alive with her writing, and her confidence grew. As her eighteenth birthday approached, she spent all her time editing, barely coming up for air or food. I'll never forget the evening of Taylor's birthday, on April 27, nearing the end of her senior year. I had ordered an advance copy of her book to be shipped to us by her printer so she could unwrap it at dinner in Park City, where we had gone to celebrate. *Infinite* (that was the title) had become a reality! As she held the book, her book, in her hands for the first time her accomplishment was real. Her dream had been realized and her self-confidence soared through the roof!

The gift of writing is certainly Taylor's gift. This fascination and talent are part of who she is. But she had to recognize it, cultivate it, and develop it over time. This process continues now as she contemplates the sequel to her first book. Sometimes she doubts her ability to write and feels inadequate. Now, at twenty-four, she looks back on her memories of herself writing at seventeen and cringes, thinking the work she produced was too naive and underdeveloped. It probably was. But she did it! She dared to dream big and accomplish her objective! To me, that is the most important thing.

She can always write more and will get better with each book or article she writes. Her writing will develop as she grows in wisdom and experience.

Thank goodness Taylor didn't think she had to be perfect, but just went ahead and made a start. Thank goodness she didn't give up. And how wonderful that her father helped her cultivate her gifts from a young age with relentless storytelling that made a difficult bedtime chore delightful. How grateful I am that we saw this gift in her and complimented her.

When she wanted to give up after losing her manuscript, we reminded her that because she had written it once, she could write it again, even better. We sometimes had to see in her what she couldn't see. We had to vocalize it and point out what wasn't always obvious to her.

The Power of Compliments

Everyone loves to be complimented. Can you think of a time when someone recognized something good about you that made you smile and feel warm inside? Or have you complimented one of your kids and seen them beaming with joy from the recognition of their best efforts? You've probably also experienced the feeling of an empty compliment—one that's generic or half-hearted. It falls flat, not really making a difference. What makes a good compliment is its specificity. When someone notices a unique aspect of you and points it out with enthusiasm or appreciation, it really brings a smile. It has a way of drawing out more of the same. We naturally want to rise to the compliment and demonstrate more of what's been highlighted. It's like we hear it and think, "Yeah, that's true, that's me," and we then show more of it. A good compliment reinforces the behavior identified and inspires more of the same.

Just like Taylor, everyone needs to be reminded every once in a while of their divine characteristics. Their unique gifts and talents. It's great to be a Pretty Sister, but it's even better when you belong to a group of amazing women who recognize your favorite attributes. Who really see you! When we began to create our Pretty Sisters community we knew we needed to make recognition a part of our initiation ceremony. The Pretty Sister initiation involves the special identification of what makes that person especially amazing or specifically "pretty" to herself and others.

In 2006, my sisters and I decided to host our first Pretty Sisters cruise and invited all of our friends to join us. Many of these women had been known as our Pretty Sisters throughout years of friendship, and some were new to our traditions. We wanted this to be a special event—not just any vacation, but one that would be remarkable, with experiences to remind them of who they truly are and how loved and special they are, where we all would be immersed in friendship and fun. To do this, we concluded each woman on our cruise needed to receive a special tribute from someone who knew her best.

In advance of the trip, we asked their spouse or the person closest to them—in some cases, a parent or family member—to write them a tribute. We provided examples and prompts to help them construct the perfect message. We also asked them to choose a single word or a few words that summarized their most cherished characteristics. This was a chance to express some creativity and personality associated with each Pretty Sister.

The ritual reading of the tributes was so much fun, better than we could have expected. What happened was nothing short of magical. In many cases, especially when a husband wrote this letter, women were reminded of their mutual love. Rather than just being glad they were away and having a break from real life (which they were), they were also filled with love and anticipation to get home and express their gratitude in return.

After the tribute letter was read, each woman attending was crowned the Pretty Sister of _____. We would fill in the blank with a special attribute. We had almost one hundred sisters on board ship that year, so it was fun to see all the variety. Among the honorary titles were the:

- Pretty Sister of Fantastical Fun and Fearlessness.
- Pretty Sister of Charming Wit and Wonder.
- Pretty Sister of Love and Selfless Service.
- Pretty Sister of Dancing and Daring.
- Pretty Sister of Adventure and Flawless Fun.

- Pretty Sister of Class and Intellect.
- And so on.

You get the idea. The list went on and on as each of a hundred women was recognized for her amazingness!

It was important to us for women to get their needed break, but not for them to engage in gossip or negative venting. We wanted to fill them with positivity and reminders of who they are, what they have, and all the things to be grateful for. Letter sharing was a chance to be lifted, together, alongside their Pretty Sisters.

The inclusion of the tribute letters worked out beautifully. It turns out we were right. Women need the occasional compliment and recognition. It goes a long way, and the more genuine, the better. Because in many cases, it was the most favorite part of a woman's trip, it is now a cornerstone of our Pretty Sister traditions. And of course, it's something that benefits from being done more than once a year.

The more we can learn to recognize and vocalize our appreciation for the special gifts of others, the more we can lift them up—and it lifts us up too. If we are generous and sincere in recognizing others, goodness comes right back to us.

In addition to the letters, we devised a Pretty Sister crowning ritual, an initiation ceremony wherein each sister raised her hand to the square and repeated the Pretty Sister Pledge line by line. After her recitation, she was crowned and then spun herself around three times while shimmying and being sprinkled with glittering "pixie dust." It ended with a kiss on each cheek from a fellow Pretty Sister.

We still do the whole ritual today whenever we get a chance to initiate a new Pretty Sister. It's fun! It's silly! Yet each part of the ritual has a special meaning and purpose that Pretty Sisters take seriously. You'll come to know about these as you read this book. By the end, I hope you will be ready to take the pledge, too, and declare yourself a Pretty Sister.

The Pretty Sister Pledge

I am a Pretty Sister.
I dare to dream.
I believe in myself!
I know who I am.
My crown reminds me.

I am a princess of divine heritage.
I am an expression of beauty, joy, and love.
I discover my dreams.
My dream dust empowers me.
My purpose is grand, and my potential limitless.

I will create my dreams.
My Pretty Sisters will assist me.
I will find the path and create the way.
I have gifts and talents and I will use them for good.
I give my best and I deserve the best.
I see the good in others, and the good in me.
I give and I can also forgive.
I can make a mistake.

I am love in motion.
I radiate a beauty deep within.
I am the joy the world is waiting for.
I will embrace my life and live each day to the fullest.
I am a Pretty Sister.

It's Easy to Forget How Fabulous We Are

The truth is, it's easy to forget our special gifts and talents, especially when life gets busy and routine. We all fall into this trap, particularly when we're in roles that involve caring for others. We also have unconscious competencies—the things we do so naturally that they don't even feel like special superpowers. Yet, these are our superpowers, and we might not realize it because they come so effortlessly to us. It often takes someone else noticing and naming them to help us recognize our personal abilities. That's why it's so important to observe the good characteristics of those around us and generously compliment and appreciate them.

A common trap is feeling inferior or competitive, thinking someone else's strength highlights our weakness. But this is flawed thinking. Other people's strengths don't diminish ours. Rather, they complement them. We need each other, and together, we flourish and grow. Celebrating others increases our own well-being and happiness. We thrive most when we work together collaboratively.

Another temptation is to shrink in the presence of others' greatness, thinking that humility means downplaying our own strengths. While humility is important, we are told, "Let your light shine." Your light is your birthright and it doesn't diminish anyone else's. The world needs your light, and only by shining brightly can you truly serve and live to your potential.

Many women don't know how to begin cultivating their gifts and talents because they think they don't have any. This is a false belief—flawed thinking. Every person is created with a unique purpose and mission in life. It's up to each of us to figure that out, and our happiness is largely impacted by our ability to do so.

Finding My Special Gifts

Even growing up with a Pretty Sister mindset, I've had days when I felt like I had no special gifts. Part of this was because I wished I could sing well. I always believed I could have been a rock star if only I had more musical talent. But I can barely carry a tune, and my musical debuts were limited to singing lullabies during late-night baby duty. Without a visible talent like singing, I wondered what else there was for me. I grew up in a family of singers and loved attending Sunday dinners that included family sing-alongs. My family's talents were fun and entertaining, and I always felt shortchanged when talents were distributed in heaven.

In high school, I received a revelatory blessing that identified some of my gifts. This was helpful, but again, they didn't seem like the ones I wanted and were quite obscure. Thankfully, the blessing was recorded, and I have a transcribed version that I refer to often. I've had to study it throughout my life to help me identify my innate gifts and discover my purpose. For me, it's been a lifelong process, changing with developing passions and different seasons of life.

Through studying this blessing, introspection, and self-discovery, I came to know that I have the gift of cheerfulness. As a young adult, being cheery wasn't the gift I wanted, but over the years, I've come to appreciate it more and more. I wouldn't trade it for anything. My natural disposition is to be happy, and the more I identify with this gift, the more I guard and protect it.

It's taken years of living with cheerfulness and using it to get through challenges to realize what a blessing it is. Especially when times are tough. Our gifts can be hard to recognize because they come so naturally. We can overlook their power because they're so easy to use. But as we recognize and appreciate them, we develop them more. That's when the magic happens—when we share our gifts with others.

One reason I'm writing this book is to share my gift of cheerfulness with you. Later, I'll dedicate a whole chapter to the principles of cultivating more happiness in your life. It's my gift, and what's easy for me might be hard for you. But it doesn't have to be because you can learn from someone who has mastered happiness. I promise you can, too!

Cheerfulness is only one of my gifts. I've also discovered I have the gift of using time wisely. I can get a tremendous amount done in a day and be incredibly productive when I want to. I honestly believe that time is always on my side.

This is a much better way to view time than feeling as if it's always "running out." Most people feel like there's never enough time, not realizing how time is the great equalizer. Rich or poor, old or young, male or female, we all have the same amount of time in a day and the same degree of control over it. It's empowering to know that we can decide how to spend our time, whether to waste it or use it wisely.

Of course, having this gift doesn't mean I'm continuously productive. I love happiness and time equally, so I prioritize both work and play. I can do either with great enthusiasm and efficiency, maximizing what I can accomplish and the joy I cultivate. Reflecting on these blessings, I have almost let go of my rock star dream . . . but a girl can still dream!

Your Gifts Will Align with Your Life's Purpose

When you think about it, it makes sense that you're designed with gifts that would fulfill your God-given purpose on earth. You are meant to have joy and success, not to be miserable and fail. This means that whatever your passions are, you have the ability to pursue them.

You can and should discover your gifts and talents. Believe that you have them and everything else you need to be successful and happy. A gift might be hidden initially, or it might need to be dusted off after a period of neglect, but all your gifts are uniquely yours. What's not visible to you may be more apparent to others.

A great way to get in tune with your gifts is to look outward and serve others. You'll do this naturally in ways that only you are capable of. And as you do this, others will notice and mirror back to you their gratitude for what you're doing well. That thing they speak of is a gift. This process will help you discover more of who you are. It's important to know this, so you can come to love and embrace the beautiful parts of you that are uniquely yours.

In college, my girlfriends and I threw a New Year's Eve party at my friend Katie's childhood house. Her parents had a mansion, a truly beautiful and inspirational place for college students figuring out their future. I vividly remember standing on the stairwell, overhearing some kids chatting about the house. They marveled at its extravagance and generosity, unaware that Katie, who they were talking to, lived there. They said, "I want to know who lives here."

At that moment, most kids would have gladly claimed the status of being the host. I know I would have. As the observer, I was about to announce Katie's awesomeness. But then, much to my surprise, I witnessed something life changing for me. Katie joined the conversation and said, "Yeah, she must be amazing. I'd love to meet her too." Then she moved on. She didn't care to be known or take credit. She was simply satisfied to bring joy to others and share. She was humble and generous. To her, it didn't matter whether or not people knew who she was, and she didn't need to feel cool because of her parents' wealth.

Wow! What a lesson! Growing up always wanting more, I imagined that being known as the host of that party would have been so cool. Yet, it turned out that it was Katie's generosity that was cool. It was her humility that was amazing. That moment of realizing the beauty of humility changed me, or at least my ambitions, and over the years, I've returned to that experience as a guiding post whenever I've been tempted to flaunt or seek attention.

It's not necessary. It's simply enough to share. When we express quiet humility, we can do a lot of good and bring people a lot of joy. That's what I've aspired to do—I want to become more like Katie in my perspectives on wealth, humility, and generosity.

I've since told Katie many times about the beauty of these qualities over thirty-five years of friendship where I've benefitted often from her special gifts. Her example has inspired me, and I've tried to emulate it in my opportunities to share. These are special qualities that come naturally to Katie and not as much to me, but I view her as a good teacher. I hope that, as I've expressed my gratitude, she's cultivated her gifts more deliberately, knowing how much they are appreciated.

This is how we help each other—by shining a light on each other's gifts.

Now, It's Your Turn to Identify Your Special Gifts

Your superpowers—or gifts—are needed by those around you. Whether it's courage, kindness, the ability to love, or wisdom, your gifts are uniquely yours to help you become who you are meant to be and serve. Embrace your gifts, shine your light, and share your brilliance with the world. You have so much to offer, and the world needs your unique talents.

So, what are your gifts? What comes so naturally to you that you might not even realize it's a superpower you possess? Here is a comprehensive list of potential gifts and talents to consider. Reflect on which of these you could claim as yours. (Additional talents and abilities may come to mind.)

Artistic Abilities

- Drawing
- Painting
- Sculpting
- Graphic design
- Photography
- Animation
- Calligraphy

Musical Talents

- Singing
- Playing an instrument
- Composing music
- Conducting
- Music production
- Songwriting

Literary Skills

- Creative writing
- Poetry
- Storytelling
- Editing
- Journalism
- Scriptwriting
- Blogging

Performance Skills

- Acting
- Dancing
- Theater production
- Public speaking
- Stand-up comedy
- Mime

Athletic Abilities

- Gymnastics
- Martial arts
- Yoga
- Dance
- Coaching
- Physical training

Intellectual Skills

- Mathematical ability
- Scientific knowledge
- Research
- Problem solving
- Critical thinking
- Linguistic proficiency
- Memorization

Technological Skills

- Coding/programming
- Web development
- Engineering
- Information technology
- Robotics
- Data analysis
- Cybersecurity

Craftsmanship & Manual Skills

- Carpentry
- Metalworking
- Sewing
- Knitting/crocheting
- Pottery
- Jewelry making
- Gardening

Business & Management Abilities

- Leadership
- Project management
- Marketing
- Salesmanship
- Entrepreneurship
- Financial planning
- Negotiation

Communication & Interpersonal Skills

- Empathy
- Active listening
- Conflict resolution
- Counseling
- Networking
- Persuasion
- Team collaboration

Culinary Arts Skills

- Cooking
- Baking
- Food styling
- Mixology
- Recipe development
- Food critiquing
- Nutrition/dietetics

Humanitarian & Social Service Skills

- Teaching
- Nursing
- Social work
- Community organizing
- Volunteering
- Mentorship
- Advocacy

Environmental & Nature Skills

- Conservation
- Wildlife rehabilitation
- Sustainable living
- Horticulture
- Environmental science
- Ecotourism

Innovative Skills

- Invention
- Strategic thinking
- Product design
- Visionary thinking

Spiritual & Healing Abilities

- Meditation
- Energy healing (e.g., Reiki)
- Spiritual guidance
- Medical practitioners
- Intuition
- Life coaching
- Care taking

Organizational & Planning Skills

- Event planning
- Time management
- Goal setting
- Task coordination
- Detail orientation
- Multitasking

Media & Entertainment Skills

- Filmmaking
- Video editing
- Sound recording
- Special Effects
- Broadcasting
- Podcasting
- Vlogging
- Acting
- Narration
- Animation

Design & Aesthetic Talents

- Interior design
- Fashion design
- Floral arrangement
- Landscaping
- Architecture

Animal Care Skills

- Veterinary medicine
- Animal training
- Pet grooming
- Animal rescue
- Wildlife photography

Exploration & Adventure Skills

- Travel planning
- Mountaineering
- Scuba diving
- Survival skills
- Navigation

Personal Development

- Self-discipline
- Resilience
- Self-motivation
- Emotional intelligence
- Mindfulness
- Goal achievement

These are just a few examples, of course, and many people possess a combination of these talents. Each individual has their own special set of gifts that can be nurtured and developed to contribute positively to their lives and the lives of others. Most of us have *unconscious competencies,* so we benefit from asking for feedback from the people who know us well when we're trying to identify our gifts. Another way is to take an online quiz that reveals your strengths and what contexts they can be used in.

There are many tools available to help you uncover your unique gifts and personality traits, and while no single test can define you completely, most can offer valuable insights into your strengths and natural abilities.

One of my favorite tools is the StrengthsFinder assessment offered by the Gallup Organization, which focuses on identifying your top strengths and encouraging you to lean into them, rather than trying to "fix" your weaknesses. I love this approach because it reinforces the idea that we don't have to be great at everything—we are meant to complement and uplift one another. Where we are not naturally strong, we can turn to collaboration and teamwork, or as I like to say, lean on your Pretty Sisters.

Once you've identified your gifts, I recommend you study how to refine them. You could start a journal in which you make note of experiences in which you have demonstrated these gifts or contemplate future activities that would require you to utilize them. Set a time each month to review and remind yourself of these qualities you have. I do this on the first Sunday of every month. I review my gifts, ponder them, and internalize how I'm using them. If I believe I'm neglecting a gift, I will ask myself questions and envision how I can improve.

It's much easier than you might think to forget how special we are. Knowing this to be true, you need to intentionally remind yourself to keep your gifts and talents at the forefront of your mind. This isn't arrogance. It's appreciation and gratitude for your God-given talents and abilities. Using, cultivating, and especially becoming your best self is the highest form of gratitude. It's always in the fulfillment of our purpose that we can do the most for the greatest number of people. It would be a shame if you didn't have enough belief in yourself to even try.

Now, pay close attention because this is important. It's tempting to think negatively about yourself—most of us do this from time to time, and sometimes too often. When you do, you aren't being respectful to yourself. Think of this . . . would you tear down or pick apart the young version of my daughter Taylor? She was an adorable little girl with long, blond hair and sparkling blue eyes. Imagine her creating stories with her father at bedtime. Sometimes they were outlandish, even ridiculous, and even as she grew a little older and started putting those stories to pen, they weren't always good. Would you criticize her for trying? Would you tell her they are bad, that she's not a good writer, that she should give up?

No, of course, you wouldn't! And of course, I didn't do that either.

Yet, we do that to ourselves all the time. We tell ourselves our attempts at things are stupid. We make up stories based on fears, of what people will think if we try or say when we do. We ridicule our looks and pull apart every aspect of ourselves with negative thinking. This must stop. It's not respectful. Instead, I want you to keep a promise that I learned from Johnny Covey's book *5 Habits to Lead from Your Heart*. You must promise to be respectful to yourself and to others. This means you accept your best, and your best is good enough. This means you recognize and stop any negative self-talk before it grows into the imaginary monster in your closet and sabotages your forward movement. We can't go about cultivating our talents and becoming what we are meant to become if the constant reel playing in our heads is negative.

So, say this to yourself and keep this promise: *"I promise to be respectful to myself and respect others."*

Do away with negative self-talk. There's no place for it in the Pretty Sister mindset. As soon as you recognize it's happening, catch yourself, and change your story at once. Give yourself grace, and as you do, you'll notice you can do it more generously with others as well. As you silence that critical self, you will slowly dissolve the critical tendencies you may have had toward others. As you give yourself grace, you'll offer more grace to those you connect with. You'll be able to become more of yourself, see your good parts, and let them shine as you do this.

After you take inventory and really figure out who you are and what makes you the "you" that you are, I promise you'll have everything it takes to lead a happy and fulfilling life of purpose and passion. To reiterate, you were designed to be great, to live happily, and to accomplish special things. If you haven't yet been living your life in a manner that utilizes your gifts to the fullest, it's not too late to start doing so now. It's never too late to figure out what makes you unique and use those gifts. You just need to get started.

Now is your opportunity.

THREE

YOU WERE MADE FOR THIS

This is your one life, so take the stage and play the lead role. You have everything it takes.

WHEN I WAS IN COLLEGE, I ATTENDED A SEMESTER ABROAD program in Israel. I lived in Jerusalem for four months, immersing myself in the study of Arabic and Jewish culture, language, history, and comparative religion. To say it was an amazing experience would be an understatement. It was life changing in every way at such a formative time in my development, and I was incredibly grateful for the opportunity to travel and study in such an immersive way.

On one of the first days at the Brigham Young University Jerusalem Center for Near Eastern Studies, which is housed in a magnificent building, while we were receiving orientation about various rules and safety protocols we were told a story that has always stayed with me. Apparently, to get a permit to build the Center, the school's sponsoring institution had to agree that students at the Center would adhere to certain rules of conduct. The primary requirement was that students would not engage in proselytizing while in Israel.

During that time of negotiating the permit, someone had asked "But what are we going to do about the light in their eyes?" knowing that the illumination of the divine inside each of us cannot be hidden.[1]

Hearing about the light in each person's eyes resonated with me. This added to my understanding of being "pretty." Now I also understood that I had a light, a spirit, that no one could diminish. You could see it through my eyes, so I needed to be sure to allow myself to be seen and also to look at others, in the eye, to truly see them. My light was sparkly and couldn't be diminished.

And so is yours! You have your own light that shines within you. I've grown to learn that we each can personally allow our light to shine (or not), depending on our level of confidence and courage. When we aren't feeling our best, either due to our thinking or due to experiences with others, we tend to dim our inner light. However, when we focus less on ourselves and more on others, our inner light shines brighter and we can impact others for good. Sometimes this happens through example, sometimes through direct interaction.

As women, we often hesitate to shine brightly, fearing we might outshine others or come across as boastful. However, it's essential to remember that our light isn't meant to dim the lights of others but to inspire and uplift them. By embracing our own brilliance, we help others see their own potential and encourage them to rise to their full capacity. When we shine, we create a ripple effect of positivity and empowerment, fostering an environment where everyone feels motivated to discover and share their unique gifts. Our light becomes a beacon, guiding and elevating those around us, rather than casting a shadow.

This light of ours has many purposes. One of the most important is to help guide us. We aren't helpless beings navigating life without direction. We have our own internal compass, our divine intuition, and an inner knowing that, if we listen and pay attention, will help us navigate our trials and lead us toward our purpose and passions. We'll talk more about how to use this inner voice for good later, but for now, know that we are meant to succeed and live a happy life, and we have the inner makings to do so. The problem is that we forget or stop paying attention or believing in our own abilities and belonging.

Pretty Sisters is a sisterhood to help resolve this. Over time, various symbols have been adopted into our Pretty Sister philosophy to remind us of our inner light, divine characteristics and the Pretty Sister mindset of thinking pretty. When my sisters and I first established this community in 2006, we launched with a line of Pretty Sister jewelry that included some of these symbols. We had a special bracelet and necklace, each featuring a silver circle with the word *DREAM* inscribed on it, from which was hanging the charms of a crown, a rose quartz stone, and a pearl. These charms hold special meaning and serve as a reminder of our shared values and aspirations.

The silver DREAM circle symbolizes our unity as sisters and the eternal nature of our bond. It represents the dreams that fuel our forward movement and the faith we have in our ability to live our purposes as individuals. The circle's unending shape is a testament to our continuous journey of growth and support for one another.

One particularly cherished symbol we give to each Pretty Sister is a crown. The crown symbolizes each sister's divine characteristics and royal nature. It serves as a reminder of our direct divine heritage, affirming that we are royal daughters of God. This symbol encourages us to embrace our inherent worth and recognize that we are entitled to blessings and prosperity directly related to our ability to live our lives according to our purpose.

Your purpose is what you were made for: *your life!*

The pearl represents the beauty that forms from adversity and trial. Just as a pearl develops from a grain of sand enduring pressure and time, we too become something soft, smooth, beautiful, and desirable through our experiences and challenges. The pearl reminds us that our struggles can lead to our greatest strengths and most exquisite qualities.

The rose quartz symbolizes each Pretty Sister's unique strength and individuality. Rose quartz is often called the Stone of Love and is associated with unconditional love, emotional healing, and self-compassion. For yoga practitioners, healers, and energy workers it is associated with the heart chakra, promoting harmony in relationships and encouraging self-love. Its rough edges and natural beauty remind us that we are all unique and strong, each beautiful in our own way. I included it in the necklace because the rose quartz encourages us to embrace our imperfections, knowing that they contribute to our distinct and valuable character.

The bracelet and necklace are intended to be more than just pieces of jewelry. They are tangible reminders, as well as symbolic reminders, of our Pretty Sister philosophy, encouraging us to dream, recognize our divine heritage, transform adversity into beauty, and celebrate our unique strengths. Together, they inspire us to live our lives with purpose, unity, and confidence, shining our light brightly and helping others to do the same.

As women who wear many hats and have numerous responsibilities, we may have the tendency to care for and nurture others well, while forgetting about ourselves and possibly even slipping into negative self-talk. While being excellent at fulfilling caregiving tasks for others is one of our important skills, neglecting ourselves is unwarranted and unhelpful. My experience as a wife, mother, and businesswoman tells me that we need reminders to help us not forget who we are, how special we are, and how important we are. Our well-being and presence matter! These symbols can serve as simple reminders to help us stay in a mindset that supports our growth and happiness.

When we remember how important we are, that God made us to be who we are and live our purpose, then we take better care of ourselves. It's easy to forget ourselves when we get busy with work, home, or community roles that demand our time and attention. If we allow this, we risk burnout and face challenges such as overwhelm, the allure of perfectionist thinking, or falling into comparisons or feelings of guilt and negativity. By prioritizing our well-being, we can avoid these pitfalls and thrive, allowing our inner light to shine brightly and positively impact those around us.

We Are Made to Accomplish Everything That We Can Imagine Ourselves Doing

When you understand that you have everything you need to be successful, because you were made for *this*—whatever you are dreaming of doing—I promise, you'll attempt to do more things. I love the question that Robert H. Schuller asks in his book *You Can Become the Person You Want to Be*, "What would you do if you knew you couldn't fail?"[2] I love it because, the only certain way to fail is not to even try. To sit it out. But how dull a life would that be?

Do you have a bucket list? Well, mine had an interesting addition: a triathlon. In theory, it sounded fantastic, but when reality hit, I discovered something crucial: I needed to learn how to swim properly.

Now, you might find this surprising, because I'm an avid water-skier and I genuinely love being in the water. I can tread water with the best of them, no problem there! Don't get me wrong; I can swim! But it's not the graceful, efficient style you'd want for a triathlon.

So, as a thirty-five-year-old adult, I made a decision that was a bit scary and somewhat embarrassing. I enrolled in swimming lessons to prepare for my race. I knew it was time to walk my talk. After all, I was always encouraging my kids to try new things, so I decided I needed to face my fear and dive in.

I remember my swim coach nicknamed me "pretty fingers" because she could spot my bright pink, painted nails poking out of the water whenever she needed to correct my stroke. Swimming lessons in the freezing Maine winter were less than enticing, and coming home with wet hair in the snowy chill wasn't exactly a treat. But hey, good things often come from stepping out of your comfort zone, even for adults.

Jumping into that pool felt like being a sinking ship, as I struggled to float gracefully. I even had to resort to wearing one of those awkward nose plugs because I couldn't stop myself from breathing through my nose. It wasn't a pretty sight, I admit.

But here's the thing: Doing something new, hard, and even a bit scary is incredibly rewarding, not just for our kids but for us adults, too. The day of the race was nerve wracking. I was pacing back and forth, feeling sick to my stomach. Swimmers enter the water in waves (no pun intended), so that there isn't a pileup. When my turn finally came, I started swimming, while chanting in my head, "Just keep swimming. Just keep swimming. What do we do when times get tough? We swim, we swim," thanks to Dory in *Finding Nemo!*

Then there was my dear friend Nicky, who signed up to do the race with me. She was a more experienced athlete and while our plan was to train together, she ended up being my trainer in every way. Our runs were like therapy sessions because we spent the whole time talking and counseling each other as friends do, and in addition, she'd keep me on pace. She would point up ahead and find a landmark and say, "OK, just run to that mailbox." Then, we'd do it, only to have her identify the next lamp post and say, "Now we are just running to that." With each new landmark as the goal, she'd get me through the training run every time.

A sprint triathlon, which is what I did that year, involves a half mile of swimming, 12.4 miles of biking, and 3.1 miles of running, in that order.

Three months after we began training, on race day, Nicky crouched at the edge of the pool, cheering me on. "You can do it, just one more lap, and you're almost there," she yelled, true to form. And she was right: I could do it! "I can do hard things" has always been my training motto, and I proved it that day. I conquered my fear and successfully completed the swimming portion of the triathlon. And I did the biking and the running, too. I did it all!

The immediate elation of accomplishment never loses its magic. Although it does require sacrifice and effort, the reward is absolutely worth it. Not only did I finish that race, but I went on to conquer even more challenges. I set goals for myself to do things that were even harder because I knew I could do them. In the process of embracing new challenges and getting them done, I got mentally tougher. I learned that pushing past my comfort zone was not only doable, but it consistently also would prove to be empowering.

When we confront our fears, rather than evading them—when we face them head on—we discover that we can achieve what we've set out to do. We learn to trust ourselves a little more and dare a little more. Consequently, we start counting on ourselves to be the creators of our dreams and realize that we really do have what it takes, despite what we may have thought previously.

Now, years later, as I look back on that triumphant swim I took during the triathlon, I'm reminded of the power of pushing through our fears and doubts. It's a lesson that extends far beyond the pool. Each of us faces our own challenges and opportunities, which are unique to us as individuals, and it's essential that we acknowledge and celebrate our small daily "wins" and bigger accomplishments along the way. Whether big or small, every achievement can be viewed as a stepping stone to a future filled with even greater successes.

So, please be sure to take a moment to acknowledge your victories, relish your hard-earned triumphs, and keep propelling yourself forward toward the amazing life destination you're striving to reach.

Your Physical, Spiritual & Emotional Health Are Key

Caring for your physical, spiritual, and emotional health is a vital factor in a vibrant, balanced, and purposeful life. When you understand how much they matter, I believe you will take better care of yourself. Regular exercise, a nutritious diet, and adequate sleep are cornerstones of physical health, ensuring that your body is strong and resilient. Prayer, meditation, pampering, and spending time in nature are equally important ways of nurturing your spiritual well-being.

Emotional health involves recognizing and honoring your feelings, seeking support when needed, and cultivating positive relationships. By prioritizing all three of these aspects of your health, you'll create a solid foundation for joy and fulfillment because they'll enable you to shine your brightest and uplift the people around you and accomplish everything you set out to do.

We must care for ourselves in all our aspects, but we typically only do this once we begin to love ourselves enough—which is based on our belief in our inherent worthiness, abilities, and being part of a divine design. Belief in a higher purpose for being alive causes us to treat ourselves with respect and also to learn to value our time, our bodies, our looks, and our very beingness. We begin to want the best for ourselves when we see that God made us this way, and who are we to disagree with God? This helps us realize that not only do we deserve care, but we can and must expect it.

Never forget that you are worthy of all the love and care you give to yourself.

By taking care of ourselves, we become the ultimate teachers to others, demonstrating how we are to be treated. Simply put, when we treat ourselves well, so will others. If we don't teach them through our own example, how will they ever know? How will they come to learn and respect us as Pretty Sisters unless we feel special and, through our actions, teach them?

When you fully understand this dynamic, you'll be able to realize that if people aren't treating you well it's either because you haven't taught them to respect you through your behavior or because their behavior is reflecting how they feel about themselves. People simply can't treat others well if they don't love themselves first.

Understanding these two possibilities can empower you to respond and free you from the shame of not feeling worthy. If you realize you haven't been feeling good about yourself and therefore haven't been taking care of your own needs, you can fix this. You can change your behavior, thus influencing those around you to change.

But if you know you are in a good place and can recognize that the disrespect is not sourced from you, but rather that the other person must not be in a place of self-love, then you can choose to influence the person and/or to set boundaries for them. Either way, you are in control of yourself, including your feelings and actions. They may not be able to treat or love anyone properly yet and will need to do some of their own inner work before you can expect more from them. This understanding is freeing because none of us should accept responsibility for others' actions—with the exception of very young children—ultimately, we only hold responsibility for ourselves.

Inevitably, someone, at some point in your life, will try to tear you down or will treat you poorly. It is critical when this kind of thing happens not to take it personally. Please know that the antagonism or meanness being expressed to you is not your fault. Remember that you have control over how you react. You can only control your own response, not another person's, and knowing or not knowing this is largely what affects your happiness. This knowledge should be empowering.

Please do your best not to let others dictate your worth. Truly, it's not up to them how you feel; it's up to you. As you begin to see yourself as a Pretty Sister and hold yourself in a place of worth, you'll become a protector of your well-being, just as you would guard a precious gem because that is what you are. Expect that type of protection, and guard yourself, and you will find that in return, others will value and protect you, too.

Four Self-Care Techniques to Help You Live Your Purpose

On the next few pages, I will describe four practices that will help you stay in tip-top Pretty Sister shape.

Self-Care Practice #1: Meditation

Meditation is a powerful self-care ritual that allows you to connect with your inner self and find peace amidst the chaos of daily life. By setting aside just a few minutes each day to sit quietly, breathe deeply, and focus on the present moment, you can reduce stress, improve your mental clarity, and enhance your overall well-being. Meditation can help you cultivate a sense of calm and balance by reminding you of your inner strength and the divine light within you. This practice is essential for maintaining your emotional and spiritual health, allowing you to approach each day with a clear mind and an open heart.

Self-Care Practice #2: Journaling

I recommend keeping a journal handy, in your purse or on your nightstand, or even using the notes application on your phone. At any time, you can take a moment to separate fact from fiction, master your thoughts, and get out of your head (where it's easy to get stuck) and into your heart, so you can much more easily move forward in the direction of your dreams.

Journaling is another essential self-care ritual that encourages self-reflection and personal growth. By writing down your thoughts, feelings, and experiences, you can gain valuable insights into your own life and identify patterns that may be holding you back. Journaling provides a safe space for you to express yourself freely and honestly, helping you to process emotions and develop a deeper understanding of your true self. This practice can also serve as a creative outlet, allowing you to explore your dreams and aspirations while fostering a sense of gratitude and positivity. Regular journaling can empower you to make more mindful choices and live a more fulfilling life.

Self-Care Practice #3: Pampering

Pampering yourself is a delightful and necessary part of self-care. Treating yourself to a luxurious lunch, a relaxing massage, or simply indulging in your favorite treats can do wonders for your mood and overall well-being. Surround yourself with beauty, whether it's fresh flowers, a new shade of pink lipstick, or a cozy blanket. These small acts of self-love remind you that you deserve to feel special and cherished. Pampering is not just about physical indulgence; it's about nurturing your soul and celebrating the unique beauty that is you. By making time for these little luxuries, you can recharge your energy and maintain a positive outlook on life.

Self-care Practice #4: Spending Time in Nature

There's something undeniably healing about being in nature. Whether it's feeling the warmth of the sun on your skin, breathing in fresh air, or taking in the beauty of a forest, a beach, or a mountain, nature has a way of grounding us and restoring our energy. Studies show that sunlight, especially in the morning, helps regulate your circadian rhythm, boosting your mood and improving your sleep. A simple walk outdoors can lower stress, improve focus, and elevate your sense of well-being.

To make the most of this practice, consider pairing your time in nature with connection. Go on a walk or hike with your girlfriends—multitasking at its finest! You'll get the benefits of movement, sunlight, and meaningful conversation all in one. Personally, I love skiing—whether it's gliding down snowy slopes in winter or carving through glassy water in summer. Nature offers endless ways to rejuvenate both body and soul, so find what lights you up and make it a regular part of your self-care routine. It's an investment in your joy, energy, and overall health.

Cultivate a Growth Mindset

If anything has been holding you back, today would be a beautiful time to venture forth and begin to tackle that challenging thing. Take the first tiny step to your objective and see how you feel about it. Then keep going. Release your fears, be patient in the process, and don't worry about others' opinions. One of my favorite sayings, which I made a point to teach my children, is "What other people think is none of your business." You'll come to realize that you are equipped to do just about anything you set your mind to, and yes, generally with a little help from your pretty sisters, like the support with my mental, emotional, and physical conditioning that my friend Nicky gave to me when we were training together for the triathlon.

Something changes when you do things you didn't think you could. A fundamental shift in belief occurs—you begin realizing you actually can do them! —that makes a transformational impact on your ability to attempt great things in other areas of your life, too.

When you fully understand that you have what it takes, that you were made for this life, and that you have a specific purpose, then you can do anything you decide you want to do.

Reading that statement, of course, you might think it promises you all the tangible things, talents, or resources you need, but that part isn't true. Each of us is born with a unique skill set, in unique circumstances, and then we have unique experiences and environments to navigate. The playing field, so to speak, isn't level or fair.

So how, then, can we all have "what it takes"?

If we look at my triathlon experience as an example, I certainly didn't begin with all the necessary skills. I had to learn how to swim properly, train for each component of the triathlon, and then put them all together and work up the stamina to complete the race on race day. I had raw potential but I needed a coach, a friend, and a cheerleader—not to mention the proper equipment—and training on how to use it. Training took time, grit, and determination.

Furthermore, I was raising five small children, so I needed help from my husband and other caretakers to watch them to give me time to fulfill this dream. I needed a lot of human support. I had to ask for and accept it, which can sometimes be very hard for a woman to do. But I learned to be open and honest with the people around me about my needs.

Embracing a growth mindset can be a game changer in our personal and professional lives. Unlike a fixed mindset, which believes that abilities and intelligence are static, a growth mindset thrives on the idea that new traits can be developed through dedication and hard work. Psychologist and Stanford University professor Carol Dweck, a pioneering researcher, explains, "The view you adopt for yourself profoundly affects the way you lead your life."[3]

By cultivating a growth mindset, you will open yourself up to new possibilities, seeing challenges as opportunities to learn and grow rather than insurmountable obstacles. By embracing this mindset, you will foster resilience, creativity, and a love for learning, which will empower you to achieve goal after goal, and continually improve in the process.

Remember, success is not about where you start but about how much and in what ways you grow along the journey. Embrace the power of a growth mindset and watch as your potential unfolds in ways you may never have imagined.

When we approach life with a growth mindset, we understand that while we may not currently have something, we can work to obtain it, whether through hard work or the pursuit of education and experience, or by networking. Whatever the challenge may be, we move forward with confidence in our ability to achieve.

Once you internalize this concept, you should have more respect for yourself. You can begin to see yourself as someone special—maybe a little rough around the edges, but a true pearl in the making.

Your Voice Matters

Have you ever felt hesitant to speak up? Maybe you've believed that your voice doesn't matter or struggled to find the courage to express your thoughts and feelings. You are not alone in experiencing this internal struggle, as many women grapple with similar challenges when it comes to self-expression. I know because I've been there.

When I was growing up, I had the privilege of having an *amazing* grandfather in my life. He commanded respect and admiration from everyone around him. Not only was he a highly successful businessman with an Ivy League education, but he also possessed an abundance of wisdom and kindness. He was, in many ways, a spiritual giant. People revered him, and whenever he spoke, it was as though pearls of wisdom were falling from his lips.

But here's the catch: My grandfather was a man of few words. He didn't believe in wasting breath on frivolous chatter. It was said that he didn't say anything unless it was worth saying, and when he did speak, you knew that it carried weight. His presence was commanding, and his words, though impactful, were few.

Growing up in the shadow of such a remarkable figure, I unconsciously adopted the belief that I should only speak when I had something incredibly profound to say. I wanted to emulate my grandfather's wisdom, kindness, and success. Consequently, I became a quiet observer, carefully choosing my words and only speaking when I felt absolutely certain that my contribution was worth hearing.

However, this approach didn't serve me as well as I had hoped. As a child, I couldn't fully comprehend the complexities of the adult world, and I placed immense pressure on myself only to speak when I had a nugget of wisdom to share. This self-imposed silence led to hesitation, missed opportunities, and a persistent fear of saying the wrong thing.

As I've matured and gained life experience, I've come to realize that my past belief system about speaking, shaped by my grandfather's example, had its limitations. I've learned that it's okay not to have all the answers and that my voice doesn't have to carry the weight of the world's wisdom. Imperfect words, spoken spontaneously from the heart, can be just as meaningful—if not more so, on occasion—than carefully crafted, planned statements.

So, why do I share this personal information? Because I believe many of us harbor a fear of speaking up, rooted in our past experiences and role models. Also many of us worry too much about what other people think. Although we may question whether our voices matter or if our contributions are valuable, the truth is that we all have unique perspectives, experiences, and insights to share.

For this reason alone, your voice, just as it is, holds intrinsic value.

It's time to recognize that your voice matters, that you matter, and that your perspective matters. Your voice is a gift to the world. While past experiences may have shaped your beliefs about speaking up, it's within your power to let go of this limitation and gather the courage to speak up. In this way, you will let your light shine brighter. Speaking up is one of the ways you can empower yourself and get your needs met. Your voice can create opportunities for you to uplift and inspire others through your authenticity and vulnerability.

And, hey, this journey of finding our voices and building our self-belief is where sisterhood plays a crucial role. Your Pretty Sisters can be your allies in boosting your confidence and encouraging you to share your thoughts, even when they may not seem profoundly perfect. Together with your friends and family, you can create a supportive environment where everyone's voice is celebrated, knowing that each contribution adds value to the collective journey of personal growth and dream realization.

Never Overlook the People Around You

In the world of belief, there's an extraordinary force that we haven't fully explored yet, and that's the power of sisterhood. Your Pretty Sisters, whether they are biological sisters, close friends, or kindred spirits you've met on your journey in life, can play a significant role in boosting your self-worth and confidence. In fact, one of the most profound ways sisterhood manifests is in the support we give each other to speak up and share our voices.

Isn't it fascinating how our childhood experiences can shape our beliefs and behaviors, often in unexpected ways? My story about my amazing grandfather illustrates the profound impact of role models and the beliefs they instill in us. This phenomenon isn't limited to childhood, however. Throughout our lives, the people we know and admire influence us.

As we embrace the power of speaking up and sharing our unique voices, we must not overlook this important aspect of human connection. We need to look up from the narrow focal points in our daily routines and truly see each other. Lifting our gaze to connect with those around us can profoundly impact our external world. When we take the time to make eye contact and acknowledge one another, we foster a sense of belonging and community that enriches our lives.

Back in junior high, I had a teacher who once told our class something that has stuck with me ever since. She said that when most kids walk down the hallway, they tend to keep their gaze fixed on the floor. Rarely, she added, would someone make eye contact with the people they passed by. "It's just human nature," she claimed.

Her challenge to us was simple: Observe this phenomenon for ourselves, and if we dared, break the pattern by keeping our heads up, looking people in the eye, and maybe even offering them a friendly smile. I was in the sixth grade at the time and a bit on the shy side, but undeniably curious about whether she was right. So, I decided to accept her challenge.

I began to pay closer attention to the hallway interactions at school, and sure enough, my teacher's words held true. Most kids did indeed keep their eyes glued to the floor, or they'd look away when someone approached. Even those who initially made eye contact would often divert their gaze as the distance closed between them. It was a universal tendency, it seemed. And I'm sure, in our age of electronic devices, the tendency to look down at a screen is even bigger.

In my case, I decided to embrace the challenge of looking up and making eye contact with other students. It was an eye-opening experience (pun intended), and it marked a significant turning point for me. This conscious effort to truly see people—strangers, acquaintances, and friends alike—became a lifelong habit that would ultimately shape my life in profound ways. I was grateful to have had a teacher who encouraged me to take this step toward greater confidence and human connection. Little did I know that a simple act could become such a powerful force for positive change in my life.

The gift of looking someone in the eye is immeasurable. When you make eye contact, you're acknowledging another person's existence, and they, in turn, recognize yours. It's a fundamental form of connection that's often overlooked in our fast-paced, digitally driven world. As I entered the workforce after college, this habit of making eye contact and engaging with people became even more vital.

Instead of strolling through school hallways, I found myself riding elevators and working in high-rise buildings. Have you ever broken the unwritten elevator code by looking at the people around you? Because I am a bit of a maverick and intensely curious about human behavior, sometimes, just for fun, I'd stand facing away from the elevator doors, daring to be different. The result was a whole new perspective—an understanding that we aren't solitary beings navigating this world independently.

We are living alongside one another, sharing this journey with people, each of whom is unique and important. These individuals have eyes—bright, expressive eyes—that represent their light inside. In people's eyes you can see that they yearn for connection, a friendly smile, or a brief, but meaningful glance that conveys "We're all in this together." I got all that from looking directly at people. From letting them see me and also see that I could see them.

If you've been missing out on human connection, I challenge you to *look up* and see who you're sharing this world with. Connect. Smile. Make a difference by lifting them up with a kind word or gesture. In doing so, you'll brighten someone else's day and you'll also gain the confidence and joy that come from genuine human connection. Acknowledging those around you could be a beautiful way to start your day. For me, it's a practice that fosters a sense of unity and shared purpose.

YOU WERE MADE FOR THIS, MADE TO UPLIFT, CONNECT, and bring light to others. Every smile, kind word, and act of acknowledgment reinforces the truth that you belong here, that your presence matters, and that the world is better because you're in it. When you step into this role with intention, you'll realize that deep, meaningful connections aren't just something you seek, they're also something you were designed to create.

BELIEF #1: I AM PRETTY

PRETTY SISTER PINKY PROMISE

AT THE END OF EACH BELIEF SECTION, YOU'LL BE ASKED TO make a Pretty Sister Pinky Promise. Since this is a serious commitment, you need to know what you are getting into.

My daughters and nieces grew up learning and living the spoken and unspoken rules about being a Pretty Sister starting when they were little girls. They knew how important the title was to me and my sisters, and understood the code of conduct necessary to claim the name, which no one wanted to lose rights to. This was helpful as a parent because when any of the girls were caught demonstrating less than desirable behavior we could simply say, "That's not a Pretty Sister thing to do," and the behavior would instantly change. It was a secret family language or code to which all the girls understood how to adhere.

Much to my delight, my daughters and their cousins added to the Pretty Sister tradition. As little girls do, they came up with their own way of knowing if someone was telling the truth or of swearing someone to secrecy. This method, which me and my sisters and our friends later adopted, too, became known as the Pretty Sister Pinky Promise. If one girl was serious about an agreement, she would make another engage in this ritual of commitment. There was a handshake, kisses exchanged, and words spoken.

It went like this: While crossing your arms and interlocking pinky fingers, the girls would both say, "I Pretty Sister pinky promise, crosses don't count," then say, "Kiss, kiss," while exchanging side kisses to each cheek to seal the deal. There was no going back; this ritual was an enacted promise.

Now it's time for you to make some promises to yourself, in the Pretty Sister manner, so there's no going back. To prepare you to do this, at the end of each Belief section, you'll have the opportunity to do some exercises that will help you internalize the belief you are being asked to adopt. There's a three-step process, and you can go through it as many times as needed until you are ready to make the commitment.

The process takes you through Spilling your TEA—examining your thoughts, emotions, and actions. This activity is based on the philosophy that we first have a thought that dictates a feeling, which then results in an action. We talked about this pattern previously in Chapter 1. It is a powerful framework for managing your thoughts and emotions, allowing you to take control of your reactions and shape your experiences more positively. This model emphasizes the interconnectedness of thoughts, emotions, and actions. By understanding and applying this process, you can create a more intentional and fulfilling life.

T (thoughts): The process begins with your thoughts. What you think directly influences how you feel. For example, if you think, "I can't do this," you might feel discouraged or anxious. Whereas if you shift that thought to "I *can* do this," you will feel more capable and willing to make the attempt to take action.

E (emotions): Your thoughts shape your emotions. Positive thoughts lead to positive feelings, while negative thoughts can lead to negative emotions. By becoming aware of your feelings, you can start to understand the root thoughts behind them. This awareness allows you to change your thoughts and regulate your emotions more effectively, leading to a healthier state of being.

A (actions): Your emotions drive your actions. When you feel positive and empowered, you're more likely to take productive and beneficial actions to accomplish different objectives. Conversely, when you feel negative emotions, you are more likely to engage in actions that do not serve your best interests in the long run. By consciously choosing to reframe negative thoughts as positive thoughts and learning how to regulate and manage your emotions, you can deliberately steer your actions toward the achievement of your goals and toward improving your overall well-being.

Being intentional is a skill you can learn. The information in this book is designed to aid you in developing this ability to the fullest extent. By establishing a positive TEA time practice, you can break any cycle of negative thinking that is impeding your progress and foster an optimistic, proactive approach to life. This pattern helps you to recognize and challenge unhelpful thoughts, regulate your emotions, and take purposeful actions. Embrace this powerful technique for self-reflection and you'll find yourself thinking pretty, which will make you better equipped to handle life's challenges and more able to seize the opportunities you get from now on.

To begin the process of strengthening your mindset, you will be asked to Spill the TEA about the belief that was covered in the section you just read. You may have many thoughts about this belief, ranging from negative to positive. It is normal to have conflicting thoughts, a state that is often referred to as *double-mindedness*, and this technique will help you uncover your internal contradictions.

To get clarity, you will be guided to go from your head to your heart. Sometimes we can get stuck in our heads, overanalyzing what we should do. While the cognitive capacity for logic and reasoning is important, when mental activity is excessive like this, our thoughts can be too fear-based, protective, and cautionary.

On the flip side, when we feel like we should be doing certain things without analyzing the reasoning for doing them, we can make poor decisions.

However, when we combine thinking from our hearts with reasoning, our thoughts become purposeful and grounded in our values and the meaning of why we are doing what we are doing. Heart-centered reasoning is based on faith, courage, and confidence.

Since we all experience a range of thinking, it's important to be able to recognize our thoughts and wisely choose which ideas to believe and which to reject. To paraphrase James Allen's words in his classic self-help book *As a Man Thinketh,* "As a woman thinketh in her heart, so is she."[1]

You have much more control over your mindset than you may realize. Now is your chance to practice managing your thoughts to create more of what you truly desire. Embrace this opportunity to shape your mindset and, consequently, your life.

You can go through Spilling your TEA as many times as you'd like. It may take more time initially, but eventually you'll get to where you can do the steps quickly to clear out mental blockages as needed and move forward.

Begin Spilling the TEA with thoughts pouring from your head—your worries, concerns, fears, and the like, related to the belief statement. Then you'll follow that through the question of how that makes you feel, and then consequently what you do when you feel that way.

Then with each thought—and this is the fun part—flip it to thinking from your heart. So, imagine now that from your heart, when letting go of those fears, what would the opposite thought be? Write down what comes to mind and then follow that through to how it makes you feel when thinking that way (with courage, confidence, and love) and what you would do. Notice the difference. This is how you Spill the TEA and turn negative patterns into powerful and life-changing ones!

Fact or Fiction?

To help you pick the thoughts to run through the process, when a thought pops into your head, ask yourself whether it's fact or fiction. Once you get smart about this, you can gain some control.

It's amazing how creative our minds are, especially in their attempts to protect us. That's our brain's primary job: self-preservation. Naturally, then, we come up with all kinds of crazy thoughts, most of which are fictitious, and we too easily believe them and allow them to influence our feelings and actions. For instance, it's common to get embarrassed and think, *Everybody's looking at me,* when in reality, that's rarely true.

Most people are consumed in their own thoughts and rarely paying attention to what anyone around them is doing. Our brains tell us we're being watched to protect us, and it typically works, but it also keeps us from daring to do more.

A key question to help you test reality is: Is this idea fact or fiction? You can unlock so much potential once you know this hack and simply filter out the fiction and begin thinking more facts.

It's TEA Time: Spill the TEA

Run through the Pretty Sister Pinky Promise process now that you've read the first three chapters, which were designed to help you internalize that you are pretty. If you need more space, pull out a pen and notepad.

When I say, "I am pretty," I THINK: _____
_____
_____
_____
_____

When I think *that*, it makes me FEEL: _____
_____
_____
_____

When I feel *that*, it makes me ACT: _____
_____
_____
_____

Afterward, ask yourself: "Is there anything else I am thinking?" Repeat the steps. Run through this process as many times as needed until you are thinking from your heart with courage, love, and confidence.

Once you feel ready, move on to make the promise.

Make the Promise

Find a fellow Pretty Sister (this can be your mom, a sister, a friend, or someone from the online Pretty Sister community), and make the following promise to her. You can also make it to yourself in the mirror.

*"I believe that I am pretty.
I Pretty Sister pinky promise—
and crosses don't count!"*

Way to go, girl, you did it! Now keep on believing, and know that you have a community of Pretty Sisters that are committed to helping remind you of how pretty you are!

BELIEF #2
YOU ARE NOT ALONE

You were never meant to walk this journey alone.
Love, friendship, and divine support surround you—
sometimes you just have to open your heart to see this.

FOUR

YOU HAVE DIVINE GUIDANCE

*"Trust in the Lord with all thine heart;
and lean not unto thine own understanding.
In all thy ways acknowledge him,
and he shall direct thy paths."*

PROVERBS 3: 5–6

AS NORMALLY HAPPY PEOPLE, IT CAN BE TOUGH WHEN life seems to be crumbling around us. The truth is, this crumbling feeling arises when our expectations are unmet. I've always found it useful to say, "It's better to aim for the stars and miss than to aim for a pile of manure and hit." But let's get real. It can hurt when life doesn't meet our expectations. What happens when we feel like our bullseye has landed us right in the middle of the manure?

It was one of those years in life—yes, I said *years*, because I've had a few tough ones—made up of days, weeks, and months that felt like I was wading through the Dead Sea with ten-pound weights strapped to each of my legs. Yet in those days, there was no choice but to move forward. (Having swum in the Dead Sea, I can report that the water is so filled with salt and other minerals that it makes swimmers extremely buoyant, so I know that adding weights would make it feel nearly impossible to move forward.)

Why was movement essential? During those particular years, I was the mother of five young kids. Also I was a wife, a business owner, and a leader in my church and community. All day, every day, I had places to be and people counting on me. Yet, I felt on the brink of collapse, as my life wasn't turning out as I had expected. Life wasn't perfect. People disappointed me. Burdens felt too heavy to bear. And because I couldn't be everything to everyone, I often felt like I was falling short—truthfully, I *did* frequently fall short.

How do you reconcile unpleasant feelings like disappointment and burden when you also firmly believe that life should be happy, and you're committed to raising your kids in a loving home, giving them the childhood of their dreams? The gap between where you want to be and where you are in regard to a particular intention or desire can be hard to reconcile. The difference can seem as wide as the Grand Canyon.

It was on one of a certain type of day when I spent more time than seemed reasonable in my closet, hiding from the chaos, and was drenched in a puddle of tears. I was praying and pleading to God for help. I felt so alone, and in many ways, I was. Dave and I had chosen to live in Maine, clear across the country from our relatives. Sure, I had friends and a church community, but during a crisis and being as private as I was, the separation from my family had a particular sting. I needed direction and hope, and the ability to keep moving forward amid what seemed like insurmountable challenges—ones I felt inadequate to face or overcome by myself.

That summer day in August, a large package arrived at my door. I examined it, unsure of its contents. This was long before we had the constant arrival of Amazon packages—back when we actually had to go to stores to shop. Getting a package was special.

When I opened the box, I was surprised to find a large, framed antique picture inside it of a little girl. Attached to the frame was a card. As I read it, more tears began to flow. I realized I was looking at my namesake, Callie Catherine Stephens.

My aunt Cynthia Thomas, who sent me the photo, had written a note explaining that when she was cleaning out her home in preparation for a move, she'd decided that I should be the keeper of this particular family heirloom, since I was Callie Catherine Stephen's namesake. She had no idea of the trials I was going through or the amount of time I'd spent on my knees lately, praying for support. Yet, mysteriously, this picture arrived on my doorstep at exactly the right moment.

I hung the picture across from my bed so I would wake up each day seeing the other Callie there, watching over me. From that moment on, I no longer felt alone. I felt the presence not only of Callie Catherine, my great-grandmother, but also of other ancestors, watching over me, helping me, and providing the divine assistance I needed to keep moving forward despite the occasional overwhelming feelings of despair. It's amazing to me how much comfort and strength is provided by knowing we aren't alone—knowing that people on earth and beyond are there to help us in our times of need.

This wasn't the only time I felt my great-grandmother's presence. As a little girl, I'd lived with Grammy (Callie Catherine's nickname) during the last few years of her life. I knew her as a wrinkled, white-haired gentlewoman who loved to be surrounded by family. I adored snuggling with her and running errands for her, as she was mostly restricted to being seated in her chair. She would call out for me with requests like "Callie, run and get me my medicine" or "Callie, I feel a draft, shut that door." To this day, all the great-grandkids laugh about the commands we knew to respond to quickly.

Before Grammy passed, as we gathered around her bed to say our goodbyes, I remember my sister Martha asking her to give us a sign from the other side so we'd know she was there. Although Grammy could barely speak, she seemed to nod in agreement when Martha suggested she flicker the lights. At her funeral, the lights flickered. From that time on, we knew

Grammy was keeping her promise with her own sense of humor, watching over us and flickering the lights when she could. There have been several sacred moments among her posterity since her passing when Grammy's presence has been unmistakably felt.

As her namesake, and being in possession of the precious family heirloom picture, to this day I feel the blessing of my name and have awareness of the special guidance it brings. Even though I've since moved across the country, the picture still resides in my home on the wall beside my bed. I see and feel Grammy's divine assistance daily and will be eternally grateful for it.

A special framed piece of artwork hangs beside Grammy's photo, representing my mother's parents, Francis and Virgil James. Francis was Grammy's daughter and, truly, the person I've grown up trying to emulate more than any other. She was fun, beautiful, kind, talented, and loved hosting parties. She always gave the impression that she loved life and life loved her.

Due to my parents' split when I was a youngster, my mother moved us across the country to Utah, where we lived with my grandparents throughout my junior high school and high school years. This intergenerational home, which included Grammy for those few years I mentioned, before her passing, presented some challenges for everyone involved, but it was mostly a blessing. I grew up cherishing my family and deeply respecting my ancestors. And I learned the value of family members taking care of one another in a loving way.

There was so much love in that household. My grandfather was a devoted husband and a true romantic. He gave my grandmother a special love poem for one of their early anniversaries, which hung by the side of their bed throughout their marriage. I remember sneaking into their room as a little girl to read it. It became my daydream as I contemplated my future love and marriage.

Somebody Cares by Edgar A. Guest (1887)

Somebody cares for you, cares so much
that the heart grows glad
at your slightest touch;

And the sound of your voice
and the sight of your smile
Make all my burdens and cares worthwhile.

Somebody cares for you, bye and bye
when the years roll on,
you will know it's I;

Then, looking back
oe'r the road we've fared,
You'll see how much for you
SOMEBODY CARED...

In my youthful naivete, this kind of love seemed both unflawed and perfect. Life has a way of correcting such beliefs as we mature, and I've learned that such love is achievable, but only if it has been strengthened through trials and challenges.

I was present when my grandfather passed away from leukemia and again when my grandmother passed from breast cancer. Both experiences were sacred, emblematic of the miraculous feeling of life passing from one sphere to another, mirroring the feeling I had at the birth of my five children. Life and death share miraculous qualities, being divinely appointed moments where heaven and earth briefly collide.

When Grandmother Francis died, the one heirloom I asked for was their love poem, which, much to my delight, no one else claimed, so it ended up in my possession. Like my grandmother, it has always hung by my bedside as a testament to the endurance of true love. I like to think it's been an anchor, helping me hold on to the ideals it expresses, even at moments when it has felt hard or impossible. These words and my memories of my grandparents' bond have been my guiding light. Even though my grandparents have been gone from this earth for a long time, their presence has always been very much with me, guiding me daily. I've just had to pay attention to realize that I'm never alone.

In quiet moments, when I feel like I'm carrying the weight of the world alone, I find solace in the pictures on my wall—especially the one of my great-grandmother as a little girl, her eyes sparkling with the promise of a future she couldn't yet imagine. When I look at that photograph, I'm reminded that I'm never truly alone because her spirit offers me a gentle nudge. I imagine her guiding me with silent wisdom. Nearby is the framed poem my grandfather gave to my grandmother, a testament to their enduring love and the boundless possibilities it symbolized.

And in the center between the photo and the poem, completing this meaningful trio, hangs a framed motto that sets the tone for my day: "Make Your Dreams Happen." It's not just a phrase; it's a call to action. I purposely placed it between these two heirloom pictures because I believe my ancestors are cheering me on, reminding me that I am capable, that I have the power to turn my dreams into reality. It's the first thing I see each morning, a daily nudge to step forward with purpose, knowing that faith, determination, and the support of those who came before me are all working in my favor. Dreams don't just happen—we create them.

These mementos aren't mere wall decorations. To me, they are like friends whose love and encouragement are woven into every challenge and triumph I face. Their presence turns my journey into a shared adventure, filled with timeless warmth and inspiration that makes every step feel like a step taken together.

You Are a Child of God

Throughout my life, I have felt myself receiving guidance and support from spirits on the other side, based on my deep understanding that, like my ancestors, I am a child of God. As such, I have divine attributes. This knowledge, along with my belief in God's unconditional love for me, has been a constant guidepost. This means God cares about me and all the little details of my life, providing me with heavenly support.

These particular beliefs have been a part of me since childhood, but it wasn't until several years ago that I truly appreciated them as a unique perspective which I am blessed to have. A new friend came to my house to help organize rooms prior to putting my house up for sale. While working in my laundry room, she picked up a pillowcase with the hand-drawn words "I Am a Child of God" on it. Ali, who lost her father at a young age and grew up without a knowledge of our loving Heavenly Father, looked at me with tears in her eyes and said, "I can only imagine how different my life would be now if I had known this my whole life." She was going through a difficult divorce and felt very alone. Her tears spoke to the power of the universal truth of being a child of God and the profound impact it can have on our lives.

Understanding that you are a child of God can be more than a comforting notion. This profound truth could reshape your entire existence if you embraced it. Recognizing yourself as a beloved child of God is a way to open the door in your heart to a deep, unshakeable sense of worth and belonging. This insight will anchor you in the understanding that you are cherished beyond measure, fueling a confidence that no challenge or setback can erode. Knowing yourself as a child of God means that His love and support are always within reach, ready to guide and uplift you through life's myriad experiences.

The divine connection is not a distant or abstract concept but a tangible reality accessible to you through personal revelation and intuition. Each of us has the ability to tap into our divine guidance, whether through quiet reflection and prayer, or spontaneously in moments of deep insight. Such moments of personal revelation act as direct lines of communication with God, which is providing clarity and direction when you need it most. It's in these sacred exchanges that you can receive inspiration and encouragement that will steer you through life's complexities.

Moreover, you're not alone in your spiritual journey; angelic supports are there to assist and comfort you. These celestial beings, often unseen, nonetheless deeply felt, are sent as companions and guardians, helping to guide your path and protect you from harm. Their presence reinforces the understanding that divine help is always available, not just from above but also through the everyday miracles and serendipities that touch your life. When you embrace your identity as a child of God, you open yourself to a network of heavenly support that offers love, wisdom, and reassurance, ensuring that you are never truly alone on your journey.

The Gift of Personal Revelation

Learning to recognize, listen to, and follow your inner guidance is a profound journey of aligning with the divine light within you. As a daughter of our loving Heavenly Father, you have a unique connection to personal revelation—a divine gift that illuminates your path and helps you navigate life with purpose and clarity. This inner guidance is a manifestation of the light bestowed upon you, reflecting your true values, desires, and instincts.

To begin the process of revelation, it is essential to create moments of stillness and reflection, allowing yourself the chance to tune in to the whispers of inspiration from a higher source. Practices like prayer, meditation, and quiet contemplation can help you connect with the divine guides and celestial beings here to help you discern a path that closely aligns with your heavenly heritage.

Listening to your inner guidance involves trusting the personal revelations you receive and distinguishing them from external pressures and fears. Your Heavenly Father's love means that the insights you gain through prayer and introspection are meant to lead you toward fulfillment and joy. This requires paying close attention to how different choices resonate with your spirit and recognizing the peace and affirmation that come from following divine direction. Your inner light serves as a beacon guiding you through life's complexities and ensuring that you stay aligned with your true, divine purpose.

Following this divine guidance means courageously stepping onto the path laid out for you, even when it diverges from conventional expectations or involves challenges. It is a testament to your faith and trust in your Heavenly Father's plan for you. Embracing your path involves making decisions that reflect your divine nature, truly seeing yourself as a Pretty Sister, and pursuing what truly resonates with your soul.

Following guidance is a practice. Nobody is perfect. As you practice, you'll become more skillful and will find that your ability to receive and act upon personal revelation grows stronger. Over time, you will navigate life with greater confidence, authenticity, and alignment with your Heavenly Father's loving intentions.

Equally important, recognizing yourself as a daughter of God enhances your ability to be a compassionate friend and support system for others. When you understand that everyone you meet is a beloved child of God, it fosters profound empathy and understanding toward those around you. You begin to see others through the lens of divine love, appreciating their intrinsic worth and offering support with greater kindness and patience. This perspective transforms your interactions, allowing you to extend the same grace and encouragement you receive from divine sources to your friends and loved ones. By embodying this understanding, you will become a conduit of divine love and support, creating a ripple effect that enriches the lives of those around you and builds a community grounded in mutual respect and compassion.

This is truly the essence of being a Pretty Sister and thinking pretty.

AS THIS CHAPTER CLOSES, I HOPE YOU FEEL A DEEP reassurance that we are never alone. The tender connections we share with those who have gone before us, the sacred gift of personal revelation, and the constant help of our loving Heavenly Father remind us that we are profoundly supported in this journey of life. Their love and guidance are woven into the fabric of our existence, offering strength, comfort, and clarity when we need it most.

But let us not forget the beautiful gift of those who surround us now—our friends, family, and relationships that uplift and sustain us. Through the love and kindness of these earthly angels, we often feel God's divine assistance in the most tangible ways. When a friend offers a listening ear, when family rallies in times of need, or when we are simply held in the embrace of someone who cares, we feel God's love manifest through their actions. These connections are His way of reminding us that He is always near. Through our friendships and our connections with our Pretty Sisters, we feel this love and divine support.

It is through all of these gifts—our ancestors, divine guidance, God's love, and the support of those closest to us—that we truly come to understand we are not alone. This knowledge buoys us up, giving us the strength to endure hardships, overcome challenges, and embrace the joy that life offers along the way. We are surrounded by love, seen and unseen, and with this understanding, we can move forward with faith, hope, and a heart full of gratitude.

FIVE

SHE'S PRETTY, TOO

Real beauty is found not only in self-love, but in honoring the beauty you see in others. Embrace and celebrate your friends' beauty, for it enhances your own.

IN HIGH SCHOOL, I HAD A TIGHT-KNIT GROUP OF GIRLfriends. My older sisters called us Callie and the Beauty Queens, and we didn't mind. My friends all knew about my nickname from my sisters and were totally fine being adopted into the Pretty Sister tribe. While we were all doing our best to be pretty inside and out, we had one particular friend, September, who was undeniably beautiful. Her reputation for being a knockout preceded her, not only because of her unusual name (she was named after the month she was born), but also because of her physical beauty. All the guys wanted to date her, and it was common for her to be asked out to our own school dances and to the dances of all the other schools in the valley.

Let's face it, during high school, self-esteem is tricky and anything but solid for most girls. The tendency is to want to be beautiful, fit in, and be known as popular. It's natural to want to belong, and it's also normal to have wavering confidence at this age as personalities and maturity are being developed. Adolescents are trying to figure out who they are, and social pressures and experiences are all a part of this development. This was no different for me growing up than it is now. However, the landscape drastically changes over time according to developing social norms and technology.

I dare say it is getting harder and harder to be a teen, and there's plenty of social proof to back up that statement—although this book is not about that. The trap most girls fall into is the flawed thinking that if one girl is popular or beautiful, it somehow takes away from another's beauty or status. This contributes to a competitive landscape, one that far too often doesn't foster kindness; instead, meanness ensues. This is contrary to everything I grew up believing, thanks to my kind sisters who created a world for me in which everyone was thought to be pretty. This was normal thinking to me and was to be celebrated, not torn down.

So naturally, when September moved into the neighborhood during the eighth grade and was, well, extremely pretty, that wasn't threatening for me—it was something I was naturally drawn to admire. We became fast friends and have been ever since, now going on thirty-eight years. What truly drew me to her wasn't her beauty; it was her kindness. She was sweet and thoughtful and pretty from the inside out, which was really what I admired. The fact that she was beautiful on the outside was just icing on the cake, and an advantage I learned was useful.

I told you, boys wanted to be where she was, so guess what that meant? They naturally wanted to be with me, too, then, since September and I were best friends. It worked to my advantage to have a beautiful friend. I didn't have to resent her for it; I learned to lead with it. I embraced her beauty, and it didn't have to diminish mine.

This concept is often lost on women of all ages, especially young women. In 2004, the movie *Mean Girls* came out. I hated the title, so I refused to watch the movie. I hated everything the concept of "mean girls" stood for and wanted so badly for girls to view themselves as pretty and understand at a deep level that kindness and sisterhood are such a better way than being mean to one another. Having a young daughter at the time, I gave it a lot of thought. And I know this consideration was why I began sharing Pretty Sisters more openly: I wanted girls to think differently and remember who they are designed to be, which is not meanspirited.

For a few years, my sisters and I put on annual cruises and shared Pretty Sisters newsletters as our tribe grew. However, I found that the demands of raising my five little kids slowed me down in my Pretty Sisters ambitions. While I continued in the Pretty Sisters lifestyle with my family and close friends, sharing more outwardly whenever I could, my bigger dreams of spreading the message were put on hold for a season.

Until the new *Mean Girls* movie came out in 2024. The title alone sparked a fire in me. The same feelings of revolution surfaced, and this time, I felt a strong determination to be a voice that protests girls being mean and promotes kindness, unity, and sisterhood. Now, with twenty years of experience raising my three daughters to think pretty, I have absolute confidence and certainty that being a Pretty Sister is better than being mean.

I believe we have to adopt a new mindset, one where we allow all girls to be pretty. It's not me or you, us or them. It's not all or no one—it's everyone. We can embrace each person for her unique qualities and contributions and see them for who they are. We can allow everyone to shine and, by doing so, give ourselves permission to shine. We can be inclusive, inviting, and respectful, and it begins one Pretty Sister at a time.

The Comparative Thinking Trap

It's a common trait for women to engage in comparative thinking. We often find ourselves measuring ourselves against others, whether it's in appearance, achievements, or life circumstances. This tendency is influenced by biological, social, and psychological factors. Biologically, women's brains are wired for holistic thinking, considering multiple perspectives simultaneously. Socially, we are raised in environments that emphasize relationships and social connections, fostering a natural inclination to compare experiences. Psychologically, our brains categorize information based on past experiences, leading to comparative assessments.

However, as Theodore Roosevelt wisely noted, "Comparison is the thief of joy."[1] This quote underscores the danger of excessive comparative thinking, urging us to focus on self-acceptance and self-love instead. It's a reminder to cultivate a healthy self-esteem rooted in authenticity and compassion, rather than striving to meet unrealistic standards or measuring ourselves against others' achievements.

Roosevelt's words resonate deeply with me, especially in safeguarding my happiness. I'm steadfast in nurturing my joy, and one vital practice is steering clear of comparisons with others. Don't get me wrong; I do observe what others are accomplishing, but not to assess my worth against theirs. My purpose is entirely different—I seek inspiration.

When I look at the achievements of others, it's not about sizing myself up against them; it's about discovering what's possible. If they can do it, why not me? Well, maybe not right away or with the same finesse, but I know I have a shot, even if it feels a bit like the optimism of the two bros in *Dumb and Dumber*.

I'm sure you've faced moments of hesitation because someone else seemed to be excelling at what you aspire to do—better, faster, with more likes or followers. It's easy to fall into the trap of thinking there's no space for you or that you won't measure up, or fearing what people might say if you try.

These are all common narratives that often play out in our minds. Trust me, I've been there too. The important thing is realizing you're not alone in these thoughts, nor will you be the last. In today's digital age, where we can easily see what everyone else is doing, it's even more tempting to compare ourselves to what might seem like our competition.

But when you stop viewing others as competitors and begin to let their presence inspire you to step up, it's a game changer.

Repeat after me: *"If they can do it, so can I!"*

When you see others pursuing what you desire, don't let jealousy, anger, or criticism cloud your vision. Instead, let yourself be inspired.

Especially when you witness others showing up imperfectly, but doing their best, offer them the same compassion you'd hope to receive. It's the courage to show up imperfectly and the resilience to disregard external opinions that propel you toward success. The path may be winding, with its ups and downs, but that's perfectly okay. Stay on course, drawing inspiration from those who've dared to pave the way before you.

Let their journeys ignite your own, and in doing so, feel a surge of joy as you begin to envision the limitless possibilities ahead. Remember, you've got this, girl!

When nurturing the sisterhood we aspire to support, one of the most crucial lessons we can impart is the value of refraining from comparisons. In this bond, we encourage each other not to measure our worth against one another. Instead, we recognize that each sister's journey is unique, and her path to fulfillment and success may differ from our own. By letting go of comparisons, we create a safe space for each sister to shine authentically and without reservation. We celebrate their accomplishments, big or small, and draw inspiration from their individual journeys, understanding that their success only enhances the collective strength of our sisterhood. In doing so, we foster an environment where each sister can reach her full potential, knowing she is supported, valued, and cherished for exactly who she is.

Choose Your Companions Wisely, for They Define Your Destiny

This story takes us back to my adolescence, when, at the age of twelve, I first met Marnee on the first day of seventh grade. It was a year filled with new faces, but Marnee stood out from the crowd. She had recently moved from California and possessed a certain charm with her unique haircut, striking green eyes, and unforgettable name.

Interestingly, Marnee happened to share nearly every class with me that day, creating a peculiar sense of fate. Though initially uncertain about this seemingly constant presence, I could never have foreseen that our chance encounters in class after class that day would evolve into one of the most enduring and cherished friendships of my life.

Our connection deepened quickly, and from that point forward, Marnee and I became inseparable. Together, we navigated the challenges of adolescence, forging a bond that would withstand the test of time and distance. Even as life led us to different states and we embraced the responsibilities of adulthood, our friendship remained steadfast.

Despite the geographical divide, Marnee and I made it a priority to reconnect several times each year, sometimes with our families and sometimes just the two of us. This friendship became a constant in our lives, an unwavering source of acceptance, encouragement, and love.

One of the most valuable lessons Marnee imparted to me was the importance of avoiding gossip. In an age where gossip often feels like an unavoidable part of growing up, Marnee's unwavering commitment to kindness and moral integrity left an indelible mark on me.

Marnee also instilled in me the significance of making wise choices and striving for excellence. She was determined to achieve good grades and urged us to aim for the honor roll. Naturally, I followed suit, adopting her ambition as my own. Her determination became infectious, propelling me to pursue academic achievements like joining the honor roll, becoming part of the National Honor Society, and actively volunteering at the Children's Crisis Center.

Our journeys continued in parallel as we pursued higher education: Marnee ventured to law school, while I pursued a master's degree in business administration. Both our husbands became doctors, and we shared a mutual passion for real estate investment. We embraced the joys and challenges of raising large families, and our children formed their own friendships.

So what's the core message of this story? It's the realization that the people we choose to surround ourselves with can significantly shape our lives. Speaker Jim Rohn famously made the remark that we are the average of the five individuals we spend the most time with, and I entirely agree. Marnee and other close friends like her have been my guiding stars, influencing my path of dreaming, believing, and creating.

I've learned that seeking out extraordinary people and learning from them can be a powerful catalyst for personal growth. I've been fortunate to follow in the footsteps of remarkable friends, and their influences have made me a better person, mother, wife, and individual. The message here is clear: Choose your companions wisely, for they will mold your destiny.

As you journey through life, be mindful of the company you keep and seek individuals who inspire and uplift you. Surround yourself with those who are more talented and knowledgeable than you, for their presence will propel you to greater heights. Remember that your friends can significantly impact your path, just as you can shape theirs. Lift one another up, shine brightly, and never dim the light of others.

This story serves as a testament to the enduring power of friendship and its capacity to influence our lives for the better. Let it remind you of the pivotal role your friends play in your own journey, and consider reaching out to those who have positively shaped your life. Express your gratitude to them for their influence and reflect on the profound impact they've had on your path to fulfilling your dreams. After all, we're all in this together, and the opportunity to uplift and inspire one another is a gift we can offer freely.

We Can All Shine Brightly

Being a Pretty Sister to others means embodying trust and kindness in your friendships. It's a value I've held dear throughout my life, as I've treasured the friends I've made along the way. These friendships have become chapters in my life story, each one contributing to the rich tapestry of my experiences.

From childhood pals and college buddies to graduate school comrades and church friends, I've cherished these connections. One fundamental principle has always guided my approach to friendship: the golden rule of never, ever gossiping.

This rule isn't just about keeping secrets; it's a commitment to respecting the trust placed in you by your friends. I recall my mother's voice echoing, "If you don't have something nice to say, don't say anything at all." Even Bambi reinforced this timeless wisdom. My childhood best friend, Marnee, exemplified this rule, never uttering an unkind word about anyone. Her integrity left a lasting impression on me, inspiring me to follow suit.

Have you ever wondered, while listening to someone gossip about another person, what they say about you when you're not around? It's a thought that often crosses my mind, eroding trust in the speaker. We all need confidants with whom we can share our innermost thoughts and frustrations, but this circle should remain small and carefully selected. It's a role reserved for those closest to us—spouses, best friends, sisters, or mothers—individuals we trust implicitly.

The challenge arises when people blur the line between confidante and casual acquaintance, oversharing with just about anyone. If you're naturally open and expressive, you may find it easy to cross that boundary. It's essential to exercise self-control and refrain from oversharing. When you do need to talk things out, be discreet, avoiding names and real stories. Instead, discuss scenarios in the abstract or, if necessary, confide in a therapist.

Breaking the golden rule of friendship by engaging in gossip is like releasing feathers into the wind; it's challenging, if not impossible, to retrieve them. Rumors not only harm others but also will return to harm you.

Once you master this aspect of friendship, you'll find that trust forms the bedrock of thriving relationships in all areas of your life. Trust isn't a one-way street; it's built through mutual respect and responsibility. Are you a trustworthy friend and confidante? Can others rely on you?

Take stock of your friendships and conversations. Are they positive and uplifting, or do they veer into gossip and negativity? If you struggle with keeping your thoughts to yourself, try flipping them around. Instead of spreading rumors or unkind words, strive to find something positive to say or practice gratitude. Remember, too, if you can't say something nice, it's perfectly fine not to say anything at all.

Being a Pretty Sister means uplifting and supporting one another, building trust, and nurturing meaningful connections. But just like in all kinds of relationships, mistakes are made in friendship. People are imperfect and generally do their best given their circumstances. We all view situations through our own lens of experience. This perspective can be tainted by our own understanding, and it's natural that everyone is viewing situations through their own varying perspectives. This is important to understand because we can all be partially correct in the way we perceive situations, and absolute truth is hard to obtain and certainly distorted.

To assist in closing the perspective gap, understanding of this phenomenon is crucial and remedied by a lot of grace. We would be correct in assuming almost 90 percent of people are going through heavy challenges at any given time, thus altering their ability to give their best in any given situation. Life is difficult and challenges are pervasive, ranging from family discord, social pressures, work-life balance, tragedy and crisis, illness and trauma. Many people are barely functioning yet have to face imminent responsibilities, so they put on a happy face and move through life almost zombie-like or, like a chameleon, have learned to cope without detection of any underlying near-explosive realities. I know this to be true because I've had to function this way on occasion myself.

As a mother of five and at varying times, the breadwinner and entrepreneur with fiduciary responsibilities and people dependent on me for their livelihoods, the brewing discord of life challenges have by necessity had to be put on the back burner, only to simmer to the point of what seemed to be an imminent explosion. I know I'm not alone in these difficult circumstances. You have been there too, and those around us are no different. This knowledge is imperative to developing our ability to view people with understanding and an amount of grace that requires us to approach situations with kindness and empathy.

The tendency to see our problems as the most important and biggest is natural, yet we are all pretty sisters, and it's helpful to deeply understand the inherent worthiness and prettiness of all our sisters. The assumption that pain and challenges are all around us and necessary in all of our developments helps. We would be more correct in assuming that even the best and most deceptively glamorous lives are in the same state of disarray. Of course, we wouldn't be fully correct, but the odds are definitely in our favor.

How do we move about life with this seemingly negative base assumption? By following the admonition to do our best, and in turn, accept everyone's best. It is a very freeing concept, doing our best. Our best is good enough, and it varies based on our circumstances. I told you before, my natural default state is to be cheerful, and this is a great blessing. Yet, even with this God-given disposition, it's hard to maintain when facing great adversity or disappointments, as I'm sure it would be for you too. When life is hard for me, I'm so grateful for those who allow me to indulge in a little sadness or even just a dip in my natural state of energetic expression of fun and optimism. At those times, I'm truly doing my best, and those who know me, whether they know the details of my experience, benefit from my deep gratitude when they treat me with love and acceptance no matter my disposition. This requires discipline in action and behavior and not jumping to conclusions.

We often want to counsel or give advice, which can sometimes be helpful. However, I learned from my father-in-law that unsolicited advice, even well-intended, is always construed as criticism. We are more successful when we can patiently wait to be asked for our opinion or consolations. Not everyone is ready to talk or explain themselves. We need to learn to sit in discomfort or in pain with others, and pointing out that they aren't acting like themselves can sometimes be grating and unwanted. Being there when they are ready to talk is helpful and takes an amount of practice and constraint, yet it's worth it in the relationship deposits that yield great rewards.

So what can we do? I have a friend who is great at checking in and asking questions. Everyone naturally loves to be thought of and cared for. No one is threatened by being asked how they are doing. It allows the person in pain to control the level of disclosure they are ready for. Sometimes, when asked, I'm in a place to share; other times, I just can't. The situation may be too tender and raw, and I may be on the verge of tears, barely able to hold it together, generally for the sake of my kids or the true need to function. Let's face it, life doesn't wait for us to be ready to rise above our challenges. And it's good it doesn't, because if we could push a pause button, I'm not sure any of us would ever resume at the pace necessary to learn and grow as we need to. Resilience is fostered this way. Life trumps us, we crash, we typically spend a minute in sorrow and contemplation, then find the strength to learn and rise above, always better and ready for the next challenge—when done right.

The opposite lands us in depression, anxiety, ruined relationships, and feeling stuck, wasting precious time and opportunities for growth. The real challenge is allowing this to happen. What most women waste is the beautiful opportunity to shortcut these steps or speed them up by allowing fellow Pretty Sisters to assist. This can be vulnerable, and we can be prideful, falsely thinking that strength resides in quiet resignation to life's barrage and that somehow we receive more points by facing life alone. We don't, as we are social creatures with the gift of communities, families, friends, and associates to assist us.

These people are our angels on earth, truly placed in our paths to assist us through life, when we allow them. Humility is required and rewarded by shortcuts through adversity and blessings multiplied by the acceptance of love and assistance. This may or may not come naturally, but it's worth the gamble and development of our ability to receive help. We often want to give help, which feels more natural to most, yet the opposite is sometimes more necessary. We find ourselves, upon occasion, on the receiving end.

If you follow the rule of only having to do your best, which, when practiced regularly, can release a lot of anxiety, life becomes a little bit easier. It feels like less pressure. You don't have to be perfect; you just have to do your best given your circumstances, which always fluctuate. Meaning, your level of best is allowed to fluctuate, too. You mean you don't always have to be happy? Of course not! It's not possible. Just like your experiences alter, so do your moods, emotions, and ability to respond and handle the stresses of life that are normal and designed for your growth.

That space between learning to handle new levels of challenges presents a gap in our ability to respond. You will eventually close the gap with the new abilities being developed and cultivated through the trial. But until then, you may need to wallow, cry, be sad, or even mad. Yes, temperance and control are required as it's never pretty to lose your marbles. Yet, when you do, a true friend and pretty sister by your side is always a soft cushion to land on, invaluable and even necessary in the deepening of relationships. Go through a crisis with a friend, and you will come to know the limits of that friendship and the depth of caring and who you can depend on. Until you have these experiences, the richness and true miracle of sisterhood are not fully expressed or understood.

When you internalize the fact that you are not perfect and your best is enough, you will embrace more challenges, dare to dream more, stop fearing failure, and cultivate more faith. It's easier to believe that life will work out for you when you know the path toward that realization may be, or in fact will be, rocky. Then, when you begin to ace this philosophy, you love the rocky path because you know the rewards are more exhilarating than the bumpy ride.

Finally, once this realization has come, you can practice the final step, allowing others' best to be enough too. Yes, you want grace, and so you must give it. If you want your best to be enough, then you can't expect perfection from others. You have bad days, and so do they. You get to be the beneficiary of friendship, but sometimes you have to be the benefactor. You can't expect what you aren't willing to give, or at least you can't for long, as others will catch on to the one-way street and find another path. Being a good friend requires this allowance and is rewarded with vulnerability and trust, which are foundational to rewarding relationships.

Seek First to Understand

Having a bias toward action is a beautiful thing and can help propel you forward. However, the ability to watch, listen, notice, and observe can help you become a better friend. Perhaps my favorite habit from Stephen R. Covey's *7 Habits of Highly Effective People* is habit 5: Seek first to understand, then to be understood. This is a habit well worth cultivating. So don't be too quick to offer your advice. Being a good listener shows people your true interest in them and helps them feel your love and concern. Ask good questions and wait to be asked for your help. Give the benefit of the doubt and be generous in your understanding and patience. Your fellow Pretty Sisters will be thankful.

When we moved to Boston for Dave's endodontic surgery residency at Harvard, we had the blessing of forming a brand-new friend group. We loved what came to be known as our Boston family, a new collection of friends who became our family away from home and our lifelong friends. This was the era of *Friends*, and our ritual of gathering on Thursday nights to watch the much-awaited thirty-minute episode of the show on TV together was a highlight of our week. Even better with this new friend group was that we were all young married couples, so not only were the wives becoming friends, but the husbands, too. This yielded an even tighter-knit group as we all, husbands and wives, developed these friendships together.

With my ninja friend-picking skills peaking, I think we landed the cream of the crop. My mom had always said to me, "I'm raising a better generation," and I knew she wanted her kids to turn out better than she was, and that was her measure of success. I loved that concept and had the same goal as a mother. I also took this philosophy into choosing my friends. I wanted to find friends that would make me better.

As I look back, this began at a young age as I understood the characteristics of a Pretty Sister, and that's what I attracted naturally. This was measured not just by outward beauty but by inward kindness and excellence and what I learned to be an energetic vibration. I was not attracted to negative people. In fact, when around them, I could almost feel the pull of their negativity and what felt like them trying to suck my positive energy from me. I felt drained whenever I came away from such people and tried to limit my exposure to what I called energy suckers. I wanted vibrant, fun, enthusiastic, energetic people to surround myself with who would challenge me and inspire me. I wanted them to help me become better. I looked for Pretty Sisters.

When you look at people this way, with a level of admiration that inspires you and doesn't make you feel less than others, you can approach them with true and authentic interest. In turn, they can feel comfortable and interested in you. We all want to be admired, but learn to admire your friends and seek to find the good in them rather than criticize or pick apart. Don't feel threatened, which you can do when you love yourself more and therefore can view people as assets to you and not there to diminish you.

I'm so grateful for my Boston friends, with whom I've been through thick and thin. I could list their talents and accomplishments that have consistently inspired me. From being wittier than me and always making me laugh to showing great empathy and always taking the time to show up. Or being what seemed to be more fun at times, more creative, more successful, or a better dancer, or smarter. When you see more in others, this is better as it only helps you yourself become more. These girls (and guys) have inspired, uplifted, and shown up time and time again for Dave and me for over twenty years now. We've raised our kids together and, while not always living near each other, have made the time to meet for vacations or get-togethers whenever possible. I am undoubtedly a better person with a richer life due to these friendships, and I'm eternally grateful. I'm glad I wasn't intimidated and instead chose to surround myself with greatness.

Remember, we all can shine. Know that you can be better with the help of your friends, not less than. I'm so grateful for September, Marnee, and my Boston Family for the ways they taught and inspired me. These are just a few examples of the many friends I've collected along the way that have made me a better person. Rather than compare yourself to your Pretty Sisters, learn from them and allow them to inspire you. Understand that while you are very, very worthy and pretty, from the inside out, so are those around you. Remember that every woman and girl is pretty too!

SIX

TOGETHER WE RISE

*The best way to find yourself is to lose yourself in
the service of others.*

I PULLED OUT OF THE DENTAL OFFICE PARKING LOT after my youngest three kids had their routine teeth cleanings. We should have been headed back to school, but a voice from the back declared that they wanted us to grab lunch first. It didn't take much convincing, so we soon found ourselves at our favorite spot: Costa Vida.

Finding ourselves eating lunch out together in the middle of a school day was an unusual experience, and I pointed this out, which led to further conversation.

Braden said, "Yeah, this is what it would be like if we were homeschooled."

Sophie piped in, "We should drop out of school, go on that RV trip we've always talked about, and be homeschooled."

Of course, Bella joined in with her enthusiastic agreement.

Always up for an adventure, I said, "Sure, why not?" And *voila!* —that seemingly uneventful lunch date turned into many more conversations, lots of planning, and within a few months, we set out on our ultimate homeschooling adventure.

During our epic, cross-country family road trip in an RV, we embarked on a journey not just through physical landscapes but also through cherished memories of the past. We had four main goals when planning our stops: visiting remarkable places, staying with important people from our lives, visiting historical church sites, and teaching health and wellness classes for one of our businesses.

One of the most heartwarming reunions was with Chrissy Morgan, my dear friend from the season of life in Louisville, Kentucky, when Dave was in dental school and I was pursuing my MBA. Those four years were a delightful blend of fun, exhaustion, and incredible experiences.

Chrissy holds a special place in my heart, and as we stopped in Kennewick, Washington, to visit her family, we were in for quite a surprise. What was meant to be a quick drop by for lunch transformed into a five-day visit. Now, that's the mark of a true friend! And did I mention that our forty-three-foot-long RV was parked in front of her house, and our dog had taken up residence in her backyard? If that doesn't define an exceptional friend, I don't know what does.

As we caught up on life, I couldn't help but notice a sign dangling from Chrissy's rearview mirror. It read, "Choose Easy," resembling the iconic red button I'd seen at Staples. Naturally, I inquired about its meaning, and her explanation left a profound impact on me.

To the Morgans, "Choose Easy" isn't about taking the path of least resistance and avoiding hard work; it's a philosophy that encourages making good choices. It means being honest, moral, kind, obedient, respectful, and living with unwavering integrity. Because when you consistently make these right choices, life becomes easy in the most beautiful sense.

I wholeheartedly embrace this perspective because Chrissy is absolutely right. By choosing to do what's right, we steer clear of mistakes that often lead to hardship and difficulty. We can sidestep hurtful relationships and the sorrows that stem from regret and remorse. When you do the right thing, life truly becomes easier. Make good choices, and you'll find yourself on the path to an easier, more fulfilling life.

So, why make life harder than it needs to be? Let's agree to make a conscious decision, right now, to *Choose easy*. Imagine the mistakes you could avoid, the path this simple phrase can guide you on—one that feels light, easy, joyful, and fun. Remember, we are meant to experience joy, and I promise you, it's easier to attain than you might think.

Choose easy isn't just a saying; it's a mindset that beautifully complements our journey of dreaming, believing, and creating with the loving support of our Pretty Sisters tribe. It means dreaming of a life that's simple and filled with joy. It's about believing in the power of making good choices aligned with our values. When we choose easy, we create a path that's uncomplicated, guided by our principles, and shared with the incredible women in our lives who inspire us to stay positive and true to ourselves. Together, we turn our dreams into reality, and life becomes even more meaningful and joyful.

You have the power to choose. So, please make it a daily practice to consciously choose for your day to be easy right from the moment you get up in the morning, and watch how it transforms your life for the better. Experiment to see if this will simplify your life and produce a ripple effect that positively impacts the people you encounter.

This brings us back to the heartwarming and empowering influence of sisterhood once again. One of the best ways to choose easy is by building great friendships.

The Special Camaraderie of Women

The impact of sisterhood is profound and multifaceted. It encompasses the transformative power of deep and lasting female friendships, the support and camaraderie that women provide one another, and the sense of belonging and understanding that comes from sharing life's joys and challenges with other women.

Just as choosing easy guides us to a more fulfilling life, the bonds we form with our sisters—whether those given us by blood or by choice—play an essential role in shaping our journey. These relationships offer us a safe haven of emotional support, empower us to chase our dreams, and provide shared experiences that validate and uplift us. Together, these principles create a beautiful, interconnected web of support, empowerment, and joy, enriching our lives in ways we never thought possible.

In essence, when we choose to embrace both the philosophy of choosing easy and the profound strength of sisterhood, we find ourselves on a path paved with love, understanding, and empowerment. This path not only leads us to our dreams but also ensures we are surrounded by those who genuinely care for and support us every step of the way.

Sisterhood becomes the easy choice and one with many benefits, including the following ones, to name only a few.

Emotional support. Sisterhood offers a safe space for women to express their emotions, share their vulnerabilities, and seek solace during difficult times. Whether it's offering a shoulder to cry on, lending a listening ear, or simply being there to provide comfort, sisterhood plays a vital role in emotional well-being.

Empowerment. Women who are part of a supportive sisterhood often find themselves empowered to pursue their dreams and ambitions. Encouragement from fellow sisters can boost confidence and self-belief, helping women break through barriers and achieve their goals.

Shared experiences. Sisterhood is built on shared experiences, from childhood memories to life's milestones. These shared moments create a unique bond that strengthens over time and helps women feel understood and validated.

Problem solving. Sisters often turn to each other for advice and guidance when facing challenges. The diverse perspectives and insights within a sisterhood can lead to creative problem-solving and offer solutions that may not have been apparent otherwise.

Celebrations of success. Sisterhood is not just about supporting during tough times but also celebrating each other's achievements and successes. It creates an environment where accomplishments are recognized and applauded, fostering a sense of pride and fulfillment.

Unconditional love. True sisterhood is characterized by unconditional love and acceptance. Sisters stand by each other's side through thick and thin, offering unwavering support and love, no matter the circumstances.

Lifelong bonds. Sisterhood often leads to lifelong bonds that transcend distance and time. These enduring connections become a source of strength and companionship throughout a woman's life.

In essence, the impact of sisterhood is immeasurable, shaping women's lives in profound ways. It provides a network of love, understanding, and empowerment that helps women navigate life's challenges, celebrate its joys, and together rise to greater heights.

Critical Traits of True Sisterhood

The core of sisterhood is trust—the foundational belief that your friend will always have your best interests at heart, and you'll reciprocate that trust in return. Loyalty stands strong beside trust, signifying your commitment to stand by your friend through life's ups and downs, reinforcing the foundation of trust.

In a supportive Pretty Sister community of women, these principles take on a special significance. Here, trust forms the backbone of the sisterhood, as women lean on each other for support and encouragement. **Loyalty** becomes a promise to stand by each other's side, celebrate successes, and offer a shoulder during tough times.

Respect is fundamental—sisters valuing each other's thoughts, feelings, and boundaries. In such a community, **kindness** and **consideration** reign supreme, even during disagreements. **Honest, open communication** becomes the glue that binds the sisterhood together, as women share their true selves without fear of judgment.

Empathy flourishes, allowing sisters to understand and share each other's feelings, and building a bridge of emotional support. **Active listening** ensures that every woman feels heard and validated, strengthening the bonds of sisterhood. **Forgiveness** is a shared understanding that mistakes can happen, but with empathy and compassion, sisters can move forward, learn, and grow.

Support is the backbone of a Pretty Sister community. Members offering emotional, and mental aid, and sometimes even physical aid, in times of need. Healthy friendships respect boundaries, communicate openly, and value equality, fairness, and quality time spent together. **Acceptance** embraces each sister's unique qualities, fostering a sense of belonging and unity.

Laughter adds joy and humor to the mix, creating a positive and uplifting atmosphere. **Conflict resolution** becomes a vital skill, ensuring that misunderstandings are addressed promptly to strengthen the sisterhood. **Celebrating each other's achievements and milestones** demonstrates genuine care and support.

The longevity of these bonds cements friendships over time, creating a sense of history and shared experiences. In such a community, effective communication ensures that misunderstandings are addressed promptly, fortifying the bond that ties these women together. Ultimately, every Pretty Sister community is unique, guided by these principles that make it special, as long as each member feels valued, respected, and loved in the sisterhood.

How Pretty Sisters Rise Together

I never truly had a dad in my life. My parents' separation when I was just ten led to our cross-country move, leaving behind the past and any semblance of a father-daughter relationship. There were awkward annual visits and strained phone calls, but it was never the kind of father-daughter bond I dreamed of. Then, when I was a young mother, taking the first steps toward mending our relationship, fate dealt me a cruel hand—my dad passed away from a heart attack at the age of sixty-three. I was only twenty-seven, a young mother with my eighteen-month-old son and a newborn baby girl, and my hopes of further reconciling with my father were shattered.

At first glance, it might seem like a sad story. Yet, as life often goes, it took an unexpected turn. I may have been without a dad, but I was never without father figures who stepped in, ready and willing, to fill that void. You see, God has a way of making things right when we allow Him. This became evident to me as I witnessed my friend Katie's relationship with her dad. To say I longed for a connection like theirs would be an understatement. What came so naturally to her was astonishing to me.

I paid careful attention to her dad's actions, the way he interacted with Katie, his treatment of his wife, and even his responses to life's curveballs. During college, I was especially struck by his unwavering support when Katie had a spectacular crash with her Ford Bronco. We were on our way to the lake when we struck the side of a bridge, sending the two new WaveRunners we were hauling careening down the street in different directions. Fortunately, we were all safe, and his first concern was, "Are you all okay?"

He then consoled Katie and calmly guided her through the aftermath, reminding her, "That's what insurance is for." He then allowed her the space to face the natural consequences of the mishap and navigate the logistics of necessary repairs.

Little did he know that from that incident I would glean lessons that would guide me through years of parenting five children.

During those formative years, I observed Katie's dad opening his 12,000-square-foot home to friends and hosting parties. He generously shared his possessions, vacation homes, and, most importantly, his time and wisdom with anyone in need. I was in need, and I clung to every morsel of fatherly leadership, advice, or example I could gather from him. Without even realizing it, he painted a vivid portrait for me of what life could be like. I was determined to create that life and reality for my future family.

Fast forward twenty-three years, and on a flight home after spending an incredible weekend with my friend Katie, her dad, and a group of girlfriends, I contemplated the many ways my life has been blessed by this association. He continues to open his heart and home—to this day filling a crucial role in my life. What made that weekend especially meaningful was that it followed my mother's recent diagnosis of Alzheimer's disease. In a way only God could orchestrate, He placed me with Katie's dad, who was in the final stages of caring for his wife, who also had AD. For one weekend, Katie generously shared her dad with me.

From the moment he picked us up from the airport, he was a father figure in every sense. Offering wise advice, providing delicious meals for us, showing tender care, and even granting us access to a multimillion-dollar beach house, he went above and beyond. The glorious weather, with beach walks featuring sunrises and sunsets that could have broken records, felt like God's way of showing off.

And that's precisely my point—life is challenging, and things don't always align with our desires. In fact, they often don't. However, God has a remarkable way of bridging the gaps. He provides stand-ins, individuals who can step in when someone else can't, serving as earthly angels. When we recognize these people, we no longer need to feel let down, inadequate, or forgotten. Instead, we can rise to our challenges with the understanding that, when we're open to it, God will always provide what we need.

I needed a dad when I was younger, and in many ways, I still do. Although I don't have precisely what I initially wanted, I've been blessed with stand-ins who have given me what I need in various moments, and for that, I'm profoundly grateful. My friend Katie, a fellow Pretty Sister, generously shared her dad with me, reminding me that we don't have to navigate life or chase our dreams alone. With the support and love of others, we can overcome any obstacle, and when we place our trust in God, all things work out for our good.

Celebrate the Wins of Your Pretty Sisters

It's essential to celebrate the wins of your fellow Pretty Sisters, and we do this with Pretty Sister Parties. Celebrating each other's achievements is more than just a kind gesture—it's a powerful way to uplift one another, inspire confidence, and create an environment where success thrives. By genuinely celebrating the successes of those around us, we contribute to a shared sense of purpose and motivation, fostering even greater accomplishments for the entire sisterhood.

Think of each win, no matter how small, as a stepping stone not only for the individual but for all of us. Every milestone reached by one of your Pretty Sisters is a testament to the power of community and encouragement. When we celebrate their victories, we not only honor their hard work but also strengthen the belief that we all have the ability to reach our dreams together.

Here are some ways you can celebrate and amplify the wins of your Pretty Sisters.

Acknowledge their progress. Take a moment to genuinely recognize how far they've come. Let them know you see the effort they've put in and the progress they've made. Sometimes, a simple "I'm so proud of you!" can mean the world.

Celebrate the milestones. Encourage your Pretty Sisters to share their smaller milestones along the way. Celebrating these moments together keeps the journey exciting and helps them feel supported in the process.

Plan a celebration. Take time to celebrate their achievements in meaningful ways. Whether it's organizing a small gathering, sending a thoughtful note, or treating them to something special, these gestures show that their wins matter to you too.

Share their joy. When a Pretty Sister achieves something great, amplify her success by sharing it with others. Post about it, tell your mutual friends, or simply make sure she knows you're cheering her on loudly and proudly.

Create shared visuals. Work together to document your collective wins. It could be a shared vision board, a journal of group achievements, or even a photo album capturing special moments. These visual reminders highlight the strength of your bond.

Speak life into their dreams. Use positive affirmations to lift them up. Phrases like "You are unstoppable," "You inspire us all," or "Your success lights the way for others" reinforce their belief in themselves and their ability to keep achieving.

Practice gratitude for their journey. Express gratitude not only for their successes but also for the opportunity to witness and support them. Gratitude fosters connection and creates a ripple effect of positivity within the sisterhood.

Celebrating the wins of your Pretty Sisters is a celebration of the collective strength of your bond. It's not about comparison or competition; it's about creating a culture of encouragement and support where everyone's success is a shared triumph.

So let's commit to celebrating every step of the journey—together. Each win, no matter how big or small, is a reminder that we rise by lifting one another. When we celebrate others, we create a beautiful cycle of love, support, and inspiration that helps us all live our most miraculous lives.

Celebrating Our Intuitive Magic

Let me share a personal story that highlights the power of recognizing and celebrating our unique intuitive "superpowers." Sometimes, we don't fully appreciate the intuitive magic we possess or how impactful it can be in helping others—especially our children—find balance and strength.

One day, my then-fifteen-year-old daughter Taylor came home from school with a face full of teenage frustration and stress. I could tell immediately that she was on the verge of an emotional storm, and I was bracing myself for the usual marathon of listening, comforting, and guiding. But this time, the timing couldn't have been worse—I had a conference call starting in minutes, and I was the one leading it. I needed a solution, and fast.

Then, it happened. In the midst of the chaos, I felt a sudden nudge of inspiration: *Give her an AromaTouch treatment.* This essential oil application technique, similar to a relaxing massage, was something my kids loved. With only moments to spare, I calmly suggested, "Taylor, how about I give you an AromaTouch, and then we'll talk?" She hesitated, but agreed, and I quickly led her to a massage table in our spare room.

While leading my call on speaker, I quietly performed the AromaTouch treatment, asking Taylor to remain still until the call was finished. My plan was to help her decompress so we could tackle her stress together later—after all, high school finals were the next day, and the pressure of performing well was weighing heavily on her.

When the call ended, I expected to hear a big emotional download. But to my surprise, Taylor sat up from the table, looked at me, and simply said, "Thanks, Mom." Then, she went to her room, studied for the rest of the evening, and aced her tests the next day.

It felt like magic. There was no meltdown, no hours-long conversation. She just needed a reset—a moment of calm to help her regain her focus and let go of the stress. The combination of nurturing touch and the calming properties of the essential oils had done exactly what was needed, restoring her balance and mindset.

This moment became a profound reminder for me: As mothers, we have an incredible capacity for intuitive problem-solving. It's a gift we often overlook, but when we recognize and celebrate it, we unlock even more of its power. That day, I didn't just solve a problem; I celebrated my ability to act quickly, follow my intuition, and provide the exact support my daughter needed.

It's important to pause and recognize these moments, not to pat ourselves on the back but to understand the power we have to create calm and connection in our families and circles of influence. Sometimes, our "wins" are quiet victories that don't come with applause, but they are no less significant. When we acknowledge and embrace this magic, we can use it more effectively, turning ordinary moments into extraordinary opportunities for connection.

In the spirit of "Together We Rise," this story also speaks to the broader importance of uplifting one another. Just as I was able to support my daughter in her time of need, we each have the power to offer guidance, love, and calm to those around us. Celebrating our "mom wins" is a way of recognizing that we're part of something bigger, a network of Pretty Sisters, mothers, and friends who are all working to rise together.

Let's take a moment to honor these wins, big or small. When we celebrate the magic within us, we empower ourselves and those around us to tap into their own strength. Together, we rise, lifting one another with love, compassion, and a bit of that magic we all carry inside.

Benefiting from Others' Service

During my early days of marriage, I benefited similarly from someone's service to me. This came at a time when Dave and I were navigating the challenges of student life. Money was tight and luxuries like shopping were not part of our budget. Dave was diligently pursuing his education, and I was working tirelessly to support us. To make matters more demanding, I had a grueling daily commute for two hours from Louisville, Kentucky, where we were living then, to Cincinnati, Ohio, where I worked at the massive public accounting firm Arthur Anderson in a specialized consulting division only housed at their larger offices.

Long hours on the road were leaving me utterly exhausted, the kind of tiredness that could lead to peculiar mishaps. One morning, I even managed to put on two different shoes without realizing it until I was already halfway through my workday—an embarrassing reminder of just how fatigued I was. We didn't have kids yet, thank goodness.

It was during this trying period that my guardian angel came in the form of my wonderful mother and her dear friend, Judy Shuley, who lived in

Ohio. Judy extended me a lifeline by graciously offering me a place to stay a few nights each week, sparing me the arduous commute.

Judy's generosity was nothing short of miraculous. She welcomed me into her home as if I were her own family, providing me with my own comfortable room, delicious meals, and, perhaps most importantly, relief from the long and exhausting commute. Judy became my second mom during that time, and I was overwhelmed with gratitude for her kindness.

One evening, after a particularly challenging day at work, Judy surprised me with an act of kindness that left an indelible mark on my heart. She took me shopping, escorting me to the mall and saying those magical words: "Pick out an outfit, anything you want!" I was astounded by her generosity and couldn't believe my luck.

As we browsed the racks and tried on clothes, Judy spent $100 on me, which, at the time, felt like an immense fortune. Her gesture left me feeling grateful, a bit bashful, and absolutely elated. I couldn't help but shower her with thank yous and promises of repayment.

However, Judy's response was simple and profound. She said, "Just promise me you'll do the same for someone else someday."

That single act of kindness and the subsequent promise I made to myself have stayed with me throughout my life. I resolved right then and there that I would lead a life of abundance, not just for my benefit but so that I could pay it forward to others. I aspired to create opportunities for others to experience the same joy I felt that day, but from the giving end.

It was a defining moment that shaped my vision for life. I've had the privilege of paying forward Judy's generosity to me in various ways since then, not necessarily through outfits but through countless opportunities to share abundance with others. What I've learned is that while helping oneself is rewarding, the true magic lies in helping others.

So, I extend this challenge to you: Consider who you might help by sharing generously in your own life. Are you living a life of abundance so that you can serve and uplift those around you? I promise you that the joy you'll discover in doing so will be immeasurable, far greater than any new outfit or material possession.

Strength in Sisterhood

In life's most challenging moments, the bonds of sisterhood reveal their true strength. When we support one another with acts of love, service, and compassion, we create a foundation of unity that carries us through even the darkest times. These moments remind us that we are not meant to journey alone but are instead called to lift and be lifted by those we hold dear.

My friend Chrissy is a beautiful example of this. Chrissy, who recently had taught me the invaluable lesson of how to "choose easy" during our RV trip, has always been a source of light and positivity in my life. When my daughter Sophie needed emergency surgery to remove an ovarian tumor, causing us to cut our RV trip short, Chrissy flew into town without hesitation, bringing treats, flowers, and the comfort only a true friend can provide.

A few years later, Chrissy faced her greatest challenge when her youngest son, Parker, was diagnosed with a rare form of bone cancer at just eighteen years old. For two years, Parker battled with unshakable hope and courage, living life to its fullest in the spaces between hospital stays and surgeries. Rather than allowing his diagnosis to define him, Parker used his journey to uplift others, sharing his story with an optimism that inspired people around the world.

Through it all, Chrissy, the queen of positivity, faced the unimaginable with grace and resilience. Her mantra, "Choose Easy," was put to the ultimate test, and though the path was anything but easy, she and her family chose to hold on to hope, faith, and love. Parker's bravery in fully embracing his final years on earth was a gift to those who loved him, and Chrissy's decision to find peace in God's plan, despite her heartache, was a testament to her inner strength.

When Parker's fight came to an end, I was honored to be there for Chrissy at his funeral. I thought I would be the one offering her strength and support, but true to her nature, Chrissy and her husband, Jeff, were the ones lifting others. Their grace, love, and humor in the face of such profound loss were astonishing. They had no regrets, knowing they had fought the hard fight, and they found solace in the love and memories they shared with Parker. Despite the years and miles that had separated us, Chrissy and I felt as close as ever—more than friends, truly Pretty Sisters.

This story is a reminder of the power of sisterhood. It's in these moments of shared sorrow and shared joy that we see how deeply connected we are. The love and support we give and receive weave a safety net that catches us when life feels unbearable and strengthens us to rise again.

As we close this chapter, let us remember the importance of celebrating, supporting, and serving one another. Whether it's through simple acts of kindness, moments of shared joy, or standing together in times of trial, we have the power to uplift one another and create a world where love and compassion reign.

Every day is an opportunity to extend a helping hand, celebrate the victories of your Pretty Sisters, and strengthen the bonds that carry us forward. Together, we can create a legacy of light, hope, and unity. Together, we rise!

BELIEF #2: I AM NOT ALONE

PRETTY SISTER PINKY PROMISE

RUN THROUGH THE SPILLING THE TEA TECHNIQUE AFTER reading the three chapters related to Belief #2. The objective now is for you to internalize that *you are not alone in the world.*

When I say "I am not alone," I THINK: _____
_____
_____
_____
_____

When I think *that*, it makes me FEEL: _____
_____
_____
_____
_____

When I feel *that*, it makes me ACT: _____
_____
_____
_____
_____

Ask yourself, "Is there anything else I am thinking?" Run through this same process as many times as needed until you are thinking from your heart with courage, love, and confidence. Once you feel ready, move on to make the promise.

Find a fellow Pretty Sister (this can be your mom, a sister, a friend, or someone from the online Pretty Sister community) and make the following promise to her. Or speak these words to yourself in the mirror.

"I believe that I am not alone.
I Pretty Sister pinky promise—
and crosses don't count!"

Way to go, girl, you did it! Now keep on believing and know that you have access to divine guidance and a community of Pretty Sisters that are committed to helping you remember that you are never alone!

BELIEF #3
YOU CAN DO IT

Believe you can and you're halfway there.

SEVEN

YOU BEGIN WITH A DREAM

"If you can dream it, you can do it."

TOM FITZGERALD, DISNEY IMAGINEER

IT WAS A COZY JANUARY EVENING AT THE FORESIDE Tavern, where Dave and I found ourselves on a rare dinner date, blissfully without the kids. We were doing what we love most: dreaming about our future and setting fresh goals for the new year. Just a few months earlier we had embarked on an adventure to explore the charm of New England's northern coast by moving our family just two hours north, from Boston to Maine; soon after, our fifth child, Bella, was born. Little did we know that this adventure, which was originally planned to last one or two years, would turn into a decade-long love affair with Maine.

Before we began talking, we established some rules for our discussion. The most important one was that anything and everything was on the table. It proved to be a perfect grounding for an intriguing conversation.

I love talking to my husband about our plans for the future because I have an insatiable appetite for business and strategy. Naturally, I steered our conversation that evening toward potential business ventures. We had recently opened a new dental practice in Maine, where we were then living, and had found that the demand for dentistry and oral surgery was so high that we were keen on establishing a second location there. We agreed on selling two other existing practices we owned in Massachusetts and New Hampshire to focus on this new opportunity for growth.

As our discussion then shifted from business to family life, a question emerged: What could we do to create something special for our family? That was when the conversation took a more exciting turn.

Dave told me he was yearning for a hunting property with ample acreage for four-wheeling with ATVs, tree stands for hunting, and a deep connection with nature. On the other hand, I harbored a dream of owning a lake house where our family could gather, reminiscent of the summer I'd spent on Lake Winnipesaukee during college. That lake, famous for being the backdrop in movies like *On Golden Pond* and *What about Bob?*, was dotted with opulent homes owned by renowned families who summered there, just like the Vanderbilt family did at the Newport Mansions in Rhode Island. Inspired by my early experience and seeing the exteriors of the extravagant lake houses, I envisioned creating our own family haven. Our dream checklist included the ability to water ski and being within a one-hour drive of home.

But what if, just maybe, we could have the best of both worlds by finding or building a lake house on a sprawling piece of land? We left that dinner with our heads full of dreams, a dream that felt like it was at least a decade away. Considering we now had five kids, the youngest being a mere four months old, it seemed like we would need much more money to make such a dream come true.

Over the few months that followed, excuses started to creep in, such as that we needed more money, more time, more everything. But we clung to hope, the precious spark that marks the beginning of every dream. Hope was enough to drive us to search for the perfect property, even if it seemed like a mere exercise in fantasy. We started looking at property online right away and spending weekends going out to look at them. It all happened quite rapidly.

Fast forward four months to April. We celebrated the purchase of a 150-plus-acre piece of property. By May, we were underway building our dream lake house and hunting property, which we named Moose Lake Ranch. One short year later, the project was complete. As a result of our commitment to taking action on this shared vision we created at New Year, our children had the chance to grow up enjoying this dream come true, instead of watching us spend a lifetime just fantasizing about it.

The accomplishment of the dream was nothing short of a miracle, and it came with a ton of hard work. But we weren't afraid of hard work, as Dave would gladly tell you—especially if you ask him about digging a trench for electrical wiring uphill both ways!

The lesson here is this: You can achieve your dreams and, as I'm here to tell you, you begin by daring to dream.

The journey to create a fulfilling life for yourself and your family begins with daring to dream and getting extremely specific about what you want. Then—and this is crucial—you must *believe* that you can achieve it, build it, or have it. Lastly, remember that *you* are the one responsible for creating *your* dream. Nobody else can do this part for you. The power is in your hands to make it happen.

Hopefully, this information makes you feel empowered. But whatever you're feeling right now, I promise you that we're going to delve into all of these concepts in detail in the three chapters in this part of the book. But in this chapter, we are going to continue to focus on the first step: dreaming.

Meanwhile, know that you can put in the work to create your dreams, and I promise you, it's *so worth it!*

Imagination and Dream Fulfillment

Imagining an outcome is not just about daydreaming; it's about harnessing the power of the mind to manifest our desires. By vividly imagining your goals and desires, you set the stage for your subconscious mind to work toward achieving them. It's a form of mental programming that aligns your thoughts, beliefs, and actions with your dreams.

So, as you cultivate the art of imagination, remember that it's not a passive activity. It's an active and transformative process that can propel you toward your dreams. Through your imagination, you can tap into your inner genius, explore uncharted territories of your mind, and unlock the boundless potential that resides within you. Your imagination is the gateway to creating the life of which you've always dreamed.

Imagination is such a powerful force that it can help us reshape our lives massively and propel us toward the fulfillment of even our wildest dreams. It's a force we can recognize in the inspiring stories of remarkable people we meet or learn about from books or documentaries.

From a young age, I have been incredibly fortunate to have wonderful role models step into my life at just the right moments, offering me invaluable guidance and revealing a vast range of possibilities to choose among that lay ahead of me. These mentors enabled me to glimpse a life beyond my current financial circumstances and to explore places and experiences that felt like distant dreams at the time. It was through their generosity that I began to envision a future for myself that was larger than I had previously imagined.

Some of the most influential figures in my formative years were the members of my early childhood best friend's family, especially her parents. The Hornes became like a second family to me, opening doors to experiences that seemed worlds away from my reality. Summer trips to Virginia became a regular occurrence, and I was welcomed with open arms. The Hornes sponsored my attendance at summer camps, took me on beach vacations, and even treated me to my very first sea cruise.

After I moved to Utah, our families began a tradition of trading summers, ensuring that we continued to create cherished memories together. With nine kids in their family, including my dear friend Christie, the household was always a whirlwind of activity and excitement. As the youngest in my own family and the only child still living at home, I marveled at the bustling energy of their home, just as Christie was fascinated by the serenity of my kid-free household.

During one unforgettable summer during college, I lived in the Horne family's beautiful Virginia home in the countryside, which resembled a Tudor castle, while completing an internship with Senator Orrin G. Hatch on Capitol Hill in Washington, D.C. I can still vividly recall the day Christie and I went grocery shopping, armed with two shopping carts. She entrusted me with the task of getting milk and I returned with a single gallon. Much to both our amusements, she went back to the dairy case and added another five gallons to the cart.

Our friendship endured through our childhood and college years, when we became roommates, and it continues to thrive today, more than four decades later, as we still routinely gather for our annual girls' trip. Christie is not just a lifelong friend, she's a very pretty Pretty Sister.

Why has this connection endured for so long? It's because the Hornes played a significant role in shaping the woman I am today. As a young teenager, inspired by their example, I made a conscious decision to become an entrepreneur, to own a magnificent home, to travel the world with my future large family, and to surround myself with beautiful things. I knew all this was possible because I had witnessed it firsthand, and even more crucially, because I understood why I wanted to create those specific things. Ultimately, my motivation wasn't personal gain, but a strong desire to impact others' lives through generosity and kindness. The act of giving, whose rewards I had experienced so personally and tangibly, became my driving force.

I will forever be grateful for the enduring friendship and the attention and love showered upon me by Christie and her family. I hope that in my lifetime, I can continue their legacy and honor the vision they planted in my heart.

Has someone in your life helped you see a grander vision and more possibilities for yourself? If the answer is yes, then take a moment right now to express your gratitude internally for their generosity. To pay the gift forward, commit to shining your light brightly and helping others see the boundless possibilities that lie before them.

Twelve Ways to Strengthen Your Imagination

With or without a mentor, you can boost your imagination to enhance your creativity, problem-solving skills, and overall quality of life. Here are twelve practical tips to help you unlock and strengthen this mental capacity. Once you find a technique for being imaginative that works particularly well for you, go ahead and apply it to imagining anything you need or want to create or find.

Read widely. Reading exposes your mind to diverse ideas, cultures, and perspectives. It stimulates your imagination by presenting you with different worlds, characters, and scenarios. Fiction, in particular, can ignite your creativity as you visualize the story's events and characters.

Explore the arts. Engage with various forms of art, such as painting, sculpture, music, and dance. Artistic expressions can inspire your own creativity and imagination. You don't need to be an artist to benefit from the arts; simply appreciating and experiencing them can expand your imagination.

Daydream regularly. Allow yourself to daydream without constraint. Let your mind wander and explore different scenarios, places, and ideas. Daydreaming is like a mental playground where your imagination can roam freely.

Practice mindfulness. Mindfulness practices, such as focusing on your in-breath and out-breath, or closing your eyes and being attentive to the sounds you hear for five minutes or more, can sharpen your awareness and focus. Mindfulness encourages you to observe your thoughts without judgment, which can help you become more attuned to your creative ideas and imaginative thinking.

Write creatively or keep a journal. Writing can be a powerful way to tap into your imagination. Write stories, poems, or just jot down your flowing thoughts and observations. Putting pen to paper can help you articulate your ideas and give them shape.

Brainstorm and collaborate. Engage in brainstorming sessions alone or with others, or collaborate on creative projects. Sharing ideas with people who have different perspectives than yours can spark new avenues of imaginative thinking. Group discussions can lead to innovative solutions and concepts.

Travel. Traveling to new places and exploring different cultures can be a rich source of inspiration. It exposes you to new sights, sounds, and experiences that can fuel your imagination. Even if you can't travel far, investigate your local surroundings with a curious mindset.

Read science fiction and fantasy. These fictional genres often push the boundaries of reality, encouraging imaginative thinking. They challenge you to envision worlds, technologies, and creatures that don't exist in our current reality.

Take breaks and disconnect. Sometimes, a change of scenery or a break from your routine can refresh your mind and encourage creative thinking. Disconnecting from devices with screens and spending time in nature can be particularly rejuvenating for your imagination. That means taking a walk without headphones on!

Ask "what if?" questions. Challenge your thinking by asking questions that start with "What if . . .?" For example, "What if I could travel back in time?" or "What if I could communicate with animals?" Such fanciful questions may encourage you to explore alternative possibilities.

Seek inspiration. Surround yourself with sources of inspiration, whether it's art, literature, music, or motivational talks. Seek out content that resonates with you emotionally and ignites your imagination.

Keep a dream journal. Record your dreams upon waking. Dreams are a product of your subconscious mind and can contain elements of your imagination. Reviewing your dream journal periodically can help you identify recurring themes and symbols that may inspire creative thought.

Remember, boosting your imagination is an ongoing process. Be patient with yourself and embrace the joy of discovery as you explore the endless landscapes of your mind. Your imagination is a valuable asset that can enrich your life in countless ways, from helping you solve problems to stimulating you to pursue your dreams with passion and creativity. So, first let your imagination soar, and then watch as it transforms your world.

The Power of Visualization and Imagination

Research has consistently shown the power of visualization in the achievement of a goal. Olympic athletes use different visualization techniques to mentally rehearse their performances before competing, because studies have demonstrated that when athletes vividly imagine themselves doing the actions that lead to success well, their performance improves. This kind of success illustrates the remarkable impact of the imagination for turning our dreams into reality.

For an advertising campaign, Tom Fitzgerald, an Imagineer for the Walt Disney Company, penned the famous phrase, "If you can dream it, you can do it," and ever since then those words have been associated with the Disney theme park experience.[1] For good reason: These words hold immense power, as they remind us that our dreams have the potential to become reality.

I remember how, when I first entered the business world, I had this quote printed on the back of my business card. I was in my early twenties, recently graduated from college, and I had a vision. It was my dream to achieve the milestone of a million-dollar net worth by the age of thirty. And guess what? It became a reality. Just after my thirtieth birthday, I secured a round of funding that valued Providio, my technology startup, at over five million dollars. For me, this was a testament to the fact that our dreams are only limited by the vastness of our imagination. I had been spending time planning and imagining that kind of moment and success for close to a decade, while working hard to implement my plan.

Let me share another example with you. Have you heard of J.K. Rowling? She's the brilliant author behind the immensely popular Harry Potter series. Before her books became a global phenomenon, she was a struggling single mother living on government assistance. But she had a dream and a vivid imagination, and she began to write a story she had in her mind. Her imagination turned into words, and those words became the foundation of a billion-dollar literary, film, and merchandising empire. Rowling's journey from hardship to success exemplifies the incredible power of dreaming big and having the courage to bring those dreams to life.

My best advice to you is not to get bogged down by the details of "how" or "when" your dreams will come to fruition. Those details will be revealed to you by your imagination as you move forward and stay committed to your vision. It can feel almost like magic, but actually this is just the way the imagination works. It gives us what we need to take the next step in our plan and fills in the gaps with suggestions. Our incredible, adaptive brain is why human beings are the most successful species on the planet.

Rowling's story is a reminder that no matter where we come from or what type of obstacles we face, we have the capacity to dream beyond our circumstances and follow those dreams to create a life that surpasses expectations. Whatever doubts she may have had, she is a model of resilience and the power of making a commitment to a dream.

Here's another inspiring success story for you. Meet St. Frances Xavier Cabrini, affectionately known as Mother Cabrini, a woman whose impact during her time rivals that of John D. Rockefeller, one of the wealthiest and most influential figures in American history. Yet, her influence wasn't built on amassing personal wealth or corporate power; it was founded on faith, service, and an unshakable commitment to humanity.

Born in 1850 in a small village in Lombardy, Italy, Mother Cabrini was the youngest of thirteen children. Despite her frail health and being told she would never be strong enough to live a religious life, she dreamed of becoming a missionary and serving others. Her determination was unwavering, and she eventually founded the Missionary Sisters of the Sacred Heart of Jesus, a Catholic religious institute devoted to helping the poor.

Her mission led her to America in 1889, where she arrived in New York City to assist the growing population of Italian immigrants struggling to find their footing in a new country. At a time when women had limited opportunities for influence, Mother Cabrini became a powerful force of change. She established schools, hospitals, orphanages, and other institutions that provided much-needed care and education for immigrants and the poor. Her efforts extended across the United States and into both Central and South America.

What's truly remarkable is the scale of her accomplishments. The wealth and property Mother Cabrini accumulated for the Catholic Church—schools, hospitals, and missions—rivaled or surpassed the wealth amassed by Rockefeller during the same era. Yet, her "wealth" wasn't measured in dollars alone; it was measured in the lives she transformed and the legacy she left behind.

Mother Cabrini's work was driven by a deep sense of faith and love. She believed in the dignity of every person and sought to provide opportunities for those who were marginalized. Her resilience and resourcefulness allowed her to overcome immense challenges, including discrimination, poverty, and her own physical frailty.

Declared the first American citizen saint in 1946, St. Cabrini's life is a testament to what can be achieved through vision, determination, and an unrelenting desire to serve. Whether your dreams are rooted in serving others, building something greater than yourself, or creating a legacy of kindness and hope, her life stands as proof that anything is possible for a woman with dedication and a heart full of love.

If Mother Cabrini's story inspires you, I highly recommend watching *Cabrini*, an incredible film about her life, starring Cristiana Dell'Anna in the title role, which premiered in 2024 to much acclaim. The film beautifully captures her unwavering faith, her tireless work for others, and her extraordinary ability to overcome obstacles. It's a reminder that no matter how daunting the challenges we face, we all have the potential to make a meaningful difference in the world.

One more example of a remarkable female entrepreneur—perhaps my favorite example—is that of Sara Blakely. As the founder and CEO of Spanx, the revolutionary shapewear brand that has transformed women's fashion and redefined an industry, her entrepreneurship is a testament to the power of dreaming big, embracing failure, and persevering through adversity. Her journey to success wasn't easy; it was filled with countless challenges and roadblocks that would have made most other people give up.

Blakely started with a simple, yet brilliant idea. She wanted to create a type of undergarment that would smooth out lines under white pants without the uncomfortable seams and bulk of traditional underwear. With $5,000 of savings, no formal background in fashion, and a lot of determination, she set out to bring her vision to life. Her imagination inspired her to create the first prototype for Spanx by cutting the feet off a pair of pantyhose.

Despite the initial excitement over her idea for a new kind of garment, getting her company off the ground was far from easy. Sara faced constant rejection from the owners of male-dominated hosiery mills and found it difficult to get store buyers to take her seriously. But she refused to let those early setbacks define the scope of her operations. She finally secured a face-to-face meeting with a hosiery mill in North Carolina after the mill owner's daughters convinced him to give her a chance. He was impressed. Even then, having solved her primary manufacturing problem, she had to work tirelessly to convince department stores to carry her products.

Blakely's breakthrough moment came when Neiman Marcus agreed to test Spanx in seven of their stores. To make sure the product stood out, she personally demonstrated its benefits to sales associates. Her hands-on approach, paired with relentless belief in her idea, ultimately paid off. Then, Oprah Winfrey named Spanx one of her "Favorite Things" in 2000, which catapulted the brand into the national spotlight and spurred its rapid growth.

Today, Spanx is a multibillion-dollar company and Sara Blakely is a self-made billionaire. But she hasn't stopped there. She is a passionate advocate for female entrepreneurs and regularly invests in other women-led businesses. Through the Sara Blakely Foundation, she supports initiatives that empower women around the world. Her story is a reminder that the path to success is often paved with setbacks and that dreaming big can lead to unimaginable heights if you have the courage to pursue your vision.

And that is what it takes, a lot of vision and imagination to get started in your dreaming. The art of imagination is a fascinating aspect of human creativity, and there's science to back its power. Let's dive into how imagination works and why it's so essential in the pursuit of your dreams.

The science of creativity is rooted in fascinating neurological processes that shape our thoughts and imagination. One of the key factors in learning is neuroplasticity, the brain's ability to biologically reorganize itself by forming new neural connections. This tangible kind of adaptability means that when you engage in imaginative thinking, you're both tapping into your current cognitive abilities and actively enhancing them. Through consistent use, over time, the brain builds and strengthens new pathways, making it easier to dream, solve problems, and be innovative.

Another significant factor in accomplishing our dreams is the role of the *reticular activating system,* or RAS, a group of neurons located in the brain stem. This part of your brain acts as a filter for the millions of pieces of information you encounter daily, deciding what should come to your conscious attention. It mediates focus and behavior. When you vividly imagine something—whether it's a goal you want to achieve or a problem you need to solve—your RAS starts to prioritize information that aligns with that imagery. Especially if it senses that you care intensely about the object of your attention, the RAS programs your brain to focus on what matters most, helping you to notice opportunities, resources, and ideas around you that will support you.

Imagination has a powerful emotional impact on us. When we picture our dreams or goals coming true, our brains release neurotransmitters, such as dopamine, which are associated with pleasure and motivation. The positive emotional response this generates in our bodies reinforces our desire to pursue our imagined scenarios, making us more willing and likely to take concrete steps to achieve them. In essence, therefore, the act of imagining an outcome can serve both as a mental rehearsal and as a source of emotional motivation, helping us take action to bridge the gap between where we are and where we want to be.

Four Applications of Imagination and Visualization

Your imagination acts as a mental canvas, where you can paint pictures of your dreams, aspirations, and goals. It's a powerful tool for formulating new ideas and shaping your future. By cultivating and intentionally using your imagination, you can inspire and motivate yourself to take meaningful action. Here are four practical ways to use imagination and visualization to improve your life.

Creative problem solving. Imagination is essential for identifying innovative solutions to challenges. When you face an obstacle, your ability to imagine alternative approaches can lead to breakthroughs. Whether it's thinking beyond the obvious or adapting existing solutions to new contexts, your imagination helps you navigate change and solve problems in creative and effective ways.

Goal setting with clarity. Visualizing your goals vividly allows you to set clear, actionable steps to achieve them. When you imagine yourself achieving a goal, you create a mental blueprint that fuels your determination and makes your path forward more tangible. This clarity transforms abstract dreams into practical, achievable objectives.

Fostering creativity. Imagination and creativity are deeply interconnected. By exercising your imagination regularly, you stimulate creative thinking, which can lead to innovation in areas ranging from art and science to entrepreneurship. Imagining possibilities expands your perspective and opens new doors for originality and self-expression.

Visualizing success. Visualization is a targeted use of imagination that helps you mentally rehearse desired outcomes. Athletes, performers, and leaders often use this technique to prepare for success and build confidence. In your own life, visualization can help you focus on what you want to be, do, and achieve, creating a sense of readiness and empowering you to take action.

What Do You Want to Be, Do, and Have? A Visualization Technique

Dreaming is the first exhilarating step on the path to embracing abundance in your life. It's the moment when you start painting the canvas of your future with the vibrant colors of your imagination. But before we dive into the realm of dreams, I want you to remember something profoundly important: *You are divine, worthy, and enough just as you are right now.*

This is not purely a platitude; it is also a fundamental truth. One that will help you lay a foundation for your journey toward being, doing, and having the things you dream of being, doing, and having. This is my definition of *abundance*. When you truly grasp your inherent worthiness, you give yourself the permission to dream and live abundantly. Permission not just to dream, but to dream as big as the boundless sky.

Maybe you have not felt this way in the past. That's okay. Life has its way of testing us all, and each of us carries our own set of scars and stories. Perhaps you've made decisions about your worthiness in response to challenging circumstances. Maybe you've had some dreams you have neglected because life's responsibilities and roles pushed them into the background. Or perhaps setbacks made you doubt their feasibility.

It also could be that someone hurt you and shattered a dream, or you decided it was too late to start dreaming or to dream a certain type of dream for yourself.

No matter the cause or situation for abandoning a particular dream, now is the time to shatter perspectives that are getting in the way and *dare to dream once more.*

Clear your mind of the clutter, release past decisions, let go of negative experiences and mistakes, and silence the noise clouding your thoughts. Close your eyes and focus inward. Picture a pristine white canvas or a limitless menu of possibilities.

I invite you now to tap into a deep place within your soul, where your creativity knows no bounds. Deep within your soul resides the power to dream, and today, we're going to awaken that dormant potential. Take this opportunity to transport yourself back to the days of childhood when your imagination knew no bounds and you believed all things were possible.

You possess an innate ability to be magnificent. It's within your very nature. And you are meant to shine in a way that no one else can. You were created for it by being born with a unique combination of talents and abilities that belongs to you alone.

So, on the blank white screen of your uncluttered imagination in the present moment I want you to begin seeing imagery related to things that you would like to be, do, and have. In this space, there are no limitations. Here you can fly or ride in the Space Shuttle. You can paint your house with purple polka dots. You can be a billionaire with a private jet and a yacht the size of a small island. You can solve world hunger and end poverty, war, and disease.

Make your dreams expansive—*as large as the universe itself.* Don't limit your dreams to what seems immediately achievable. Dream bigger, bolder, and brighter than you've ever allowed yourself to dream before.

And when you've reached that level of ambition, dream even larger.

Start by asking yourself four crucial questions.

Who am I?

What do I want to be?

What do I want to do?

What do I want to have?

As the renowned business trainer Zig Ziglar wisely said, "You've got to be before you can do, and you've got to do before you can have."[2] So, let's embark on this extraordinary journey together, my friend, with your boundless dreams as our guiding stars.

I recommend that you pause after you ask each question so that you can receive the answers which may come to you in a flood. Turn on a voice recorder and record your answers aloud so you won't forget them. Or keep a pen and paper at hand and jot down notes.

As you embark on this incredible journey of self-discovery and dream fulfillment, one of the most profound questions you'll ask yourself is, **"Who am I?"** This question goes beyond the surface and dives deep into the core of your being. It's an invitation to explore your identity, your values, and your unique essence.

Remember, Pretty Sister, you are not defined solely by your past experiences, your roles, or your circumstances. You are a magnificent masterpiece of dreams, talents, and aspirations waiting to be unveiled. Discovering who you truly are is like finding the key to unlock the door to your limitless potential, and it's a journey well worth embarking on.

The second question, **"What do I want to be?"** will help you to delve deep into your values, ideals, and whatever inspires the very best in you to show itself. The goodness that resides within you wants to emerge.

After you ask yourself the question, take a moment to reflect on the people who inspire you, those "shining stars" in your life whom you look up to. What is it about them that moves you? What qualities, accomplishments, or values do they possess that resonate with your soul?

Your positive reaction to the thought of these people is not accidental. They are guiding lights, showing you a glimpse of what's possible. Let them inspire you to become the best version of yourself. Whether it's the aspiration to become a bestselling author, a celebrity chef, a high-ranking earner, a spiritual leader, an award-winning entrepreneur, the world's greatest mother, or even a professional athlete, let your imagination soar.

As you ask your third question, **"What do I want to do?"** think about what brings you true peace, ignites your passion, and gives you a profound sense of purpose. No one can tell you what to do with your life except for you. Wouldn't it be wonderful to wake up every morning and feel like what you're doing has value? Well, this is your chance to imagine yourself as someone with a destiny.

Now, here's a thought experiment for you: If money were not a factor at all in doing things, what would you want to do?

Also, imagine that you have all the time in the world. What would you choose to do? The truth is that you have significant control over the twenty-four hours in your day.

And where would you be doing this wonderful thing that you would be doing? If you could travel to any place on Earth, where would that be? Picture yourself there, absorbing the sights, sounds, and experiences.

And who would you be with while you're doing the fabulous things you're picturing yourself doing? Think about the people you would like to surround yourself with if you could be with anyone in the world. With whom would you choose to share your time and your life?

A lot of us are motivated by an altruistic desire to be of service to our communities and humanity. If you could devote time to serving someone or some cause, what would you like to do? Remember, service is rewarding.

As you give of yourself, you will receive immense joy and fulfillment in return. Who would you serve if you were doing what you wanted to do?

And finally, have some fun with the fourth question, **"What do I want to have?"** Imagine your fairy godmother magically appearing before you, waving her wand to grant your deepest desires. What would you ask for?

This is the moment to let your imagination run wild. Picture yourself in your dream home, going on an extravagant shopping spree, or standing in Willy Wonka's Chocolate Factory with the coveted golden ticket. Think as big as the universe itself and let yourself tap into the exhilarating energy of having all your material dreams come true.

Remember, Pretty Sister, your dreams are more than fantasies. They are the blueprints of the extraordinary life you can create. So, dream boldly and dream often, for in your dreams lies the road map to your abundance and happiness.

Really, all these questions are leading you to discover what you would like your purpose in life to be. A purpose aligned with your values will become a driving force that fuels your existence.

Combine Emotion with Specificity When You Daydream

As you unleash your inner dreamer and begin to explore the limitless possibilities of what you want to be, do, and have—given the person you identify yourself as *being*—be sure to be super specific. To become actionable, your dreams and desires should be clear and vivid in your mind's eye. Think of the process of clarifying a goal as adding details to a painting. With every new brushstroke, you are adding depth and definition.

Equally important to articulating the specific details of your dreams and goals is defining the way you feel about them. As you consider your dreams of being, doing, and having things you need and want, be sure to imagine how you will FEEL when they come true.

Close your eyes and tap into that emotion. How you feel is the true spark of your soul, so it's critical to connect with this feeling for motivation.

Let me share a personal story that illustrates the power of combining clarity and emotion in our daydreaming. As a little girl, I vividly imagined my future husband. He would be tall, dark, and handsome, much like my beloved grandfather. But I didn't stop there. I also envisioned the qualities of his character. I imagined him as being deeply spiritual and highly intelligent, just like my grandfather, who was an Ivy League-educated man. I carried this dream in my heart for years, unwavering in my belief that I would find this mystery man.

It wasn't a surprise to my family when I eventually married Dave, who is the man of my dreams. What they didn't know was that he would go on to be an active leader in our church, graduate from Harvard University, and become a doctor. The more specific I got with my dreams, the more powerful they became, and the likelihood of realizing them increased.

That's the magic of combining specificity and emotion in your dreaming process. When you can see the details and feel the emotions associated with your desired outcomes, it feels like you're creating a magnetic force that is drawing those dreams closer to you. It's as if you're sending out a clear signal to the universe, saying, "This is what I want, and I can feel it in my core." There is a scientific reason for this, hardwired into our neurological processes, which we'll get into shortly. But I like believing in magic and sparkly pixie dust, too.

My point is this: As you define your dreams, hold nothing back. Be specific about what you want to be, do, and have. Imagine the colors, the sounds, the scents, the textures, and most importantly, the emotions that accompany your dreams. Whether it's the thrill of achieving a personal milestone, the joy of making a positive impact, or the contentment of living in your dream home, those feelings will guide you to the fulfillment of your dreams. Also be specific about your emotional state.

Remember, you're doing more than setting goals; you're creating a road map. If you are clear about your desires and then connect deeply with the emotions they evoke, the more you'll soon find reality aligning with your dreams.

A Step-by-Step Guide for Working with Your Dreams One by One

You've decided to embark on a journey to awaken your dreams and create your happily ever after—whatever that looks like for you. When you are ready to fully embrace a particular dream, there is a six-step process you can use to realize it. This process will empower you to love yourself unconditionally as you step into your own brilliant light.

Congratulations on making it this far and being ready to take the important steps to implement your dreams! I believe you'll find that this process is filled with promise and potential, and the possibility of boundless joy. Your confidence in your ability to bring your dreams to life will increase as you work toward success. Ultimately, you will identify a larger purpose that will make you feel happy and fulfilled. That purpose will emerge as you peel away the layers of smaller goals.

Working toward any goal will reveal information to you about what inspires you. You can repeat the same steps to achieve any dream you dare to dream. But you'll be most successful if you tackle dreams one at a time.

Step 1. Clarify your dream. Take a closer look at the dreams you've uncovered through visualization. Is there any one that particularly excites you, tugs at your heartstrings, or ignites your passion? This is the one to focus on first. Clarify your vision for this dream by describing it in detail. Visualize what it would look like if it were already a reality.

Example: Let's say your dream is to become a published author. Clarify it by specifying the genre of book you want to write, your target audience, and the impact you hope your books will have on readers.

Step 2. Break it down. Dreams can feel overwhelming when viewed in their entirety. That's why you need to distill smaller goals from big dreams. Break your plan for how to proceed into bite-sized, manageable actions. What are the specific things you need to do to move closer to the achievement of this dream? Create a road map, outlining the different milestones you want to achieve. And remember, these actions can be tiny.

Example: For the dream of becoming a published author, your road map might include steps like outlining your chapters, writing a certain number of pages each day, or going online to research literary agents.

Step 3. Set SMART goals. The acronym SMART stands for s̲pecific, m̲easurable, a̲chievable, r̲elevant, and t̲ime-bound. Apply these criteria to your dream as a whole and to the individual actions you plan to do to ensure they are well-defined and actionable. SMART goals will provide you with a clear path forward and help you stay motivated.

Example: Instead of setting a vague goal like "write a book," make it SMART: "Write a 300-page novel in the romance genre within one year." For an action like writing 500 words a day, a SMART goal could be: "Sit down in front of my computer in the kitchen between 10 AM and 11 AM on Tuesday to knock out the first scene in Chapter 15."

Steps 4–6 will be discussed in detail in the coming chapters, but here's a sneak peek to get you started.

Step 4. Believe in your dream. The power to bring your dreams to life lies within you. Cultivate a deep belief in your ability to achieve your dream. Visualize your success, and use positive affirmations to reinforce your belief. Surround yourself with people who support and encourage your dreams.

Example: Visualize yourself holding a published copy of your book, signing it for eager readers, and receiving heartfelt letters of gratitude from fans.

Step 5. Take the action. Accomplishment requires concrete action. Start by doing the first action you've planned, no matter how small and insignificant it may seem. Progress often comes one step at a time. Embrace the process, and don't be discouraged by setbacks or challenges. Hold yourself accountable to this commitment.

Step 6. Refine and repeat. As you work toward your dreams, you'll encounter obstacles, learn valuable lessons, and from this, refine your approach. It's okay to iterate and adjust your plans as needed. Be persistent and resilient in the face of setbacks.

Example: If you face writer's block or receive rejection letters, use those experiences as opportunities to grow and improve your craft. If things go well, congratulate yourself and then do more of the same. You might find in the case of the daily word count that you're capable of writing 1,000 words in an hour—more than you guessed.

Remember, your dreams are uniquely yours, and they hold the potential to bring immense fulfillment and joy into your life. Embrace them, cherish them, and take deliberate steps toward making them a reality. You have the power within you to create the change you desire. Keep believing, keep trying, and watch as your dreams transform into tangible achievements.

Identifying a Larger Purpose

For me, your clues to finding a larger purpose come from looking back at things that made your life seem worthwhile in the past, and looking around you at what brings you a sense of purpose today.

I'm sure you've had moments in your life when everything felt just right, moments when you were bursting with joy and wished time could stand still so you could savor every second. Do you remember any occasions like that when you couldn't contain your pride, love, or excitement, and felt like you were on top of the world? These moments gave you glimpses of the extraordinary, of the joy, beauty, and miracles that surround you every day, waiting for you to recognize them, didn't they? I encourage you to dream a dream that makes you feel as great as those moments did.

Other times, you may be guided by a feeling of discontentment, or frustration. Sometimes, the longing for something more—the quiet ache of discontent—isn't a sign that something is wrong, but rather a divine nudge pointing us toward a greater purpose. This **divine discontent** is not meant to discourage us, but to awaken us. It's a clue, a whisper from our souls, urging us to grow, to step into something bigger, to pursue the life we were meant to live. Instead of simply feeling frustrated by what's missing, we can learn to recognize this feeling as a sacred invitation to seek more meaning, stretch beyond our comfort zones, and create a life that aligns with our highest potential. When we listen to these inner promptings, they become a guide—leading us toward the dreams waiting to be realized.

Here, I'm urging you to dare to dream of a purpose in life that you believe will bring you immense satisfaction. If you do not feel ready yet to define such a vision for your future, the time to figure it out will be after you work on several of your smaller goals.

You'll know you are ready to chase the larger dream when it feels as if you've arrived at a crossroads, a place where choosing the right road to follow depends on knowing where you want to go. Without a dream, you cannot find the right road. You can only wander aimlessly—maybe having some nice experiences by accident—but not ensured of arriving at a destination. By comparison, with a dream in mind, you have the equivalent of a destination, and now the path to get there will become clear.

Some Pretty Sisters have more than one thing they could do that speaks to them on the soul level. Because in fact, we've all got options. Having used the previous exercises in this chapter to dip your toes into a vast sea of possibilities, to create a dream that has purpose, it's time to narrow down your focus and choose one to three goals that resonate most strongly with you.

Large dreams won't typically emerge fully formed but will grow out of the seeds of doing things that are meaningful to us. Selecting these kinds of goals is the initiating step in a longer process.

Let's Dream Together: The Power of Sisterhood

As we reach the final pages of this chapter on daring to dream, there's one more invaluable aspect of dream manifestation that we must touch upon: the incredible potency of sisterhood when it comes to the fulfillment of our dreams.

Imagine how nice it will feel to sit down with your Pretty Sisters and have your hopes and aspirations acknowledged, respected, and welcomed—not ridiculed or dismissed. And also how fascinating and rewarding it will be to listen as they unveil their own dreams and you honor them, similarly. A beautiful synergy occurs when women dream together. It's as though the universe pays extra attention when hearts aligned with purpose unite.

Here are several reasons why dreaming together can be so impactful.

Support and encouragement. Your Pretty Sisters will be your biggest cheerleaders. They'll celebrate your victories, no matter how great or small, and lift you up if you stumble. Their encouragement will be like the wind beneath your wings when you're chasing your dreams.

Accountability. Because of sharing your dreams with others, you'll be likely to stay committed to them. Your Pretty Sisters will hold you accountable, gently nudging you back on track if you stray from the path to your goal and celebrating your progress in hitting various milestones with you.

Inspiration. Hearing your Pretty Sisters speak about their dreams may spark new ideas in your mind, ignite new passion in your heart, and help you to expand the scope of your dreams. Together, you and they can establish a wonderful cycle of inspiration, where one dream feeds into the next and then the next, creating a stunning blend of brilliant colors, like a sunset that grows more beautiful as each hue merges into the next.

Shared resources. Within your sisterhood, you'll find a wealth of knowledge, skills, and resources that can aid you in achieving your dreams.

Whether it's advice, connections, a loan of a tool, or hands-on practical assistance, your Pretty Sisters will be there to lend a helping hand.

Safe haven. Pretty Sisters often create nonjudgmental safe spaces and occasions where friends and family feel free to express their wildest dreams openly. Sisterhood is a relationship in which vulnerability is accepted and cherished, and where the power of collective belief is understood to move mountains.

Remember, sisterhood doesn't have to be limited to blood relations; it's a bond formed by kindred spirits, shared values, and common dreams. So, whether you're surrounded by your biological sisters, dear friends, or members of an online community, nurture these connections and watch how much they enhance your dreaming journey. You'll be amazed.

The Sky's the Limit

In the chapters that follow, we'll delve deeper into the elements of belief, creation, and the ongoing journey of dreaming together. But for now, embrace the beautiful sisterhood that surrounds you and revel in the power of dreaming together. Your dreams are more within reach than you can imagine, and with your Pretty Sisters by your side, you'll go far.

Late August, on my fiftieth birthday, I found myself at our family lake house in Maine, surrounded by close friends and loved ones. As the day turned into night, a group of us ventured down to the dock for some late-night stargazing. Lying there under a blanket of stars, we indulged in my favorite activity—dreaming. One by one, we each took a turn sharing the first dream that came to mind.

When it was my turn, I hesitated. I had held a particular dream close to my heart for seven years. But something about the setting of being wrapped in the warmth of family and friends, gave me the courage to say it out loud. "I want to finally create a magical backyard—a place where we can all gather, play, and enjoy life together. I dream of a backyard with a pool, a beautiful pool house, and even a pickleball court," I declared. It was a big, bold dream, the kind that makes your heart race a little when you say it out loud. But I knew that speaking it meant I had to give it my all.

Fast forward to a year later when, for my birthday, I threw myself a fabulous summer celebration at what is now affectionately known as "Callie's Kingdom." We gathered in my newly renovated backyard—complete with a sparkling pool, charming pool house, and yes, a pickleball court. The very same dream I had dared to voice under those Maine stars had come true, and I couldn't have asked for a more magical setting to share with the people I love.

Fulfilling this dream wasn't without its challenges, of course. The project was far from smooth sailing. It faced setbacks at almost every stage. The budget stretched beyond what we had originally earmarked, requiring us to find creative funding solutions. Town zoning laws initially prohibited us from building the pickleball court, sparking a series of neighborhood meetings, zoning discussions, and, eventually, a town zoning code rewrite. During construction, a surprise water line owned by a neighboring town was discovered right where the pool was meant to be, forcing us to shift plans and relocate the pool entirely, which had already been dug.

Every time we hit an obstacle it felt like a test of Dave's and my commitment. Were we willing to dig deeper—literally and figuratively—to see this dream through? The answer, time and time again, was a resounding *yes*. We adapted, persevered, and believed in our vision for our backyard renovation until each piece of the plan fell into place.

All along the way, speaking to my Pretty Sisters about the challenges I was navigating lifted my spirits and kept my focus aligned with the dream that had been the seed of the project.

Whenever I look out the window at the landscape we created behind our house, I'm filled with gratitude for the process. It took determination, collaboration, and a belief in something bigger than the setbacks to keep us motivated along the way. This experience reminded me that dreams, no matter how impossible they may seem, can come true with hard work, faith, and the emotional support of my Pretty Sisters. OK, and a little magic too. After all, that's what it means to truly *dream, believe, and create.*

Look, dreams come in all sizes and shapes. They are related to our relationships, our hobbies, and things like the conservation of nature in the midst of climate change, just as much as they are to our income levels and careers. What's meaningful to one women is not going to be meaningful to every other woman. Stay true to yourself. Live authentically. Your genuine interests and desires are the source of the magic.

Whatever you've been dreaming about lately, please nurture the dream. Our dreams are the seeds of our futures, the blueprints of our destinies, and also the source of great joy.

Have you ever heard the adage "Enjoy the journey." The journey is life. This is your life and life is the true destination. The idea is to make yours abundant.

Are you ready to embrace your dreams, nurture them, and watch them blossom one by one until you are living a truly meaningful life you love? Dare to dream. Your journey to greatness can begin with the seed of a single, beautiful dream.

EIGHT

YOU MUST BELIEVE IN YOURSELF

A dream is only the beginning. Belief is the fuel that helps it take flight. It's what gives you the courage to try, to keep going, and to work your magic—one brave choice at a time.

THE AIR WAS FILLED WITH LAUGHTER AND ANTICIPATION as my sisters and I gathered around, preparing to initiate another Pretty Sister into our fold. It was a tradition we cherished—creating a magical moment where girls, young and old, could step into a space of self-worth and possibility. The ceremony that day wasn't just about the glitter, the crowns, or the laughter that always followed our playful shimmy; it was about something far more important.

Every time we placed a crown on a new Pretty Sister's head and asked her to repeat the pledge, something magical happened. As she held up her right hand and spoke the words affirming her worth and potential, you could see a spark ignite in her eyes. It was as if she was seeing herself clearly for the first time, and in that moment, the crown wasn't just a fun accessory—it was a symbol of belief.

After the pledge, we waved our magic wands, sprinkled glittering pixie dust over our friend's head, and dubbed her a Pretty Sister. We watched as one by one the women spun around, giggling, embracing the silliness and the joy of the occasion. But the most important part of the initiation wasn't the fun—it was the shift in the participants' hearts.

The Pretty Sister initiation ceremony has always been special because it reminds each of us of the powerful truth that we have the ability to believe in ourselves and to create our own magic. The ritual may be playful, but the meaning behind it is profound. It reminds us: *You are capable, you are enough, and your belief in yourself is the key that will unlock your dreams.* The crown we place on a woman's head during the ritual is a physical manifestation of an inner truth: She is worthy, she is beautiful, and she has the power to dream big.

It's one thing to crown someone a Pretty Sister, but it's another thing entirely to *believe* that you are one yourself. But believing in yourself is the foundation of everything we do. When you don that crown, it's not just about pretending to be royal for a moment—it's about stepping into your own sense of self-worth and claiming your place in the world with confidence.

Belief is the magic that turns dreams into reality. Just like sprinkling sparkly pixie dust on each other during Pretty Sister initiation ceremonies makes them feel magical, belief is the delightful ingredient in our hearts that lifts our dreams off the ground and sets them soaring. As I watched each woman take her first spin in her new crown that day, it became clear that the most magical part of the initiation wasn't the glitter or the wand—it was the belief that followed. But belief isn't something that happens by accident— it's something we must cultivate, nurture, and strengthen over time.

The Power of Belief

When you truly *believe* in yourself, you step into a power that can move mountains. Belief is what will make your dreams possible to achieve.

Remember the story of *Peter Pan* and his magical flight lessons with Wendy? The process starts with her thinking a happy thought. As she holds fast to it—believes in it—that thought lifts her off the ground.

This whimsical formula isn't just for Neverland—it actually works in our real lives too. Any joyful notion holds a kind of magic power over us if we hold it as an intention in our hearts. Then the real magic begins! For if we give a thought our faith and trust, it transforms our dreams into vibrant, living experiences. This is how belief plays an indispensable role in achieving success. It's like a bridge between desire and accomplishment.

Belief is slightly different than thought. Belief is a fixed idea that molds your more transient thoughts and shapes your actions. The ability to change your beliefs gives you the power to take control of your thinking and move it in a new direction. It can turn fleeting ideas into focused intentions, and from there, into action. It's what takes the sort of "happy thoughts" written about in *Peter Pan* and multiplies them into a force strong enough to help you soar like you have wings.

Now, you might be wondering, *How can I cultivate unwavering belief in myself and my dreams?* The answer is that you must build belief in the same way you build a muscle, through repetition.

Belief in my abilities is a gift I was fortunate enough to receive from my mother. She instilled in me the belief that I could do literally anything I set my heart to. Not everyone is so lucky. We all come from different family dynamics and have had life experiences that shape our levels of self-belief. Even if you were blessed to have confidence instilled in you early on, the challenges you encounter in your life could shake your belief system. That's why it's not enough to simply declare "I believe" once and expect it to stick forever.

Belief, like faith, needs nurturing. It ebbs and flows like the wind, so we must continually strengthen it, especially during life's storms.

One of my favorite aphorisms is "The secret to having it all is believing that you do." I keep it displayed on a plaque in my home as a constant reminder of the power of belief. A way you might build your own belief is by choosing to visualize your dreams "as if" with unwavering certainty. Plan your life *as if* your dreams are already unfolding before your eyes. Pretend that you believe until you actually do. Find evidence around you.

The goal is to come to believe in your visualization so completely that your every thought and action begins to align with your vision. When they do, before you know it, you'll be living out the affirmation: "Everything I need comes to me at the right time and place."

Think of visualization as a process of planting healthy seeds in your mind. Your thoughts are seeds, and your belief is the soil, the water, and the sunlight that will help them grow.

When you nourish beliefs in your capability to accomplish the things you are dreaming of, you create fertile ground for your dreams to flourish. Pretty Sisters can help one another have more confidence in themselves.

Faith and Trust: The Building Blocks of Belief

Like any muscle, belief needs to be exercised. It grows stronger when you show it evidence. Every time you set a goal and achieve it or show up for yourself and work toward it, and every time you overcome a challenge or show up for yourself and face it, you are strengthening your belief in yourself. This kind of evidence enables you to trust your skills and abilities, which gives you confidence, and builds your faith in your capacity to dream.

Faith and trust are a dynamic duo that can reshape your life and steer your destiny in the direction of your dreams because, together, they build your strength. Together, they're like the wind beneath your wings, propelling you toward the life you desire and are destined to live.

Let's dive deeper into how these powerful forces work.

Faith:
The Fuel of Achievement

Faith isn't just a belief; it's unwavering trust in the unseen, a deep knowing that your dreams are bound to happen. When you possess faith, it's not about wishful thinking or hoping things will work out by chance. Faith is about being entirely and confidently convinced of a future reality, even when the evidence isn't there yet.

Operating on faith is like surrendering to the mysteries of the universe and trusting in divine timing. When you fully embrace faith, you allow yourself to let go of doubts, place your trust in the journey, and focus on the bigger picture of your dreams becoming a reality.

Faith is the rocket fuel that propels our dreams. Consider the audacity of the astronauts who originally set foot on the moon. They didn't land there by accident; the engineers who built their rockets succeeded because they had unshakable faith in the possibility of sending people over 200,000 miles into outer space. But without that rocket fuel, even the best designed rocket wasn't going to get an inch off the launch pad.

In the same way, you must have unwavering belief that you can accomplish your dreams if they are to lift off—out of the planning phase—and go the distance. If you believe something is impossible, your disbelief will turn into a self-fulfilling prophecy. Any obstacle will serve as a reason to give up. It is our faith that is the driving force behind the implementation of our dreams. Faith makes taking action much, much easier.

Faith means trusting in the unseen and knowing, deep down, that your aspirations are achievable, even when the road is unclear. It's an internal conviction that transcends obstacles and setbacks, keeping you aligned with your purpose. Faith cannot be faked. It comes from a combination of repetition and visualization, which ultimately wires your subconscious mind so that the belief is your default mode of thought. Once faith is real, it is effortless to maintain it.

Faith is a paradox. Faith leads to action. Action leads to faith.

To get the evidence you need to be faithful enough to take a big leap may mean starting small and building up evidence. Ultimately, you want to have sufficient faith in your dreams that you believe your success isn't a question of "if" but "when." This degree of certainty, when you attain it, transforms how you act. When you *know* something will happen—that it is inevitable—your behavior follows suit. The person who believes they are going to succeed approaches challenges differently than a person who fears they will fail.

This level of conviction can be the engine that powers your dream into reality. But do not worry if you do not have conviction yet. We all must begin in the same way when we are starting something new. We must supply faith until the evidence to back it up exists. Martin Luther King, Jr., famously said, "Faith is taking the first step even when you don't see the whole staircase."[1] The desire to develop faith and be uplifted by it requires us to move forward, even when the path is unclear.

So, without faith, we may remain paralyzed by fear. But if we are hesitant to act and risk nothing, then for sure we fail. Faith without action is merely a wish. It's crucial that your belief in the value of your dream is reflected in your actions. Take steps that correspond to the reward, not the risk.

Think of a person expecting a child. Their entire life adjusts in preparation for that arrival—because it is inevitable. Similarly, when you *know* your dreams are coming true you will prepare and act accordingly, setting the stage for their manifestation.

A secret is that you can take steps and start getting results *before* you have complete faith.

Overcoming Fear, Faith's Counterpart

Fear is the direct opposite of faith. Fear can paralyze us, keeping us stuck in doubt and uncertainty. When we allow fear to flourish, it creates a barricade, blocking us from taking action and our dreams from being realized. Fortunately, faith can dispel fear. Thus, we have a choice of which reality to commit to—the one built by fear or the one built by faith.

Fear isn't something we can eliminate entirely; it's part of the human experience. However, in the pursuit of our dreams, understanding how to manage fear and replace it with faith is vital. The key is nurturing your faith until it becomes the dominant force in your life. As faith grows, fear shrinks. Then, with every step we take, the path to our dreams becomes clearer.

A Personal Story of Fear and Worry

To truly grasp the significance of faith over fear, let me share a personal story about worry. My grandmother, despite being one of the most fun-loving people I've ever known, had a tendency to worry—a trait she shared with her sister, my Aunt Pauline. When these two got together, they could turn the smallest issue into a full-blown catastrophe. If someone wasn't home on time, they'd quickly spiral into dramatic scenarios, imagining accidents, kidnappings, you name it.

Time and time again, their worries would amount to nothing as the person they were concerned about would show up safe and sound. Watching this pattern repeat left me puzzled. I realized that all their worries were for nothing. Worrying didn't change the situation, solve any problems, or make anything better. It was a futile waste of time and energy.

As a young observer, I made a conscious decision not to allow worry to consume me. Little did I know at the time this decision would be one of the greatest gifts I could give myself. Worry, in most cases, does nothing but steal our peace and clutter our heads. Life will go on, with or without our worry, and if feared outcomes do come to pass, then the challenges we face will still be there with or without having worked ourselves into a tizzy. Worry only magnifies problems by feeding fear and uncertainty into any situation. By making my choice always to focus on faith instead of fear, I learned to trust that things generally work out pretty well, even when I cannot control the outcome.

Yes, I worry on occasion. For example, when I became a new parent, worry crept in with questions like, *Am I capable of raising this child?* or *Will I be a good parent?* But I quickly reminded myself that life doesn't wait for our worries. Time moves forward whether we're anxious or calm. So, I figured: *Why not choose faith over worry?*

I developed a simple habit. Any time a worry arose, I would ask myself, *Can I do anything about this?* If the answer was yes, I'd take action. If the answer was no, I'd release it into the hands of fate, knowing that everything eventually works out for the best. I leaned in to the belief that everything happens for a reason. And I shifted my energy from stressing about the things I couldn't control to focusing on the things that I knew I could do, like eating well, reading books on infant care, setting up the baby's crib, and shopping for supplies.

In every situation, even the hard ones, there is something we can do, even if that thing is simply to be kind to ourselves.

Taking Control of Your Thoughts

Faith can become your guiding light in moments of fear and uncertainty. When you feel overwhelmed by life's challenges, stop and remind yourself to express some faith in the situation. For example, show faith that everything will work out in the end, even if you can't see how. Let the world and invisible forces meet you halfway.

If there is nothing else to believe in, choose to trust that every trial serves the purpose of helping you grow and preparing you for the fulfillment of your dreams.

By replacing worry with faith, you'll find peace every time. That's a reason to make the effort, isn't it? I believe that with a little practice, shifting your mindset can become a habit you rely on.

As you move forward, it's essential to address how you think. Faith and trust are not just abstract concepts; they are rooted in thoughts. If you want to strengthen them, you must actively manage the way you think.

We all have moments when our belief in ourselves falters and we are not thinking pretty. Maybe you've caught yourself comparing your progress to someone else's or doubting your ability to succeed. Such self-limiting thoughts are like weights that keep your dreams grounded. To release the ballast so your dreams can take flight, you will need to disrupt and rewire old thought patterns that don't serve you. Thought patterns you absolutely *must* let go of include:

- Comparing yourself to others.
- Criticizing yourself or feeling inadequate.
- Dwelling in a victim mentality and feeling sorry for yourself.
- Fixating on life being unfair.
- Worrying about things you can't control.
- Holding on to regrets and past mistakes.
- Speaking negatively about others.
- Feeling sorry for yourself because life is hard or unfair.
- Thinking nothing ever works out for you.
- Believing you're not lucky or that success is beyond your reach.
- Making excuses because you feel afraid.
- Feeling like no one cares about you.
- Convincing yourself there's never enough time.
- Thinking it's too late to chase your dreams.

We've all been there. These thoughts creep in, sometimes unnoticed, and begin to take control, and they're not pretty. But here's the thing: *You have the power to take back control of your thoughts. You have the power to think pretty.* Negative thinking is often automatic—your mind responds to conditions without you even realizing it, much like driving a familiar route home in your car without needing to think about it. But just because it's automatic, doesn't mean it can't be changed.

Disrupting Your Old Thought Patterns

So, how can you change your subconscious thought patterns and begin thinking pretty? Start by being mindful of your thoughts and catching yourself having a moment of negativity. Awareness is a powerful tool. When you find yourself entering a cycle of negative thinking, stop in your tracks, take a deep breath, and then *disrupt* the pattern by consciously choosing a new thought. (Yes, this may feel weird. It's going to seem awkward the first several times you do it.)

Shifting your mindset can be challenging, especially if you've held on to a particular pattern of thought for a long time. But disrupting old thinking is a necessary step if you want to build a new belief system that aligns with your faith in your dreams and trust in God's plan for you. By breaking the cycle you will create room for more positive, empowering thoughts.

Instead of letting negative thoughts weigh you down, replace them with affirmations of your value and competence. For example, you could remind yourself: *I am worthy. I am capable. I am a Pretty Sister with the power to create my dreams.*

Elevating Your Vibration

One of the most powerful ways to reset your thinking is by raising your energetic vibration. This might sound unfamiliar, but it's simpler to do than you might initially think. Every thought and feeling carries its own energy, and this energy either attracts positivity or negativity. Positive thoughts generate positive outcomes, while negative thoughts generate negative outcomes.

The fastest way to elevate your vibration when you're experiencing negative thinking is to express gratitude. Gratitude shifts your focus away from what's going wrong to what's going right. It's a simple, profoundly effective tool that can immediately lift your spirits and bring you back into alignment with your dreams and beliefs.

Start bringing gratitude into your experience by listing a few things you're grateful for each day—no matter how small—and watch how this practice transforms your overall thinking.

Trust:
The Divine Partnership

God is the most steadfast partner we could ever have. God is entirely trustworthy. While faith is about believing in the unseen, trust takes it a step further. Trust is about having confidence in the integrity, strength, and timing of a greater power that is in operation in your life—whether you call it the Divine, the Universe, or God. When you trust, you're handing over control to this higher force, knowing it understands your deepest needs and desires even better than you do.

Divine intelligence doesn't operate on the human timeline. It orchestrates events in alignment with our ultimate peace and joy. This typically involves the moving around of many parts that are unseen to us. All we can do is trust.

Trust means having the confidence that everything will unfold exactly as it should, even if the timing doesn't match our expectations. It's about letting go of control and embracing the natural flow of life, understanding that challenges are part of the journey, not roadblocks to our dreams.

Building Trust: A Bridge to Your Future

Your trust is like a sturdy bridge that connects your dreams to reality. It's built not only in faith but through consistency, integrity, and perseverance. Trust begins with you knowing that you yourself are capable of navigating challenges and uncertainties. Each time you set a goal and achieve it you're reinforcing your trust in your own abilities.

Trust also extends to the relationships around you. Trusting others allows you to form meaningful connections and create a network of support. Collaboration with your Pretty Sisters or likeminded individuals on a similar journey as you, enables you to pool resources, gather wisdom, and stay inspired.

Moreover, trust in the process is essential. Setbacks are part of every manifestation journey, but trusting that you're on the right path and that each step is contributing to your growth and ultimate success will help you persist through your difficulties.

Trust, in this sense, is the bedrock upon which the grandest dreams are built. With trust in yourself, your relationships, the unfolding process, and your higher power, you will find that the road to your dreams becomes not only clearer but also more meaningful and rewarding.

Your Pretty Sisters Will Help You Build Your Trust in Yourself

Building self-trust is deeply personal, but the support of your Pretty Sisters can amplify your efforts. When your sisters cheer you on, offer guidance, and celebrate your victories, they help you maintain faith in yourself, especially during moments of doubt. Having a network of individuals who believe in your dreams just as much as you do can be a powerful motivator.

Sharing your dreams with your Pretty Sisters allows for mutual accountability. When you're surrounded by those who uplift you, your commitment to your own goals will be strengthened and your belief in your ability to achieve those goals will flourish.

Setbacks, of course, are part of the journey. But with your Pretty Sisters by your side, even the hardest moments can become opportunities for growth. They'll remind you of your worth and capability, helping you shift your perspective from failure to learning. With this support system, your belief in yourself will soon become rock solid.

Three Tools for Anchoring Your Belief in Your Worth

When you consciously choose to think positive thoughts and act as if your dreams are already coming true, you uplift yourself and elevate your vibration. Just as Peter Pan flew by holding on to a happy thought, focusing on the good inside you is transformational. Your thoughts are the key to unlocking your potential. By nurturing self-belief, elevating your energy, and filling your mind with faith in possibility, you create the conditions necessary for your dreams to take flight.

During a Pretty Sister initiation, a woman or girl is surrounded by her friends who tell her she is fabulous, intelligent, beautiful, and beloved. We also use physical symbols, like crowns and sparkling pixie dust (glitter), to remind her of her worth and potential. We shift her emotional energy by anointing her with the fragrance of natural essential oils. And finally, we have her speak the self-affirming words of the Pretty Sister Pledge, which is the ultimate acknowledgment of everything wonderful that she embodies.

While the entire ceremony is fun and whimsical, it is also deeply meaningful and serves to anchor the woman or girl's belief in her dreams and capabilities. These five elements of the ceremony help her transform abstract ideas—like confidence, self-love, and empowerment—into something tangible and memorable.

These delightful anchors become powerful reminders that you can carry with you and use to guide you back to your center any time doubt creeps in—as it inevitably will at some point. Whether it's the glimmer of pixie dust to remind you of the magic in believing, the regal weight of a crown symbolizing your inner royalty, or the uplifting scent of essential oils sparking a reconnection to your dreams, these anchors are more than simple tokens.

Symbolic Anchor #1:
Embracing Magic and Possibility with Pixie Dust

First, let's talk about pixie dust, a playful glittering powder that symbolizes the magic of belief and possibility. In the Pretty Sister initiation, pixie dust is sprinkled over each initiate's head as part of the ceremony, signifying the magical moment when she steps into her potential. But beyond the glitter and fun, there's a deeper meaning behind this whimsical dust.

Pixie dust serves as a reminder that magic doesn't just exist in fairy tales—it exists in the everyday moments of our lives when we choose to believe in something greater than ourselves. When we dare to dream, hope, and believe in the impossible, we sprinkle a bit of that same magic into our own lives. Pixie dust symbolizes *faith in things unseen*. It's that extra something we tap into when things seem tough—when dreams seem out of reach, or life's challenges feel overwhelming. When we sprinkle pixie dust on a newly initiated Pretty Sister, we are not only celebrating the beauty of her spirit but also reminding her that she has all the magic she needs inside of her to make her dreams come true.

Belief, much like pixie dust, can take many forms: It can be the childlike wonder that opens our hearts to new possibilities, or the determination that helps us keep going even when the path ahead is unclear. Pixie dust is that special touch of hope and optimism we add to our daily lives. It encourages us to approach life with a sense of adventure, knowing that no matter what happens, there's always something good waiting to unfold.

As you move through life, remember to carry a bit of your own pixie dust—whether that's in the form of gratitude, optimism, or faith that things will work out. When life gets difficult, or when you find yourself doubting your own abilities, reach for that pixie dust. Let it remind you that you can rise above any obstacle and soar toward your dreams.

And don't keep the magic to yourself. Share it! Much like how, in the Pretty Sister initiation, we sprinkle pixie dust on one another, you can sprinkle some belief on the people around you—your family, friends, and fellow Pretty Sisters. Your belief in them might be just the magic they need to chase their own dreams.

Symbolic Anchor #2: The Crown Is a Symbol of Worthiness and Self-Sovereignty

Next, let's talk about the crown, a symbol that's rich with meaning and deeply personal to every Pretty Sister. When we place a crown on a new Pretty Sister during the initiation, it's not just a playful gesture. The crown represents the acknowledgment of her divine worth, her inner beauty, and her sovereignty over her own life. It's a reminder that she is a queen in her own right—worthy of love, respect, and all the good things life has to offer.

For centuries, crowns have been symbols of royalty, power, and leadership. They are worn by those who are entrusted with great responsibility, but more importantly, by those who carry themselves with grace, confidence, and self-worth. In the Pretty Sister tradition, the crown serves as a daily reminder that each of us is deserving of the best in life simply because of who we are.

Wearing a crown—whether a real one or a symbolic one—means recognizing your own value. It's a way of affirming that you are not defined by external circumstances or the opinions of others. Instead, you are anchored in your inherent worthiness. This belief is foundational to achieving your dreams. After all, if you don't believe you're worthy of your dreams, how can you expect to reach them?

The crown also reminds us to carry ourselves like queens. This doesn't mean being haughty or feeling superior to others, but rather, standing tall with dignity, self-respect, and kindness. It means walking through life with a sense of purpose and treating others with the same respect and worth that we desire for ourselves. Every time you picture yourself wearing a crown, let it be a reminder to hold your head high and believe in your own power to create the life you want and deserve.

As a symbol, the crown also speaks to self-leadership, the ability to guide your own life, make decisions that align with your values, and take responsibility for the consequences of your actions. When we crown a new Pretty Sister, we are celebrating her ability to show up, do the work necessary, and lead herself toward her dreams, even in the face of challenges. The crown isn't just for show; it's a testament to the strength and resilience that live within her.

Throughout history, crowns have been decorated with jewels, each representing something important, such as wisdom, courage, love, and strength. In the same way, you can imagine your own crown being adorned with the qualities that define who you are and what you stand for. Every time you face doubt or insecurity, remember that you are wearing an invisible crown, filled with the jewels of your experiences, lessons, and strengths.

Collect crowns, real or symbolic, and let them remind you daily of your worthiness and divine potential. Hang a crown from your rearview mirror, place one on your desk, or wear a piece of jewelry that makes you feel regal. Every glance at it will reignite your belief in your own power to create, to lead, and to thrive.

Symbolic Anchor #3: Anoint Yourself with Essential Oils

Essential oils are natural aromatic compounds extracted from various parts of plants, such as their leaves, flowers, bark, stems, and roots. These potent oils have been used for thousands of years across different cultures for their therapeutic, medicinal, and aromatic properties, and they continue to play a significant role in supporting emotional and physical well-being today.

One of the most powerful oils when it comes to anchoring your belief and dreams is wild orange, often referred to as the *oil of abundance.* This vibrant, citrus-scented oil has been celebrated for its ability to uplift the mood, encourage creativity, and inspire a sense of joy. Its connection to abundance and positivity makes it a powerful tool in helping you stay centered on your dreams.

When you use wild orange or any other essential oil intentionally, you're engaging your mind and body in a sensory experience that helps ground your thoughts and emotions. The olfactory system—the part of the brain responsible for our sense of smell—is closely linked to the limbic system, which governs our emotions, memories, and moods. This is why inhaling a familiar scent can instantly transport you to a specific memory or evoke a certain feeling.

When you smell wild orange, it triggers a response in your brain that can elevate your mood and help you refocus on the positive, abundant possibilities ahead. As you breathe in the citrusy aroma, you may find yourself feeling more hopeful, optimistic, and energized. This is not just about positive thinking—there is science behind the connection between scent and emotion—using essential oils is a powerful way to elevate your vibration and shift your mindset.

Imagine starting your day by inhaling the scent of wild orange while repeating an affirmation like "I am worthy of abundance. I believe in my dreams." The combination of scent, affirmation, and intention creates a powerful trifecta for building your belief in yourself. As the scent anchors the affirmation in your mind, it becomes a daily ritual that helps to cement your belief in your ability to manifest your dreams.

Additionally, wild orange isn't just about abundance in the material sense. It's about abundance of the heart, feeling full, content, and joyful in the present moment. It's a reminder that abundance begins with gratitude, and when you practice gratitude daily, you align yourself with a higher energetic vibration, opening the door to even more blessings.

Of course, wild orange isn't the only essential oil that you can use to anchor positive beliefs in your nervous system. Oils like lavender are known for their calming and soothing properties, helping to reduce anxiety and stress when self-doubt creeps in. Peppermint is invigorating, boosting mental clarity and focus, perfect for days when you need extra motivation to work toward your goals. Frankincense, often referred to as the *king of oils,* promotes a sense of spiritual connectedness and grounding that can help you stay aligned with your higher purpose.

By incorporating essential oils into your daily routine, you create a simple but effective way to anchor your belief in yourself and in your dreams. Whether through aromatherapy, applying oils topically, or using them in your environment, these oils serve as powerful reminders of your intentions and your capacity to create the life you desire.

Just as the crown and pixie dust in our Pretty Sister initiation help anchor the beliefs of worth and possibility in your mind, essential oils give you another layer of support for your pursuit of your dreams. Oils are anchors that remind you of the power you have to shift your thoughts, change your emotional state, and stay grounded in your belief, no matter what challenges arise.

Remember, belief is not a one-time event, but a daily practice. And having physical reminders like essential oils can help you stay committed to that practice. So, the next time you're feeling uncertain, reach for your bottle of wild orange, take a deep breath, and let its scent bring you back to the truth: *You are worthy. You are capable. You are a Pretty Sister, destined to achieve your dreams.*

So, my dear dreamer, let the magic of pixie dust, your crown, and essential oils be a reminder of the power you hold. Let them remind you to have faith in your dreams, trust the journey, and embrace the magic within. When you choose to believe, you open the door to a life filled with boundless possibilities, joy, and the wondrous fulfillment of your deepest desires.

The Journey of Belief

Believing in your value and future success is a journey, and like any journey, it has its ups and downs. But just as each new Pretty Sister is crowned by her sisters with a sense of magic and possibility, you can crown yourself with belief every single day. It's a choice to make a commitment to see your worth, to trust in your dreams, and to have faith in the journey.

When you believe in yourself, you unlock the door to a life filled with magic, possibility, and purpose. So today, I challenge you to crown yourself with belief. Wear it proudly. And just like the newly initiated Pretty Sisters, spin around, shimmy, and let yourself dream big. You are worthy of your dreams, and with belief, you have the power to make them come true.

So, today, choose to believe. Let go of the thoughts that no longer serve you, disrupt the old patterns, and replace them with more empowering ones that align you with your highest potential. Your dreams are waiting for you. Are you ready to embrace them?

NINE

YOU CREATE YOUR REALITY

"Whatever you can do or dream you can, begin it; boldness has genius, power, and magic in it."

WILLIAM HUTCHISON MURRAY

IT ALL STARTED ONE DAY IN MY HIGH SCHOOL HISTORY class, when my teacher, Mr. Ward, introduced us to the Close Up Foundation program. This program offered an extraordinary opportunity: an educational trip to Washington, D.C. A weeklong adventure of touring the nation's capital, soaking in its rich history and culture with my friends. The prospect felt magical, and I was immediately drawn to it.

For me, this wasn't just about visiting Washington. It was a chance to return to my roots. I had been born in Vienna, Virginia, just outside the District, and lived there until my family moved out west. The idea of visiting my hometown and reconnecting with family and old friends added a deeper sense of purpose to my dream. I had to go.

But there was one significant hurdle: the cost. The trip was priced at $1,000—a small fortune for a sixteen-year-old making just five bucks an hour at a part-time job. Financing the trip seemed like an insurmountable goal at first. Yet, this experience would become my first real lesson in how to turn a dream into reality, a lesson that's shaped my approach to every challenging goal going forward.

Filled with excitement, I rushed home to tell my mom about the opportunity. As always, her response was supportive: "Yes, of course you can go!" But then she added the condition that would change the way I saw obstacles forever. "But you'll have to find a way to make it happen," she said.

At that moment, I didn't realize the full impact of her words. She could have easily listed all the reasons why it might be too difficult or too expensive. But she didn't rain on my parade. Instead, she handed me the greatest gift a parent can give a child, belief in my capability. She believed that I could make this dream real, and her confidence lit a fire in me. I began to see the challenge from her perspective, not as a roadblock, but as a puzzle to solve.

With advice from Mr. Ward, I learned that the Close Up Foundation could receive tax-deductible donations from businesses as it was a nonprofit organization. This opened a door I hadn't thought of before, and soon, I was reaching out to local businesses, sharing the story of my upcoming trip, and asking for contributions. I worked harder than I ever had and more than met my initial goal. I surpassed it. By the time I left for Washington, I had raised enough funds to cover both the basic expenses of the trip and some extra spending money.

But the true lesson wasn't just about the money I raised. It was about realizing that when you truly desire something and commit to it with action, anything becomes possible. Finding the cash necessary to pay for my airfare, hotel, and meals wasn't the goal; it was the journey. Fortunately, where there's a will, there's a way. My mom's faith in me taught me to look around to find more pathways and options to get something done. She taught me that dreams aren't passive. They require intention, belief, and most importantly, action.

Taking Action: The Key to Creation

Now that you've taken the bold step to dream and firmly believe in the manifestation of your dreams, it's time to move forward and create your dream life. This is where the real magic happens. *Action* is the key, and through your actions, you're not only claiming your power but also demonstrating your unwavering faith in your ability to create the life you desire.

Some manifesting experts may guide you through the dreaming and believing phases but leave you hanging after that. You might hear phrases like *Just surrender and let the universe handle the rest.* While surrendering is an essential part of manifestation, there's more to actively creating your dream life. You possess far more power than you may realize.

You're not just a bystander in the grand theater of your life. You're the star of the show, the director of your destiny. You hold the incredible power to shape your path, cocreate with God, and turn your dreams into reality. Your actions, your choices, and your unwavering belief in yourself are the driving forces behind the scenes, working in perfect harmony with the divine plan.

Own Your Expectations

As you embark on the journey to create your dream life, it's important both to set goals and to own your expectations. To declare and claim them. Getting clear and being intentional about going after what you want, rather than leaving your desires to chance, makes a world of difference in achieving any vision.

Let me share a personal story from early in my marriage about the importance of owning our expectations. This crucial lesson has stuck with me throughout my life and crops up again and again when I'm doing business.

Have you ever heard the saying *Don't assume, as it makes an ass out of you and me?* (It comes from an episode of *The Odd Couple.*) Well, case in point. This story is about how assumptions led me and my husband astray.

My first birthday as a newlywed was approaching, and I mistakenly *assumed* Dave would know exactly what I wanted. He, well-intentioned, but still unaware of my preferences, gifted me a fishing pole. While thoughtful from his perspective—because he loved fishing and had a vision in his head of us enjoying fishing standing side by side in a stream—fishing wasn't something I had ever expressed interest in.

In fact, I had never communicated any of my expectations. The day arrived, I opened the package, and my palpable disappointment on receiving this gift was a direct result of my oversight.

That birthday taught me a valuable lesson: If you want something, you need to be clear about wanting it. I couldn't assume that Dave or anyone else could read my mind. I had to claim my desires and expectations and express them.

As a result of this lesson, I became an expert at throwing birthday parties for myself. I quickly learned that if I wanted a specific type of celebration or gift, it was up to me to make it happen. One milestone birthday, my thirtieth, stands out. We had just emerged from the financial struggles of Dave's surgical residency, and my business was thriving. So, I had some cash to play with and decided to pamper myself with a birthday extravaganza at my favorite salon in Boston, Àcôté on Newbury Street. I booked almost the entire salon for myself and my friends, catered delicious food for everybody, and we indulged in a day of mutual self-care. The outdoor rooftop patio was adorned with jewelry for my friends to shop as we enjoyed our rooftop lunch. It was a birthday celebration to remember.

Whether it's a birthday gift or your life's biggest dreams, the lesson remains the same: Make your desires known. Do not make assumptions. Take responsibility for articulating what you want, and don't be afraid to ask for help when needed.

This idea translates perfectly into the process of creating your reality. Clarity is key. By communicating your goals clearly—to yourself, to others, and to God—you will take charge of the energy surrounding your desires. Instead of relying on assumptions and random chance, you make the path to achieving your dreams more direct and actionable.

In fact, communication could be one of the action steps you name in your six-step plan!

Daily Inspiration: Seeking Guidance from God and Within

As you work toward creating your reality, one of the most transformative habits you can develop is the habit of seeking daily inspiration. This habit isn't just about checking a task off your to-do list; it's about employing a practice, such as prayer, contemplation, or journaling, to align yourself with your higher purpose and your inner wisdom. God will work hand in hand with your inner guidance to illuminate your path forward, giving you clarity, strength, and focus as you move closer to your dreams.

Think of the time you spend doing whichever practice you choose as your *daily spiritual training session.* Just as an athlete seeks guidance from a coach to excel in their sport or an actor works with a director to find the right way to bring the lines in a script to life on stage or screen, you can seek guidance from God and your own inner wisdom to excel in life.

In my experience, the more we practice listening to, and acting on this guidance, the stronger and clearer it becomes.

How to Seek Daily Inspiration

Start each day with a moment of quiet reflection. Whether it's through prayer, meditation, or journaling, this is your opportunity to connect with God and your inner self. Use this time to ask for guidance, aligning your actions with your higher purpose.

Here are two questions to help guide your practice.

What am I doing that I should *continue* to do? This question helps you recognize the positive steps you're already taking toward your dreams, affirming the actions that keep you moving in the right direction.

What am I doing that I should *stop* doing? Here, you identify habits, behaviors, or thoughts that are holding you back, allowing you to let go of the things that no longer serve your goals.

After reflecting on these questions, listen to the inner guidance that comes through. Trust the gentle nudges or strong impressions you feel and act on them. Seeking inspiration is not just a practice of asking, it's also about listening and acting.

By seeking daily inspiration, you create a direct channel for guidance that will help you make the small adjustments necessary to stay on track.

Why Daily Inspiration Matters

Daily inspiration, whether from God or your own inner guidance, is essential to staying aligned with your higher goals and maintaining a clear path forward, especially when life becomes complex and overwhelming. Wisdom acts as a spiritual compass, helping you recalibrate your actions so they remain connected to your dreams and divine purpose. Each day, when you seek guidance, use it as a chance to ensure you're on track so you can avoid unnecessary detours. Being in alignment with your purpose will help you make more meaningful progress toward your current goals.

Just as physical exercise strengthens the body, regularly seeking divine inspiration strengthens our connection with God and our inner wisdom. Over time, this daily practice becomes second nature, empowering us to navigate our challenges with confidence and clarity. As we seek this guidance consistently, our spiritual muscles grow, making it easier to face life's twists and turns with resilience.

Life is full of unexpected moments, and that's why daily inspiration practices are so crucial. They allow you to make small course corrections that will keep you aligned with your highest purpose. Like the GPS in your car adjusts its map to your position when you're driving, this guidance ensures you stay on the most efficient path toward your dreams. Instead of going miles out of your way after making a wrong turn, you can recalculate your route, continuously realigning with the bigger picture of your goals.

Throughout history, countless individuals have experienced life-changing moments as a result of their practice of daily inspiration. Mother Teresa, for example, was known to begin each day with prayer, relying on God's guidance to fuel her mission of serving others. It was through this daily connection that she found the strength to carry out her work, even under the most challenging circumstances.

Similarly, founder Steve Jobs often credited intuitive hunches with shaping the trajectory of his company, Apple. He believed that those moments of inspiration came from a deep connection to something beyond himself, helping guide his creative and business decisions.

Now, it's your turn. Think about a time when you felt a sudden insight or "knowing" that nudged you in the right direction. Whether it was acting on a gut feeling that opened up an opportunity or avoiding a challenge thanks to a quiet internal nudge, that was your inspiration at work. Were you doing something special that enabled you to hear your inner voice? If so, I suggest that you do more of the same thing.

Such moments, however subtle, are the result of staying open to daily inspiration and allowing God and our inner guidance to lead us forward. By making daily inspiration a habit, we create a powerful foundation for staying aligned with our dreams and purpose.

Incorporating Inspiration into Your Daily Routine

Whether it's through morning prayer or meditation, or through a few moments of reflection or debriefing before bed, a habitual daily action to connect with yourself and your higher power will keep you focused and inspired as you work to improve something in your reality. Over time, you'll notice that your thoughts and actions naturally align with the guidance you receive, allowing you to make meaningful progress to realize your dreams.

Life and inner work aren't about perfection; they're about showing up consistently and being open to the direction that comes to you. Some days, the guidance will be subtle. Other days, it will be commanding, a clear and possibly urgent call to action. Either way, trust the advice. If you doubt it, check it against other sources.

Developing Habits to Create Your Reality

Creating your dream life isn't about wishful thinking alone. It's about taking action consistently, making intentional choices, and developing habits that are in alignment with your goals and values. Action is the driving force behind manifestation, but, in particular, habitual action is the foundation for creation.

Let's dive for a few pages into the power of habits, the role of consistency, and how your small daily choices have shaped your present and will shape your future.

One of the most important principles I learned while fundraising for my trip to Washington, D.C., was that consistency is key. Each day, I dedicated time to writing letters reaching out to potential donors, and tracking my progress. At first, the idea of raising $1,000 through donations felt overwhelming, but by focusing on bite-sized steps—like setting daily fundraising goals—it became achievable. Raising $20 to $100 at a time felt manageable. I wasn't afraid to make requests of the adults I knew in that financial range.

The same goes for any habit you want to develop. Whether you're working on a fitness goal, learning a new skill, or even trying to stay more organized, the power lies in repeating an action consistently—one that you will not shy away from doing. If the idea of walking 10,000 steps in a day makes you want to sit on the couch, but you are willing to walk 500 steps, then walk 500 steps. The more you do something, the more automatic it becomes.

Once you are comfortable at the initial level, stretch to go further. In the case of walking, next after 500 steps is 1,000 steps.

Surrounding yourself with a supportive environment can bolster your consistency. Our surroundings play a critical role in supporting or hindering us from forming new habits. For instance, if you're trying to develop a habit of working out in the morning, having your gym gear ready to go in a bag by the front door the night before can help you succeed.

One powerful technique to build new habits is to stack them on top of existing ones. This technique is especially effective for integrating smaller changes into your routine. For instance, you could stack a new habit like daily journaling with your morning wakeup routine, making it more natural to adopt. Wake up, go to the bathroom, wash your face, brush your teeth, get dressed, then write in your journal for five minutes. You're already doing five of those things, adding a sixth could become part of your routine very quickly.

Creating habits is like building a muscle. It takes time and repetition, but once the habit is established, it feels effortless. The key is to stay consistent, even when the results aren't immediately visible. Every small effort adds up, and over time, the impact becomes undeniable.

As you grow and evolve, your habits should too. Stay flexible. The goals and habits you have today may change in the future as you continue to build your dream life. It takes time to build lasting habits. Research shows that habits can take anywhere from eighteen to 254 days to become automatic.[1] Be patient with yourself. The same principle applies to creating your dream life. If it takes time, keep going—you're building something worthwhile.

Remember, the habits you develop are tools for transformation. The process isn't about perfection, but about progress. You don't have to get everything right the first time, and that's okay. What matters is that you're showing up every day, committed to the life you want to create.

Book recommendation: If you're ready to dive deeper into the power of habits, one of my favorite books on the topic is *Atomic Habits* by James Clear. This book offers practical tools to help you develop habits that align with your dreams.

Small Changes, Big Impact

You don't need to make giant leaps in realizing your goals to see signs of progress. In fact, significant changes often come from making small, manageable adjustments that are consistent. Take one step at a time, and soon, those steps will compound into substantial progress. While fundraising $1,000 in a single month seemed overwhelming to me at first, breaking it down into $100 increments made the goal seem achievable. And within a week, I could already see in my bank account that I had brought in donations of $480. Internally, that made me feel more confident, and I now had a different goal of $520 to raise. I could do it!

The same concept applies to any goal you set. If you dream of writing a book, for example, you don't need to sit down and write an entire chapter in one sitting. Start by dedicating fifteen or thirty minutes each day to writing. Over time, those daily efforts will add up, and before you know it, you'll have a finished manuscript. In fact, you may find the thirty-minute interval is so manageable that you really would rather sit and write longer. That's what happened to me. By the end of writing this book, I was devoting whole days to writing and editing every chapter and thoroughly enjoying myself as I was doing it.

The secret to success isn't in the big, dramatic actions, it's in the small, consistent efforts that enable you to build momentum over time. This phenomenon is often referred to as the *compound effect,* borrowing a term from the world of banking where the interest that accumulates on savings grows exponentially over decades. Small, seemingly insignificant actions, when repeated over time, can lead to massive results.

Whether it's saving money, improving your health, or working toward a career goal, the key is consistency. It's not about doing everything all at once, but about doing the right things many times in a row.

Accountability and Tracking

One of the most effective ways to stay consistent is to hold yourself accountable. During my fundraising efforts, my older sister Becky played a critical role as my accountability partner. She regularly checked in on my progress and encouraged me to keep going, even when it seemed to me like I wouldn't reach my goal. Having someone to share your journey with, such as a friend or mentor, dramatically increases your chances of success.

Tracking your progress is also an important tool for accountability. When you track your actions in a journal, on a habit-tracking app, or using a simple checklist of to-do items, you will be able to see the progress you're making in concrete terms that help you acknowledge your progress as real. This will give you a sense of accomplishment that fuels your motivation and keeps you moving forward.

Another of my favorite techniques for maintaining progress is to break my tasks into smaller, more manageable steps. Dividing a large goal that could take months to accomplish into daily or weekly tasks makes it possible to feel accomplishment regularly. The sense of accomplishment I derive from completing these smaller tasks helps me to maintain my forward momentum, even when my life gets busy. I love checking items off my to-do list and rewarding myself with mini celebrations.

Another example of the practicality of this approach comes from the many times I have moved my family. Each time Dave and I packed up our home, we have done so without professional movers. My strategy is simple, but powerful: Pack a few boxes each day, no matter what. Some days, especially when I was exhausted, I would make the choice to pack something easy, like a box of books, blankets, or pillows. The important thing was that I stuck to my plan of packing a set number of boxes before I allowed myself to go to bed. Acting on my commitment took discipline and dedication, but it was these small, daily efforts that ultimately brought me to the finish line on moving day.

It's just like the old joke, "How do you eat an elephant? One bite at a time." Small actions may seem insignificant in the moment, but every action is essential. Each box packed, each word written, each dollar saved, each task completed brings you steadily closer to your goal. Consistent, incremental action is how big dreams are brought to life.

Decisive Action and Momentum

As we've discussed, your dreams won't materialize on wishful thinking alone. It's through consistent, intentional actions that your reality begins to take shape. But what often holds people back from creating their dream life is indecision. Overthinking the rightness of an action and second-guessing yourself leads to inaction.

This is where decisiveness comes in. When you build the habit of making decisions quickly and then confidently act upon them, you set your life in motion. One powerful tool to help with this is the *five-minute rule.*

The five-minute rule is simple: If a decision isn't life-altering, never spend more than five minutes deliberating on it. Successful people don't analyze every small decision. They act. Whether it's choosing which task to tackle first or deciding whether to say yes or no to an opportunity, limit yourself to five minutes of reflection (if that much!) and move forward. Why? Because small hinges swing big doors. The more decisively you act, the faster you create momentum. Also, this approach will prevent you from developing decision fatigue.

Decisiveness doesn't just help you move quickly; it gives you control over your life. Each decision made in five minutes reinforces your sense of personal agency, saves you energy, and helps eliminate your mental clutter.

When you're decisive, you build forward momentum, which is crucial for achieving goals. But it's not about rushing. It's about trusting your instincts and understanding that action leads to progress.

When being decisive, you may make a mistake, but mistakes are not the end of the road. Think of them as stepping stones on the path to ultimate success. Fear of failure often leads to perfectionist thinking, which can paralyze our decision-making and stifle growth. But when we embrace the idea of "failing forward," we shift our mindset. Each misstep becomes an opportunity to learn, grow, and refine our direction.

Mistakes aren't fatal; they're inevitable, and they play a crucial role in moving us closer to our goals. With each error, we gain valuable insight that equips us to make better choices and ultimately reach success.

Decisiveness doesn't mean that every choice will be perfect. It means you trust yourself enough to act and course-correct if necessary. This is where our humility becomes a powerful tool. Pride can keep us clinging to a poor decision longer than we should, compounding the mistake and making it harder to recover. Humility, by contrast, allows us to acknowledge when we've taken a wrong turn and make the necessary corrections early.

The key is to focus on making the next best decision. If you realize you've erred, adjust quickly to minimize the impact, and then keep moving forward. Progress isn't about never making mistakes—it's about learning to pivot gracefully and confidently when they happen.

Focus on What Really Matters: The Pareto Principle

But there's another key to taking decisive action: focusing on what truly moves the needle in your life. This is where the *Pareto principle*, also known as the *80/20 rule*, comes into play. The Pareto principle suggests that 20 percent of our actions produce 80 percent of our results. In other words, not all tasks are created equal.

This principle is a game changer when it comes to goal achievement. Instead of spreading yourself thin across numerous small tasks, focus on the few actions that will yield the biggest results. The key is to ask yourself: *What are the top three things I can do today that will move me closer to my dream?*

By focusing on those three actions, you will magnify your efforts. Over time, as you watch what happens by doing this repeatedly, you'll find that the majority of your progress comes from focusing on the most impactful tasks. So, rather than feeling overwhelmed by all the things you could be doing, home in on the few things that truly matter.

For example, if you're trying to build a new business, instead of getting lost in minor tasks like tweaking your website design or endlessly updating your social media profiles, focus on the core actions: building your product, connecting with customers, and securing key partnerships. These are the 20 percent of actions that will lead to 80 percent of your success.

Swallow the Frog: Tackling Your Biggest, Ugliest Challenge First

There's another key to maximizing your effectiveness: doing the hardest, most important task first. This is known as *swallowing the frog*. Imagine starting your day by knocking out the most intimidating task on your to-do list. When you handle that toughest thing first—the thing you would rather avoid, for whatever reason—you free up mental space and build momentum for the rest of your day.

In my own life, I've found combining eating the frog with the Pareto principle invaluable in overcoming procrastination. Each morning, I identify the three most important tasks for the day, placing a special focus on the one that seems most daunting. Whether it's tackling a big work project, having a difficult conversation, or pushing myself through a workout, swallowing the frog frees me from procrastination and gives me a sense of accomplishment.

Even on tough days, when my energy is low and life feels overwhelming, I find that I will take an action once I remind myself, *Just do three things*. Whether they are big or small, it doesn't matter, I can see that progress is progress. Confronting those three tasks without delay, especially the biggest, ugliest, most uncomfortable one, keeps me moving forward, no matter how challenging I anticipate my day will be.

Combine these powerful tools yourself: the five-minute rule for decisiveness, the Pareto principle for focusing on impactful tasks, and swallowing the frog to tackle your hardest challenge first. With them, I predict you will create a momentum-building system for success. These strategies aren't about working harder, but about working smarter. That's how to turn your dreams into reality.

Go All In:
Burn the Boats and Move Forward

As you are creating your dream life, there will be moments when you'll need to take small, consistent daily steps. But there will also come times when you must take a bold leap—a step so committed that there's no turning back from it.

There's a famous story about Spanish treasure hunter Hernan Cortes who, upon reaching the shore of Veracruz in 1519, ordered his men to burn the ships. The message was clear: There would be no retreat. They either would conquer the Aztec Empire and return home in Aztec ships or perish trying. And conquer, they did. Sometimes in life, we're faced with similar moments—where the only option left is to go all in.

This happened to our family a few years ago. We were living in Maine at the time. My son, nearing the end of his junior year in high school, approached me with a big decision. He wanted to move to Utah and live with my sister Martha for his senior year. For him, it was an opportunity to pursue what he felt was the next right step. But for me, as a mother, it felt like losing a piece of our family. He would be leaving behind his friends, the football team he loved playing for, and our life in Maine. Yet, his conviction was clear. He knew where he needed to be, and he was ready to go all in.

Soon, the rest of our kids and Dave and I were also on board with this life-changing idea. Dave and I had always imagined returning to Utah at some point with our family, but neither of us had expected to leave Maine so soon. What had once been a distant possibility became a reality. And it turned out to be a significant leap.

To make the move with all our kids would require us to both sell a house and buy a house, but also to find buyers for the multispecialty professional practices we'd spent the last ten years building. We wanted to make the move in time to enroll our children for school in the fall. Also we had to pack and move every-thing. In its entirety, our chore list seemed impossible. The logistics felt overwhelming, but we knew it was time to burn the boats. There would be no turning back. The decision had been made, and we were fully committed.

I remember the day we put our house up for sale. The weeks that followed were filled with packing and planning, and had a sense of urgency. My initial plan was simple: Pack a little each day and take things slow. But as you might imagine, life had other plans. By the end of the summer, the house hadn't yet sold, and we still hadn't found a new one. The surgical practice—with several locations—hadn't been sold, and our children had missed the tryouts in their old school for the sports and dance teams they had long been a part of, so there was no point in staying for another school year anymore. We had already said our goodbyes to our friends and community, and we were determined to move forward no matter what.

On the very last possible day, we loaded ourselves and a pile of luggage into an RV and began a cross-country journey. Where was our first "home" in Utah? A Walmart parking lot across the street from the high school, as we scrambled to get everything sorted.

Although the challenges were immense, we pushed through them because we had made a commitment and gone all in. Today, looking back, I realize how vital that decision was. Our kids thrived, and as a family, our bonds grew stronger through the shared experience.

Going all in on this dream of relocating to Utah taught me that the power to create your reality lies not just in the small, daily steps but also in those bold moments of unwavering commitment when you burn the boats and never look back.

Where Are You Holding Back?

Is there an area of your life where you've been holding back, unsure whether to commit fully? Sometimes, creating a new reality requires taking a big leap. It means making the decision to burn the boats, fully commit, and face whatever comes your way. Life will present you with opportunities and obstacles, and if you move forward with determination, you will find a way to conquer the worst, say yes to the best, and thrive.

So, ask yourself: *Where can I go all in? Where can I take a decisive step that moves my life in the direction of my dreams?* Today is your chance to stop holding back and embrace the path forward, no matter how difficult change may seem. Like my family's sudden bold move across the country between school years, your bold decisions may be exactly what you need to propel your life toward new heights.

The Importance of Hard Work in Creating Your Reality

Dave and I have always shared a love for hard work, viewing it as a form of play and an opportunity to engage fully with life. This shared belief shaped our approach to life and to parenting from the beginning. We had a clear goal: to raise children who valued industriousness and understood the deep rewards that come from a strong work ethic.

As young parents, we didn't always have a detailed plan, but we did have determination and a "we've got this" mindset. As life unfolded, our commitment to instilling a strong work ethic in our children was tested in ways we didn't foresee. Amid the hustle of raising five kids and building our dream lake house, Dave introduced an unexpected element to the mix: cows. Yes, cows! Pregnant cows, to be precise. His reasoning was simple: "The kids need to learn how to work."

Although I agreed in principle, the timing was overwhelming. Our oldest was only eight, and our youngest was just a baby. Yet, we embraced the adventure of teaching them about cows together—and did a lot of chores and chasing cows around ourselves.

What followed were unforgettable lessons in responsibility. The cows constantly tested our patience, escaping from their pen and requiring us to chase them down. Dave even performed an emergency calf delivery one summer with the help of our son Chase. Although the mother didn't survive, Chase spent his summer bottle-feeding and raising her baby calf. It was tough, but it was the kind of hard work that leaves a lasting impression on a young mind.

Dave and I often look back and laugh at those days—at our audacious parenting goals and the chaos of life on a makeshift farm. We can see that the lessons stuck. Chase, now an adult, took those early experiences with him throughout his life. After doing a two-year mission in the Philippines, he continued to embody the value of hard work. What's more, all of our other kids followed in his footsteps. Taylor served a mission in Chile, Braden in Argentina, and our fourth child, Sophia, is currently serving in Mexico. Bella, our youngest, plans to serve a mission in the future. None of them has shied away from doing hard things.

Dave's objective to teach our children the value of hard work succeeded. Our kids have grown up with a deep appreciation for putting in effort, for showing up even when things get tough, and for recognizing that hard work is the backbone of any dream worth achieving.

So, What Can You Start Working on Today?

The path to success isn't always easy, but it's through our willingness to roll up our sleeves and do the hard things that we create the lives we desire. Hard work doesn't just apply to large goals, but to daily tasks, challenges, and decisions. It's in these moments that we lay the groundwork for the futures we want to build.

As you reflect on your dreams and the kind of life you're creating, ask yourself: *What small, daily action can I take to move closer to my dream?*

You don't need to make drastic changes overnight. Instead, focus on the small, consistent actions that lead to progress. A little hard work never hurt anyone—in fact, it's often the very thing that makes our dreams come true.

BELIEF #3: I CAN DO THIS

PRETTY SISTER PINKY PROMISE

RUN THROUGH THE SPILLING THE TEA TECHNIQUE AFTER reading the three chapters related to Belief #3. The objective now is for you to internalize that *you can do it*, knowing that you have the power to envision, believe in, and actively create the life you desire.

When I say "I can do it," I THINK: _____
_____
_____
_____

When I think *that*, it makes me FEEL: _____
_____
_____
_____

When I feel *that*, it makes me ACT: _____
_____
_____
_____

Ask yourself, "Is there anything else I am thinking?" Run through this same process as many times as needed until you are thinking from your heart with courage, love, and confidence. Once you feel ready, move on to make the promise.

Find a fellow Pretty Sister (this can be your mom, a sister, a friend, or someone from the online Pretty Sister community) and make the following promise to her. Or speak these words to yourself in the mirror.

> *"I believe I can do it.*
> *I Pretty Sister pinky promise—*
> *and crosses don't count!"*

My Pretty Sister, you really can do it! By daring to dream, believing in your inherent worth and abilities, and taking deliberate action to bring your dreams to life, you've laid the foundation for a future built on confidence, purpose, and possibility.

BELIEF #4
YOU ARE MEANT FOR JOY

You weren't made to simply get through life; you were made to delight in it. Joy is your divine design, the spark that reminds you you're alive and the quiet signal that God is near. You don't have to wait for it. You were meant for it.

TEN

LIFE IS HAPPENING *FOR* YOU, NOT *TO* YOU

There are only two ways to live your life.
One is as though nothing is a miracle.
The other is as though everything is.

LET ME TAKE YOU BACK TO A SUMMER SPENT IN EUROPE, a time when what seemed like an obstacle turned into one of the most cherished memories of our lives. Dave and I had the incredible opportunity to live in Austria that year while he pursued an oral surgery externship. At the time, we had two young children, ages one and two, but we were fearless and full of adventure. Our spirits were high, and we were ready to conquer Europe one destination at a time.

We stayed in a convent in Graz, Austria, a setting right out of *The Sound of Music*. Our room sat above the chapel. Each morning, we would wake to the beautiful sound of the nuns singing hymns. While Dave worked at the hospital, I spent weekdays exploring the city with the kids and planning weekend getaways. It was the era before smartphones with GPS, so paper maps and Eurail Passes were our trusty companions as we navigated planes, trains, and automobiles.

It wasn't always easy, though. There were the inevitable challenges—like when our son Chase managed to escape the ropes during our group tour and ran straight for King Ludwig's bed, leading to us being politely escorted off the premises. There were missed trains, lost bottles, and diaper changes in the most inconvenient places, as well as moments when we found ourselves hopelessly lost. But even in the midst of these challenges, we cherished every second.

One of the most memorable experiences of the trip came when Dave accidentally filled our rental car with gasoline instead of diesel. We drove for miles before the car sputtered to a stop high in the Swiss Alps. Stranded with no idea of how far we were from the nearest town, Dave set off on foot, while I stayed behind with our two little ones. Miraculously, we stumbled upon a small, picturesque town nestled in the hills—complete with a repair shop for the very car we had rented. Though the repairs were costly and the whole situation put a serious dent in our plans, we decided to embrace the unexpected turn of events.

We spent a few days in that little town, completely adjusting our itinerary, and that sojourn turned out to be one of our favorite memories. We stayed at a cozy bed and breakfast, and each day, we'd wander around the town, letting the kids explore and enjoy the serenity of the countryside. There was something magical about the simplicity of it all. We strolled among the animals, admiring the chickens and cows, and even wandered through an old cemetery where the weathered headstones seemed to tell their own quiet stories. Time seemed to slow, and the usual hustle and bustle of travel faded into the background.

Of course, we could have chosen to feel impatient or frustrated. We could have focused on the fact that our plans were disrupted, the repairs costly, and we had to miss out on visiting our original destinations. Instead, we chose to focus on what we were grateful for: the peacefulness of our surroundings, the kindness of the locals who helped us, and the repair shop that came through when we needed it most.

We trusted that this unexpected detour was exactly what we needed. It was as if life had something better in mind for us—something that couldn't have been planned. Instead of seeing the situation as a burden, we saw it as an opportunity to slow down, embrace the simplicity of life, and revel in the little miracles that surrounded us.

That summer left a lasting mark on me. Even though that particular Switzerland experience was far from what we expected, it became one of the most meaningful parts of our journey. It taught me that sometimes the detours—the unexpected moments—are exactly what we need to find joy and peace in the present. Two decades later, I still travel extensively, often with my five adult children for company, and I cherish those unplanned moments that allow us to decelerate and truly experience the world around us.

We have the power to choose how we experience each situation we encounter. Our perspective—how we view the world and react to it—shapes our experiences. We can choose to see life as happening *for* us, not *to* us. If we adopt the mindset that everything works out for us, that's exactly what will happen. Life, with all its twists and turns, is constantly shaping us into who we are meant to be, and when we choose to see it that way, we can embrace each experience as a step toward something better.

This perspective can be difficult to embrace, especially when things aren't going our way. It's easy to feel frustrated, disappointed, or overwhelmed when life doesn't unfold according to our plans. But let's face it—life rarely goes exactly as we expect. That's just part of the journey. So, how do we maintain our optimism and happiness, particularly when our subconscious paradigms are filled with limiting beliefs?

Master Your Thoughts

Your thoughts are the top deck from which you captain your life. Like the steering wheel of a ship, they determine the direction in which you sail. This concept is both empowering and challenging. Empowering because it means you have the power to steer your life in the direction you desire; challenging because it places the responsibility squarely on your shoulders.

If you indulge in thoughts of worry or fear, those thoughts lead to anxiety, which often gets suppressed and may turn into depression eventually. Over time, this negativity can manifest in physical and emotional erosion and drifting off course.

On the other hand, if you train your brain to think in terms of faith, the belief that all things work together for your good, and you put your focus on positivity and your future dreams, your mindset will be like a strong wind that propels you forward. These thoughts lead to inspired ideas, spur action, and, eventually, the realization of those dreams. Our lives end up unique because our thoughts are exclusively our own.

One example of the power of an intentional mindset can be seen in the story of Viktor Frankl, who endured unimaginable suffering in a Nazi concentration camp. Despite the horrors surrounding him, Frankl held on to one aspect of his humanity that remained under his control: his thoughts. In the darkest moments, he chose to focus on gratitude for small blessings, even in the midst of chaos. This choice not only helped him survive but also allowed him to thrive even under the most harrowing circumstances.

So, how do you harness the power of your thoughts, especially when you find yourself in a funk or facing difficulties? It all begins with making and keeping three essential commitments to yourself that Johnny Covey teaches in his book *5 Habits to Lead from Your Heart*.

Commitment #1. Be respectful of yourself and others. So often, we are our own harshest critics. We berate ourselves for our imperfections and mistakes, which only fosters negativity. To love yourself fully, you must first be respectful in your thoughts. Treat yourself with kindness and compassion, as you would a dear friend. Extend this respect to others as well, avoiding criticism or negativity. Recognize that respect is the foundation of every healthy relationship.

Commitment #2. Be your best and accept others' best. Perfection is unattainable, and yet many of us strive for it, harshly judging ourselves when we fall short. The truth is that your best is enough. Embrace your imperfections and love yourself for who you are right now. Extend this acceptance to others too, recognizing that they, too, are doing their best. When you let go of the need for perfection, you free yourself to love and appreciate yourself and others more deeply.

Commitment #3: Be present and don't worry about the past or future. Regret for past mistakes and anxiety about the future can steal the joy of the present moment. Life unfolds in the now, and that's where your power lies. Commit to being fully present in every moment. When you do this, you'll notice how often you catch yourself dwelling on the past or worrying about what's to come. This awareness is the first step toward letting go of unnecessary stress and finding peace in the present.

Mastering these commitments may not be easy, especially in challenging times, but it's a journey worth embarking on. Just like a ship's captain must navigate rough waters, you can steer your life toward happiness and fulfillment by taking control of your thoughts. As you commit to these principles, you'll discover that even in the most stressful situations, you have the power to decide how you perceive and react to life's events. Embrace this power, and you'll find happiness in your ability to take control of your thoughts, and ultimately, your life.

Practicing the Three Essential Commitments

Let me take you on a journey through one of those moments when mastering your thoughts and living in the present truly shines. It happened during a flight from Porto Alegre to São Paulo, Brazil, a flight that almost became a tale of disaster.

About an hour before our flight, Dave and I arrived at the airport, excited for upcoming meetings in São Paulo. But as our Uber pulled up at the terminal, it hit me like a lightning bolt: Our passports were still safely tucked away in the safe at the hotel we'd just checked out of. It is impossible to get through security without them in an airport anymore—especially when traveling inside a foreign country! Panic set in instantly. Missing the flight was simply not an option because of our planned business meetings, and the clock was ticking.

With determination, we sprang into action. Dave, who is fluent in Portuguese, stayed behind at the airport to check us into the flight, while I rushed back to the hotel in Porto Alegre with the Uber driver to retrieve our passports. The stakes felt high—on top of the stress of being late, I couldn't communicate with the driver, as I didn't speak the language, and my phone was malfunctioning. The possibilities of things going wrong were endless.

At that moment, two choices presented themselves. Option A was to succumb to frustration, blame, and worry. Options B was to embrace the challenge and put into practice the three commitments: Be respectful, be your best, and be present.

I chose Option B. Instead of letting my frustration take over, I committed to staying grounded and mindful. This wasn't the time to blame myself or Dave for forgetting the passports or to indulge my irritation with the situation. Instead, I focused on the task at hand, which was having the staff at the hotel help me get back into the now empty room to retrieve the passports, and then making our flight.

During the ride back to the hotel, I reminded myself to be present. While I could have stressed about the fifteen- to thirty-minute drive each way, depending on traffic, I chose to let go of worry. I soaked in the sights outside the window, appreciated the warm sunshine, and felt grateful for the speedy Uber driver who was getting me to the hotel as quickly as possible.

And then, miraculously, everything began to fall into place. Dave, with his quick thinking, had managed to secure an agent at the airport who checked us both in and took care of our luggage. He even managed to get us an upgrade to the front row of our section in the plane, a stroke of luck and his problem-solving brilliance.

Meanwhile, Dave was on the phone with the hotel I was headed back to, explaining our situation and setting me up for a positive experience with the safe. By the time I arrived, the concierge at the front desk was ready to hand over our passports.

I thanked the concierge, grabbed the passports, and, with the help of the same skillful Uber driver expertly navigating some back roads, I made it back to the airport in the nick of time. Dave and I raced through security and made it to the gate with mere minutes to spare, and in the end, we were able to board the flight together, relieved and grateful.

This moment was the perfect example of the three essential commitments. Through our thoughts, Dave and I both consciously shaped our perceptions of the situation, and, in doing so, ultimately influenced the outcome. Had either of us allowed frustration to take over, we might have missed the flight or let the stress cloud our experience. But instead, by embracing the commitments, we were able to turn what could have been a disaster into a triumph.

So, are you ready to master your thoughts? Then I challenge you to adopt the three commitments. When your life takes its next unexpected turn, you'll be amazed at the happiness that washes over you when you take control of your thoughts and your life by being respectful, doing your best, and staying mentally present.

Affirmations:
A Powerful Tool for Shifting Our Thoughts
and Shaping Reality

In addition to making commitments, we need technology to manage our thoughts.

Imagine having a magic wand to dispel negativity, summon confidence, and manifest your heart's desires. The truth is that you already have access to a magic wand of sorts that can do these things, with the inner technology known as *affirmations*. Affirmations are spoken or thought statements in which you declare to yourself and God that an outcome you want has already happened. Through their repetition, you program your mind—and the reticular activation system (RAS) we talked about in Chapter 7—to open up your mental filters and get the help of your whole being to work toward the accomplishment of the outcome you are affirming.

One of my favorite affirmations is "Everything always works out for me." When I'm feeling stressed and overwhelmed, speaking this affirmation reminds me that I am capable and have been blessed with incredible goodness in my life. I've faced hard things—harder even than catching a plane when my passport is back at the hotel—and come through them.

Much more than words, affirmations are personal magic spells that can bring about positive change. And they are not just wishful thinking; they actually do have the potential to help us reshape our thoughts, beliefs, and ultimately, our lives.

I would like you to think of your chosen affirmations as being like guiding stars in your sky, illuminating your path and leading you toward the fulfillment of your deepest desires. Once you select and begin working with them regularly them, they will shape the way you view the world and yourself. And they will uplift you emotionally, by giving you a sense of control and intentionality. These simple statements will help you to align your mind with a positive vision for the future. When you adopt this technique for creating magical change in how you think and feel, you're more likely to manifest the images and outcomes behind those words in your reality.

The simple yet profound affirmation "Everything works out for me" has been my anchor through many twists and turns. No matter the challenges I've faced, this affirmation has never failed me. Life may throw me curveballs, and situations may not unfold the way I expect, but my unwavering belief in this affirmation ensures that everything eventually falls into place.

Let me share a little personal magic that happens every time I park my car. (Yes, it sounds whimsical, but it holds an important lesson about the power of belief and positive affirmations.) Every time I drive somewhere, I believe that the best parking spots are reserved just for me. I've held on to this belief for years, and it continues to amaze me how often it matches my reality. I know it might sound small, but here's the key: I firmly believe that those spots will be there for me, and most of the time, they are. It also gives me a positive sense of expectation that lowers my stress levels considerably.

Now, let's be clear. I don't actually have a reserved spot in every parking lot, and I'm well aware that sometimes the prime spots will be occupied. But when I arrive someplace, I actively seek the best spot, confident that it's waiting for me. And more often than not, a decent spot is available when I'm looking for it.

Even when the spot isn't there, I don't let it frustrate me. I simply park wherever else is available and move on, knowing that my "parking fairies" are just waiting for a different lot to surprise me.

Recently, my daughter playfully teased me about this phenomenon when we were at Disney World. The parking lot was packed, and she jokingly said, "Guess your parking fairies aren't here today."

I smiled and replied, "Oh no, this isn't the lot I want. I prefer to park over there." I drove to a different lot, and to her surprise (but not mine), I found not one, but two prime spots to choose between right up front.

A story about success in parking may seem trivial in the grand scheme of world affairs, but it illustrates a profound principle: the power of belief and affirmations. When you believe something is possible—even something as small as finding the perfect parking spot—it often manifests in your life. For me, this kind of success is a small, daily reminder that life works out when we trust it will.

By expecting the best and actively seeking it out, I predict that you will start to notice miracles, big and small, unfolding around you, too.

Affirmations are expressions of our expectations. When we choose to believe in the truth of them, we open a door for positive changes to occur.

The Science Behind Affirmations

While affirmations may sound like mere words, their impact goes far beyond the surface. When you repeat affirmations regularly, they influence your subconscious mind, shaping your beliefs, attitudes, and behavior. This process is rooted in the phenomenon of *neuroplasticity*, the brain's ability to form new neural connections. Essentially, your affirmations will help you rewire your brain by replacing old, negative thought patterns with positive, empowering ones.

The more you repeat affirmations, the more your brain begins to accept them as the truth. Once it does, this shift in mindset changes how you react to situations, how you feel about yourself, and how you perceive the world around you. Affirmations don't just change your thoughts, they change your brain, making it more resourceful in creating the life you envision.

Crafting Effective Affirmations

Now that you have a general understanding of how affirmations work, let's talk about how to make them as effective as possible. To get the most out of your affirmations, it's important to align them with the brain's natural

tendencies for positive change. Any time you're inventing an affirmation to support a new goal, the guidelines are to:
- **Be positive.** When creating affirmations, always use positive language. Instead of saying "I'm *not* a failure" say "I *am* successful."
- **Be specific.** Specificity also enhances an affirmation's intensity. The more detailed your affirmation, the more your mind can focus on it and help bring it into your reality.
- **Use the present tense.** Affirm your desire in the present tense, as if it is already true. Saying "I *am* confident and successful" is far more effective than saying "I *will be* confident and successful." This creates a sense of immediacy that helps you internalize the belief that your affirmation is already a reality.
- **Add emotion.** Infuse your affirmation with emotion. Feel the outcome of your desire as if it is already happening, as if it is part of your present experience. The more emotionally charged an affirmation is, the more effective it becomes; by helping you connect deeply with your desired outcome.

Also remember that the ultimate key to effective affirmations is consistent repetition. By repeating your affirmations, they become ingrained in your subconscious mind. Consistency is crucial. You are repeating them to train your brain to believe in them and to build neural networks that support you in thinking and doing the things you need to do.

Ten Affirmations for Every Pretty Sister

The following affirmations are some of my personal favorites.
- **"Everything works out for me."** This affirmation lays the foundation for trusting that life is unfolding exactly as it should.
- **"I am enough."** In a world that often makes us feel inadequate, this reminder helps us realize our inherent worthiness.

- **"I can do all things."** This one boosts our confidence and empowers us to face our challenges head on.
- **"I am loved."** A beautiful affirmation that reminds us of the love surrounding us—both from within and from others.
- **"I am adventurous and I overcome fear by following my dreams."** This encourages bravery and a spirit of adventure in pursuit of our goals.
- **"I am in charge of how I feel, and today I am choosing happiness."** A reminder that we control our emotions, and we have the power to choose joy.
- **"I am my own superhero."** This affirmation taps into our inner strength, reminding us that we have the power to overcome obstacles.
- **"I can, and I will."** Simple, but powerful, this declaration reinforces our determination to succeed.
- **"I have the power to create change."** This one empowers us to be the catalyst for positive transformation in our life.
- **"I let go of all that no longer serves me. I deserve the best, and I accept the best now."** An affirmation of abundance, inviting you to release what no longer serves you and embrace the good things coming your way.

Never forget that affirmations are like seeds you are planting in the soil of your mind. As you repeat them over and over with emotion and conviction, they will sprout and then come to fruition through your thoughts, choices, and actions. The more you repeat them, the faster they'll transform your life. Then, stand back and watch as your world begins to shift in miraculous ways.

Whichever one you choose to begin with, enjoy the experience of listening to yourself make this meaningful declaration. Let it affect your heart and bring imagery into your mind. Permit yourself to *believe* it.

As you continue to embrace the belief, for example, *Everything works out for me,* you will begin to realize that life is full of miracles that you can see if you open your eyes to see them. Each day, miracles unfold around us, sometimes in the smallest of moments. But the key to recognizing them is gratitude.

Develop a Gratitude Practice to Cement Your Results in Reality

A gratitude practice is an activity that invites us to shift our focus from what we lack to what we have. It's about seeing the beauty and goodness that already exist in our lives. When we embrace a gratitude practice, we open ourselves to a symphony of miracles just waiting to be discovered. Starting your day with affirmations followed by a gratitude practice honoring the results you receive is like planting seeds that blossom throughout the day, filling your heart with appreciation and opening your mind to all that is working in your favor.

One of the most transformative practices I've adopted is my daily gratitude ritual. Each morning, I set aside a few quiet moments to reflect on the blessings in my life. I consciously express thanks for the good I have now and for the good that's yet to come.

I've been doing this practice for more than a decade and I have found that the more deeply I feel the gratitude on a particular morning, the better my experience feels throughout the day. It gives me resiliency and joy.

During these moments, just as I do when I'm speaking my affirmations, I visualize my dreams as if they have already come true and then allow the feeling of joy to permeate my being. Over time, this visualization has helped me become more aware of the miracles around me—small and large—that I might have otherwise overlooked.

This practice is not just about saying thank you for the big things, but also about acknowledging the small everyday miracles that make life so extraordinary. I aim to look around me and notice at least three miracles every day, whether they are the kindness of a stranger, the beauty of nature, or the warmth of a shared moment with a loved one. A miracle could be the sun breaking through the clouds or the support of a friend when you need it most. With practice, I wired my brain to see many miracles. And the more of them I see, the more I'm filled with gratitude. In this way, being grateful sets up a virtuous circle.

The big shift in your mindset comes from focusing on the abundance in your life instead of what you don't have. The simple act of pausing to acknowledge your blessings invites goodness into your experience.

Gratitude has been shown to improve mental health, reduce stress, and boost physical well-being. Because of this, when we focus on the positive our resilience to adversity increases. When things feel tough or life doesn't seem to be going our way, stopping to do a gratitude ritual can give us a lifeline. It won't eliminate our difficulties, but it will help us see them through a lens of possibility. This shift in perspective is key to finding the silver lining in every situation.

Now, let me share a story that perfectly exemplifies the magic of gratitude and how miracles often show up in the most unexpected ways. A little over ten years ago, my husband Dave and I made the decision to host a Brazilian exchange student. Dave had spent several years in Brazil, and his connection to the country made a lasting impact on him. I, too, was drawn to the idea of sharing that experience with our family. With our busy household, it seemed like a distant dream, but then one day, an idea hit me: *Why don't we host a Brazilian exchange student?*

It felt like divine inspiration, as if God was giving us a nudge. I reached out to a friend who ran an exchange program, and the process began. We sifted through profiles of potential students, hoping to find the perfect match for our family. One student, Leonardo, stood out immediately. There was something about him that felt like he was *our kid*. The connection was undeniable. We submitted our choice and eagerly awaited confirmation.

However, when the placement letter arrived, it wasn't as we expected. We had been assigned a different student—someone we hadn't chosen. We tried to accept it, but deep down, we felt it wasn't the right fit. After much thought, I decided to call my friend and explain the situation. A mix up was confirmed, and with a little work, Leo was assigned to our family.

What began as a simple decision led to one of the greatest blessings of our lives. Leo arrived, and from the moment he stepped through the front door, he was more than just an exchange student. He was part of our family. Over the course of the year, we all grew incredibly close, and Leo quickly became an integral part of our lives. What we had originally planned as a semester-long stay turned into a full year, and by the end of it, we couldn't bear to say goodbye.

Now, more than a decade later, Leo lives near us in Utah with his wife and two children. We get the joy of being the American grandparents to their little ones, filling a role that has been so rewarding for our family. As Leo and his wife's only family members are in Brazil, we get to be their support system here, and this relationship has become one of the greatest blessings in our lives. We never could have imagined that this one decision would lead to such deep, lasting bonds.

Leo's story is a beautiful testament to how life can surprise us in the most unexpected ways. The decision we made all those years ago has changed both of our families for the better. God saw the bigger picture we couldn't —from our limited perspective we never imagined the incredible depth of connection that would come from this decision. But that's how miracles work.

When we have the courage to ask for our desires to be given to us and trust in the divine timing of when they will be realized, then wait patiently, what comes may be the fulfillment of our desires—or something even better. That's the beauty of miracles: The way they unfold is often far more beautiful and meaningful than we have ever anticipated.

For me and Dave, the presence of Leo and his family in our lives is a constant reminder that God wants to give us everything.

As you navigate your future, remember that miracles will be all around you, sometimes in the form of an unexpected phone call, a new friendship, or a seemingly random opportunity. Trust that when you open your heart to gratitude, God will bring you exactly what you need. And when the miracles come, as they always do, embrace them with gratitude and joy.

Life isn't always fair—but fairness was never the promise. Growth, strength, and resilience are. Instead of measuring life by what's "fair," measure it by the joy you choose to find within it. Challenges will come, but so will beauty, and it's up to you to decide which lens you'll see through.

This is the power of thinking pretty: You were born with the ability to shape your world by shaping your thoughts. You can't always control what happens, but you can choose how you think about it. And this choice? It changes everything. So when life feels unfair, hard, or uncertain, remind yourself: Life is happening for me. Because of that, I will grow, I will rise, and I will find joy along the way.

Life Is Happening for You, not to You

Let's take a moment to reflect on the powerful truths we've explored in this chapter. First, life is not happening *to* you—it's happening *for* you. This understanding is the key to fully embracing the richness of every experience, whether it's joyful or challenging. No matter what comes your way, there is always a silver lining to be found. Sometimes it's hidden beneath the surface, but if you choose to look for it, it will appear.

One of the most powerful ways to discover the silver linings in your life is through affirmations. These simple, positive statements can transform your thoughts, how you channel your energy, and as a byproduct of your choices and actions, ultimately, your reality. By using affirmations, you will begin to shift your focus away from problems that crop up and toward the opportunities, solutions, and blessings that are unfolding in your life.

Through consistent, dedicated practice, affirmations will help you train your mind to see the good in every situation—even the most difficult.

Life isn't always easy or fair. This is a truth I've embraced, especially as a parent. I've taught my children that fairness isn't the measure of a good life; instead, life is good when we choose to find joy in our circumstances. Life can be messy, unpredictable, and challenging, but it's also filled with miraculous moments and blessings. The key is to recognize these precious gifts when they appear. Life, when seen through the lens of gratitude and the belief that everything works out, becomes an enriching collection of experiences that shape and mold us into the people we are meant to become.

Whether it's a beautiful sunrise, a kind word from a friend, or an unexpected blessing that shows up at just the right moment, there is a miracle close at hand. They are always there.

ELEVEN

YOU MIGHT AS WELL BE HAPPY

The secret to happiness isn't waiting for the right circumstances, it's realizing happiness has always been yours to unlock from within.

SOPHIE'S SIXTEENTH BIRTHDAY WAS FAST APPROACHING, and she had been dreaming about it for months because it meant that she could get her driver's license. One day, weeks before her birthday, she came to me with a request: She wanted a new car. Naturally, I said no. None of her siblings had gotten a new car for their birthdays, and I wasn't about to make an exception. Instead, I told her she could drive the Jeep that had been passed down through the family. It wasn't new, but it was a cool-looking, reliable car that had served her three older siblings well.

To say that Sophie wasn't thrilled with my response to her request is an understatement. She was disappointed and frustrated, and stormed off to her room in a huff after hearing it. I knew she was upset, but would get over it quickly because Sophie has a remarkable way of dealing with her emotions. And I was correct; she didn't stew for long.

Sophie has what we now affectionately call her "flipping her switch" process. It's a skill she's developed over the years. When life doesn't go her way, she retreats to her room to think, reflect, and work through her frustration until she's able to "flip her switch" and come out with a completely new attitude. And that's exactly what she did.

When Sophie emerged from her room a little while later, calm and collected, she had a new request: "If I have to drive the old Jeep, can you at least clean it and put a big red bow on it?"

I couldn't help laughing, but I agreed. "Sure, I can do that!" I said, knowing I'd need to put in a little effort to make this happen.

In the days leading up to Sophie's birthday, I had the Jeep detailed. And honestly, it looked amazing. By the morning of her birthday, the vehicle was in the driveway, adorned with a shiny red bow. When Sophie emerged from her room, she acted like she had no idea what was waiting for her. I led her out to the car with her eyes closed, her anticipation growing with every step. When she opened her eyes and saw the Jeep, you would have thought she'd won the lottery. She squealed with excitement, jumping for joy at her "new" car. She was incredibly thrilled to have a car to call her own.

I smiled throughout the entire process. I knew Sophie had more than an inkling of what was coming, yet she still managed to manufacture so much joy from the gift of an old hand-me-down car that wasn't *supposed* to be a surprise at all. The whole thing was nothing short of adorable and became a life lesson for me in how to embrace what we have with gratitude and a positive attitude.

Later that day, we went to pick up her driver's license. Afterward, Sophie wasted no time filling the car with all the essentials for the lifestyle of a contemporary teenage girl—lipstick, deodorant, snacks, gum, you name it. Her car quickly became her own personal convenience store, stocked with everything she or a passenger could possibly need.

Sophie's sweet sixteen story is one I will never forget because it beautifully demonstrates her ability to adjust her expectations and choose happiness, no matter what the circumstances. No one I know has the ability to flip their switch and adapt to life's realities more brilliantly than Sophie. She teaches the whole family that we don't have to have everything go exactly the way we want to be happy. Sometimes, happiness is found in how we respond to the unexpected—and Sophie's ability to adjust, embrace what she has, and find joy in it is a perfect example of that.

Your Happiness Matters

Your potential is intricately tied to the choice you make of how to approach life. If you embrace happiness as your guiding principle, your potential increases. If you lead with resentment, the opposite is true.

I wholeheartedly believe that life is meant to be happy and each one of us is destined to lead a life brimming with joy. For this reason, happiness isn't something we should wait for. It's something we can choose to feel now.

When we consciously choose to be happy, we set a powerful precedent for embracing our full potential. Instead of seeing life as a series of challenges and obstacles, we begin to view it as a journey filled with opportunities for growth, success, and fulfillment. When we make happiness our constant companion, we can unlock doors to new possibilities, transform our relationships, and become the people we were meant to be.

The belief I strive to live by is that happiness is not an external condition, but an internal choice. Being happy is something I commit to daily, and in doing so, I've discovered that the accumulation of happy moments is the key to an overall joyful life and a gateway to limitless potential.

Happiness is a treasure we all seek, yet it's also something that can slip through our fingers when we least expect it. The curious thing, however, is that happiness isn't all that elusive; it's a choice we can make for ourselves on an average day. So, why is it that we sometimes choose to be *unhappy*? (Of course, sadness is normal when we experience a loss or trauma. I'm not talking about times like those, but about how we feel in the course of our routines.)

The truth is that happiness is not bestowed upon us by situations or circumstances; it is a gift we give ourselves. I have learned to protect my happiness fiercely because I understand now that it's within my power to choose it, and I believe it's a choice that is always available regardless of external conditions. Though I would never judge another woman for her feelings unless I had "walked a mile in her shoes," as the adage goes, I also believe that signs of dissatisfaction—which I don't let cloud my happiness—should be interpreted as information about what we need and how we want to grow, going forward.

If you're feeling sad or upset, like Sophie did with her sweet sixteen request, aim to answer the question: *What do I need to restore my happiness?*

Being able to choose happiness is not exclusively my skill—it can be yours you, too. I believe that you can be happy. I believe it's within your reach. Happiness isn't reserved for the lucky few; it's a choice for everyone, and it's a choice that can transform your life in ways you never imagined.

Embracing the Joy of Life

We are meant to have joy in this life. We have a loving God who wants to give us everything, to help us succeed, and to see our desires fulfilled. When we grow to truly understand this, we can stop resisting the natural flow of life. We can learn to cultivate happiness, regardless of the circumstances, as we journey toward growth and development.

Choosing happiness doesn't mean pretending everything is perfect; it simply means choosing to focus on the positive, even when things don't go as planned. Life isn't fair, that's the reality we all face. Things don't always turn out the way we think they should, and sometimes tragedies occur, but that doesn't mean our lives can't still be joyful underneath all these events. We can still find peace, contentment, and—yes—joy amid the trials we face.

People often bristle at the idea of *choosing* happiness, especially when life is tough. It might seem trite or even impossible when we're in the middle of hardship. But it's exactly when life feels hardest that we need to acknowledge this possibility the most. Because in those moments, choosing happiness can be the very thing that helps us push through. We might as well choose to be happy, right? Why not?

The first step in choosing happiness is awareness—accepting life as it is without labeling it as good or bad. Everything just *is*. The second step is to find the good in the situation. There is always something to harvest joy from, even in very difficult and trying times.

The third step is forgiveness—meaning, letting go of the rest. We'll discuss this in detail in the chapters associated with Belief #5.

In the end, happiness is not a destination, but a mindset and a lifestyle. Even in the hardest of moments, I promise you it's possible. And more than that, it's worth making an effort to feel this way.

So, the next time you're faced with a challenge, ask yourself: *What would it look like if I were to choose happiness right now?*

The Formula for Happiness

One of the most powerful tools for maintaining happiness comes from a mathematical formula that has greatly influenced my life.

Happiness = the events of your life – your expectations

This formula, developed by Mo Gawdat, author of *Solve for Happy*, was designed to help us understand that our happiness is determined by how we view the events in our lives in relation to what we expect. When our expectations are aligned with reality, happiness follows. But when our expectations exceed the reality of the situation, we open ourselves up to disappointment.

Think of it this way: There's always a gap between what we want and what we have. This gap is natural, and it's something we have to "mind" so we don't fall into a funk. We need to remind ourselves to step lightly just like the signs on London's underground tube stations remind us to "mind the gap" before stepping on to a train car.

In life, we need to be aware of this gap between our desires and our reality. But we don't need to eliminate the gap. In fact, it's necessary for our growth.

It's in the gap, in the pursuit of what we desire and the lessons we learn along the way, that we generate joy and fulfillment. We're meant to be challenged. We're meant to learn, adapt, and grow into better versions of ourselves. So, doesn't it make sense that growth and joy are linked? That even in life's trials, which seem harsh and challenging, we can find joy? When you stop to think about it, it makes perfect sense.

To help illustrate this further, let me add an analogy: Imagine you're in London, where rain is expected. If you expect rain and it happens, you're not disappointed. But if you were hoping for sunshine for a special event and it rains instead, you might feel frustrated. This is how our expectations shape our happiness. It's not the rain itself that makes you unhappy, but the fact that it didn't meet your expectations.

This is exactly what Gawdat's formula shows us. We need to manage our subjective response to the gap between what we want and what we get in life. The gap itself is an inevitable part of the human condition, so we have to create workarounds. If we can adjust our expectations and accept life as it comes, we will experience peace and contentment in the present moment.

Remember, with a growth mindset, the gap is something you can master. In fact, mastering your expectations is a very worthy endeavor that can lead to profound happiness and fulfillment.

Integrating Happiness with Wealth Creation

When we adopt the mindset of *thinking abundantly* and align it with Gawdat's formula for happiness, we see how they complement each other perfectly. By adjusting our expectations and creating our happiness, we unlock the power to create not only more joy in our lives but also more abundance. When we expect to live a joyful life, regardless of circumstances, and when we choose happiness as our baseline, the cycle of wealth creation naturally follows. We are in a constant state of flow, and we attract everything we need—not just to meet our own needs, but to fulfill the higher purpose of serving others and making the world a better place.

So, as you think about your own happiness and your finances, remember that it all begins with your perspective. The wealth we create is directly tied to the mindset we cultivate. And when you approach life with the intention of doing good, serving others, and embracing your purpose, the universe will respond in kind, opening doors for you to prosperity and joy that you never thought possible. And when you add the formula for happiness into the mix, you've got a recipe for a truly fulfilling life.

The PERMA Model: A Formula for Cultivating Happiness

As we continue to explore how to embrace the abundant joy that life has to offer, let's dive into the PERMA model, a foundational theory from the field of positive psychology that can help guide us toward a happier life. Developed by psychologist Martin Seligman, this approach identifies five essential elements that contribute to human flourishing, providing a framework for cultivating long-term happiness.

PERMA is an acronym. The *P* in PERMA stands for **positive emotion.** This is the foundation of happiness, where you focus on cultivating feelings of joy, contentment, and gratitude. By actively choosing to experience positive emotions and savoring the good moments, you can build a solid base for happiness. Positive emotions don't just make us feel good in the moment; they also contribute to our overall well-being and physical health.

The *E* represents **engagement.** The word *engagement* refers to the sense of being fully absorbed in an activity, a condition often referred to as "being in the zone." Whether it's pursuing a hobby, work you love, or quality time with friends, engaging fully with what you're doing leads to a greater sense of meaning and satisfaction. Engagement helps us grow, develop our skills, and feel deeply connected to the world around us.

R stands for **relationships.** Perhaps the most important element of the PERMA model, relationships are central to our happiness. The long-running Harvard Study of Adult Development, known colloquially as the Good Life Study, has shown that strong, supportive relationships are the single most important factor in determining our happiness and longevity. The study, which is ongoing, has followed participants for over seventy-five years and consistently found that people with deep, meaningful relationships—whether with family, friends, or romantic partners—live happier and healthier lives. It's clear that happiness is not a solitary pursuit.

We are all in this life together, and who we choose to share our lives with, and the degree of effort we put into those relationships, plays a large part in our happiness. The more we invest in others, the greater the dividends we receive in joy and fulfillment.

The *M* in PERMA represents **meaning.** *Meaning* refers to the sense that our life is purposeful and that we are contributing to something greater than ourselves. When we align our actions with our core values and serve others, we create a deeper sense of satisfaction. The pursuit of meaning brings clarity to our life's goals and helps us stay focused, even when faced with challenges.

A stands for **accomplishment.** Having a sense of accomplishment is a key driver of happiness. Whether it's completing a project, hitting a personal goal, or simply making progress, accomplishment boosts our self-esteem and reinforces the belief that we are capable of creating success. The sense of achievement, no matter how big or small, fuels our desire to keep striving.

When we focus on these five elements—positive emotion, engagement, relationships, meaning, and accomplishment—we unlock the potential to create a life filled with happiness and fulfillment. This model serves as a powerful tool to help us not only understand happiness but actively cultivate it in our lives.

Relationships:
The Heart of Happiness

As we just discussed, relationships are a key pillar of happiness. The findings from the Good Life Study underscore the importance of our connections with others. This long-term research project shows that individuals with strong, supportive relationships have higher levels of happiness, better physical health, and greater life satisfaction. These relationships provide us with a support network during tough times, increase our sense of belonging, and add meaning to our lives.

In my own life, relationships have been the cornerstone of my happiness. One example that comes to mind is the story I've shared before about my family's time in Austria. That summer abroad was filled with joy, yes, but it was also challenging. Traveling through Europe with young children and living on a tight budget meant we had to rely heavily on each other. That's when the strength of our relationship as a family became so clear. We leaned on one another, found humor in our mishaps, and celebrated our victories together.

It wasn't just about the places we visited or the sights we saw, it was the time spent together, making memories as a family, that made the experience unforgettable. The relationships we nurture with friends, family, and our communities are the ones that matter most. They are the foundation of our happiness, and they pay the greatest dividends over time. The more time we invest in these connections, the more joy they bring into our lives.

Happiness Hacks:
Choosing Joy in the Everyday

It's important to recognize that happiness isn't a passive experience or a single resolution. It's a series of active decisions we make every single day. Every time you come to a fork in the road—so to speak—aim for joy.

This kind of navigation requires self-awareness. One of the most profound happiness hacks is recognizing that *we get to choose our thoughts.* We may not always have control over events, but we always have control over how we think about them.

Through learning to choose our thoughts, we create a resilient mindset that can weather any storm. This doesn't mean we won't face difficult or painful moments. Life has its fair share of challenges. But when we master the ability to shift our thinking, we open the door to a more joyful experience, even in the midst of turbulence and adversity.

Another great happiness hack is *living in the present moment.* When we place our attention on the present moment, rather than ruminating about the past or future, we can give ourselves some much-needed relief. The stratagem of paying attention to what you are actually doing will remove a significant amount of stress and anxiety from your life.

Living in the present allows us to fully enjoy the experiences that come our way, no matter how big or small.

The Joy of Work: A Happiness Hack for the Whole Family

Another happiness hack I've found incredibly helpful is to *decide to love work.* It could sound strange, but learning to love the process of doing hard work—not only the end result of our effort—can truly change our experience of life. As parents, we may need to instill this idea in our children as well as ourselves. My kids grew up in a large home, and keeping it in order required a lot of hands on deck. We needed everyone to pitch in, and yes, it always took a little more time for me to teach them how to do the chores at first, but I knew that taking the time to teach my children these important life skills would be worth it in the long run.

Many dividends were paid by teaching my kids to appreciate work. Not only did my kids learn how to take care of themselves and their surroundings, but they also learned the value of a job well done. They learned that there's a sense of accomplishment and satisfaction that comes with work, and that in the process of doing necessary things, we grow. They understand now that work is a chance to develop new skills, and it can bring a surprising amount of joy when we approach it with the right attitude.

I've made sure to model this mindset for my children. Even when chores seemed tedious, we found joy in knowing that we were contributing to the greater good of our family. When we stop resisting work and instead look for the joy in it, we begin to feel a sense of pride in our efforts and a sense of connection to our purpose.

A Dance Through the Chaos

Not long after having my fifth baby, Bella, I found myself struggling with some postpartum baby blues, compounded by the exhaustion of caring for a fussy, colicky baby. The days were long, the nights were filled with tears (both the baby's and mine), and I was on the verge of feeling completely defeated. Bella cried constantly, and I often found myself crying right alongside her, wondering how I would make it through the day.

One evening, Dave came home to a sight that stopped him dead in his tracks. There I was, with Bella strapped to me in the BabyBjörn carrier, bouncing her up and down to calm her while I tried to cook dinner. The house was a mess, with toys and kids' belongings scattered everywhere. Dishes were piled up, and the chaos of the evening "bewitching hour" was in full swing. You know, that super hard part of the day right before dinner when you and the kids are tired and hungry and ready for a meltdown. But despite all of that, I was *dancing*. The music was blaring, and I was bouncing Bella to the beat, tears streaming down my face.

Dave wasn't sure whether to rush to comfort me or join in on the dance. Was I happy or was I at my breaking point? Okay or losing it?

In that moment, I realized how messy and complex life can be, especially when we're trying to balance multiple roles. But rather than getting caught in the struggle, I chose to accept what was and do what I could to find joy in that moment. My happiness hack that night was to dance. With each beat, I bounced the frustration out of my body, dancing myself into a place of peace and acceptance. It was hard, yes. But I wasn't submitting to defeat—I was submitting to the flow of life, to the reality of where I was at that moment.

The joy I derived from that moment didn't come from pretending everything was perfect; it came from choosing to make the best of things. By dancing through the chaos, I was able to remind myself that life has its pleasures, and I had options even in the hardest times.

Mindset, Joy, and Abundance: The Keys to a Fulfilling Life

All of these happiness hacks come down to a single truth: *We get to choose how we experience our lives.* Life isn't perfect, and we certainly don't have control over everything that happens to us. But we do have control over how we respond, and how we choose to view the world. Whether it's dancing through the chaos of parenting, deciding to love work, or simply choosing happiness, we hold the power to shape our experiences.

When we embrace a mindset of growth, positivity, and service, we open the door to greater joy, abundance, and fulfillment. And when we use tools like the PERMA model, or embrace simple happiness hacks like living in the present and adjusting our expectations, we create a life that is not only meaningful but full of joy.

So, let me leave you with this advice: *Choose happiness.* Embrace the tools that will help you get there. Dance in the mess. Love the work. Adjust your expectations. And remember just to think pretty. Every moment holds the possibility of joy, and every challenge is an opportunity for growth. You have the power to shape your reality—so you might as well choose to be happy.

TWELVE

IT'S NOT THE END YET

*"The future belongs to those who believe in
the beauty of their dreams."*

ELEANOR ROOSEVELT

GROWING UP, I ALWAYS ENVISIONED HAVING A LOVE LIKE that of my grandparents. Their marriage was the epitome of the one I dreamed of for myself, a partnership built on respect, love, and shared values. My grandmother, Francis, was the life of every gathering—talented, warm, and full of laughter. My grandfather, Virgil, was a wise, charming figure who made everyone feel at ease. Together, they were a dream couple, and I aspired to create that same kind of enduring relationship with my future spouse.

When I met Dave, now my husband of twenty-nine years, I couldn't help feeling like I had found my version of Virgil. He embodied all the qualities I had always dreamed of: He was tall, dark, handsome, and brilliant. I was excited to begin a life with him, building our own version of the classic type of fairy-tale romance I had always admired. Little did I know that the journey ahead would not always be as smooth as I had envisioned, but every moment of struggle would teach me invaluable lessons about love, resilience, and the true meaning of the phrase *Happily ever after.*

Our story is not unlike that of many couples. It's been filled with its share of challenges and hardships. As we've journeyed through life together, we've faced trials that tested our love and commitment, but with each challenge, our bond has only grown stronger. It's been a reminder that the real magic of a good marriage isn't just about the perfect beginning; it's about putting in the work, effort, and devotion required to make it last.

The Hard Work of Happily Ever After

The fairy tales make it seem so easy, don't they? The storybook ending is simple, because fairy tales end at the beginning. That's why the hard work of maintaining a relationship is glossed over. The reality of what happens next is different. A lasting marriage, like the reality of any good thing we do in life, takes patience, commitment, and resilience.

The challenges Dave and I have faced over the years, which are both personal and professional, have tested us as individuals and as a couple in ways we never anticipated. But through it all, we've held on to our belief in each other and in the future we're building together.

Our fairy tale is about the "after," the part where the work really begins. It's about sticking together through thick and thin, learning and growing alongside one another, and continuing to choose to love each other every single day, even when life isn't as easy as we'd hoped. Our marriage reflects a fundamental truth: *The most rewarding things come from persistence and a willingness to keep going, even when it's hard.*

You see, when life doesn't unfold exactly as you've envisioned it, this doesn't have to signal the end of your dreams. As we've discussed previously, the gap between our expectations and reality is an opportunity for growth. It's in the process of working through challenges (which will enable us to close the gap) that we discover our strengths and find the meaning that makes the dream seem even more worthwhile. The reward of realizing a dream is not only in the result but also in who you become through having experienced the journey. You gain a new level of ability.

Given this dynamic, I encourage you to think about your own journey moving forward. Are you holding back in your career or your marriage because it seems hard? Are you about to give up on a dream because the path feels steep? Please don't. Dreams, like love, require patience and perseverance. They're worth the effort, and they're worth the endurance.

In retrospect, there were times I had to set aside business dreams (including my Pretty Sister activities, like the cruises) to focus on the kids—I put it off until recently, when it felt like better timing. However, I did pursue other career opportunities while parenting.

The whole of life involves giving and taking, the juggling of roles and responsibilities, and making compromises and sacrifices along the way.

Your happily ever after is still possible. It might just look a little different than you imagined, and that's okay. It's the journey, not just the destination, that makes it all so meaningful.

Visualization: A Tool for Perseverance and Reward

This brings us back to the importance of visualization and how it can help us put our focus on an end goal. We've discussed the concept of visualization before, but it's essential to revisit it here because, without this ability, we can easily lose sight of our dreams when we face obstacles. Visualization is not just about seeing our dreams in our mind's eye as concluded, it can also be about seeing ourselves as confident and capable of staying the course when things get tough.

There are always going to be bumps in the proverbial road, moments when the reality of our journey feels hard. But it's during these moments, when things seem like they might fall apart, that it's most important to hold on to the vision of where we're going. *When something is a little hard, it's a little rewarding; and when it's very hard, the rewards are even greater.*

Just like in fairy tales when little kids are trying to get through the dark forest, the path of life is predictably filled with unexpected twists. The trick is to stay focused, to keep visualizing your dream destination, and to understand that the difficulties you encounter are not signs of your failure. Visualize yourself growing so you are capable of achieving something truly worthwhile. Also visualize yourself finding the right kind of support.

Mindset, Growth, and the Pursuit of Dreams

So, what happens when life throws us curveballs? When we take a swing and miss, or things don't go exactly as planned? It's important to remember that the reward of the "game" is often found in the "playing" itself. Stepping up to the plate to face our challenges, while sometimes scary or difficult, allows us to grow, learn, and appreciate the fulfillment of our dreams even more when it happens.

We build resilience, patience, and strength by persisting in moving toward our goals when times are tough. Confronting our problems, even when it's a struggle, helps us understand the depth and value of what we're working toward. We may need to run and jump to catch our equivalent of a pop fly to the outfield or to field a ground ball to third base in life.

Any time you're struggling and feel like giving up, remind yourself, *This is not the end yet.* And it's true. Even when things don't go as expected, there's always the opportunity to grow, learn, and persevere until you have what you need to overcome your obstacles and complete the task at hand. Keep your focus on your dreams and trust that everything you're going through now is preparing you either to do this or something greater.

In the next sections of this chapter, we'll continue to explore how to embrace life's challenges with grace and resilience. We'll dive deeper into the importance of commitment, perseverance, and the unwavering belief that the "happily ever after" we want isn't just something that happens at the end. It's something we create, day by day, choice by choice.

Keep going because *it's not the end yet.* Your dream life is still unfolding, and you are right on track.

Rinse and Repeat: The Ongoing Journey

Life has a way of adding complexity to our daily routines. It's easy for the mind to overthink and complicate things, but here's the secret to maintaining momentum on the path to your dreams: *Keep it simple.* Complexity can lead to confusion and stagnation, and that's not what you should want. You should want to be in a constant flow of happiness and progress. For this, simplicity is the key.

Success isn't some mysterious, convoluted process. It's the result of maintaining inner focus and directing your thoughts toward a specific, straightforward target: *your dreams!*

Consistency Is Key: Maintaining Momentum in Pursuit of Your Dreams

Welcome to the heart of the ongoing journey—the land of *consistency.* This is where dreams are truly cultivated, where belief is reinforced, and where creation becomes a natural rhythm. Consistency is the secret that transforms ordinary actions into extraordinary results.

Think of it like this: A single raindrop may not seem like much, but when you have a constant downpour, it can carve rivers through rock to create canyons. Similarly, your daily efforts, no matter how small they seem, have the power to shape the grand landscape of your dreams.

Consistency isn't about doing something once and expecting an immediate, mind-blowing transformation. It's about showing up every day, week after week, and year after year with unwavering dedication. It's about making small, intentional choices that may not yield instant gratification but will, over time, accumulate into profound achievements.

Or here's a different analogy. Imagine you're building a bridge. Each day, you lay a single brick. At first, it may seem insignificant, but over time, you've built a sturdy, reliable bridge from where you are now to your dream destination. Consistency ensures that each brick in this structure is perfectly placed, forming the strong foundation for your dreams to rest upon.

The beauty of consistency is how it makes achievement of a goal less overwhelming. Instead of trying to conquer monumental tasks all at once, you break them down into manageable steps and tackle these steps one by one, a day at a time. It's not unlike climbing a mountain a step at a time. Before you know it, you're standing at the summit and enjoying a breathtaking view of your accomplishments.

Consistency also builds trust, both in yourself and in the process. When you commit to consistent action, you reinforce the belief that you're capable of achieving your dreams. You prove to yourself that you can depend on yourself, and that your dreams are worth pursuing. And you get to see increments of progress occurring, which will boost your confidence.

So, as you continue on this journey of dreaming, believing, and creating, remember: *Consistency is your faithful companion.* Embrace it, nurture it, and let it guide you toward the realization of your most cherished dreams.

The Power of Endurance: Life's "Thirty Seconds"

For years, when my kids were younger, I had a sanctuary: the local YMCA. This was a place where I could drop them off at daycare and spend two blissful, uninterrupted hours doing what I needed to do. At the Y, I could exercise, shower, and just breathe without constant interruptions.

But what should have been a time of relaxation often turned into something much more complex. It was a torture chamber in disguise—especially during my favorite exercise class.

The class was taught by Paige, a trainer with a drill sergeant persona, and it was intense. Think lots of shouting, sweating, and a workout that felt like military boot camp. But there was one phrase she used that has stuck with me: *"You can do ANYTHING for thirty seconds!"* Every time I wanted to quit during those grueling intervals, that phrase would echo in my mind.

At first, I didn't believe her. Thirty seconds? Her thirty-second drills seemed to last forever. But it turned out she was right. The hardest part of the workout was not the thirty-second intervals, but the mindset behind them. Once I realized this, I started applying that mindset to life.

This simple lesson became an enduring principle in my life. Life, like those intense workouts, throws challenges at us, but it's not all difficult all the time. Accepting that there will be tough moments and then pushing through them becomes easier with practice. The more we endure, the stronger we become. And just like the cooldown at the end of each class, there's a reward waiting for us at the end of the hard moments.

One of my favorite quotes is from Friedrich Nietzsche: "What doesn't kill you makes you stronger."[1] I can't think of a truer statement. So much of life is about endurance. When we face challenges head on and accept that these difficult moments will pass, we come out on the other side not only stronger but also more capable.

In every hard moment, there's an opportunity to grow. And just like a workout at the gym prepares your muscle for tests of endurance and strength, each difficult experience prepares you for the next. So, what's holding you back because it seems too hard? Make a commitment today to face it head on, even if it's just for thirty seconds. You'll be amazed at what you can accomplish and how much you'll grow through the experience.

And before long, you'll look back at your toughest moments with gratitude for what they taught you and how they made you stronger.

Learning from Setbacks: Embracing Challenges as Opportunities

Setbacks and challenges are inevitable parts of life, but they offer incredible opportunities for growth and transformation. They aren't roadblocks; they are stepping stones. How we respond to these trials shapes our character and our future. Life's most difficult moments can become the crucibles in which our strength, resilience, and wisdom are forged.

A diamond, one of the Earth's most precious gems, is formed under immense pressure. Similarly, life's challenges shape us into something beautiful and resilient. Rather than expecting life to be easy, we should embrace challenges as opportunities to grow. They test our character, refine our strength, and ultimately help us become who we're meant to be.

The night before my wedding, at a small, intimate dinner with close family and friends, I received a special gift. The evening was filled with joy, love, and laughter, but it was what my father said during his toast that would stay with me forever.

My father stood up, raised his glass, and expressed how proud he was of me. As he shared his excitement for my future with Dave, he added something that would profoundly impact the way I viewed my life and challenges moving forward. He said, "I've always believed that you carry a silver-lined cloud above you. No matter what happens, you'll always find the good in any situation, and everything will work out for you."

In that moment, it felt like time slowed. I wasn't just hearing words. I was receiving a gift more precious than any material possession. My father was giving me a belief, a conviction, that would serve as my constant companion. It wasn't just a toast, but a profound truth that I would carry with me through every storm, every hardship, and every joy.

His words became my silver-lined cloud, a belief I clung to like a lifeline. From that moment on, I knew I had a tool to navigate life's inevitable challenges. His confidence in me gave me strength, a certainty that no matter how difficult the circumstances, I could find the silver lining. As the evening continued and the wedding celebrations unfolded, his words stayed with me—not just as a comforting thought, but as a practical reminder that even in life's storms, I always have the power to seek out hope and resilience.

Over the years, that toast has become a personal mantra and more. It's something I've passed on to my sisters, especially when they've faced their own trials. We often joke that whenever life threw them a challenge, they would call and ask to borrow my silver-lined cloud. I'd always happily send it their way, knowing that they, too, would emerge from their struggles stronger and wiser.

It's become a family tradition that no matter how difficult life gets we always have the ability to find something good in our circumstances, something that will help us grow, learn, and move forward. Now, I'd like to extend that same tradition to you.

Life's challenges are here to refine you, not defeat you. When setbacks arise, look for the silver lining in your situation. Find the good.

Life may bring storms, but with the right mindset, you can weather them. I know you have this ability because I've never met anyone who doesn't. When you respond to adversity with resilience, you'll discover the sunlight of your inner strength shining brightly behind the cloud, ready to illuminate a brilliant future.

Dreaming BIG:
The Power of Resilience

My brother has been battling a severe illness for years, enduring countless close calls and years of unimaginable pain. He must have nine lives, like a cat, because every time he seems to reach the brink of disaster, he bounces back. A few years ago, during a routine family gathering to celebrate my mother's birthday at his home, he experienced one of the most harrowing moments of his life. He went into diabetic shock and suffered a severe tetany attack. This involves painful, involuntary spasms and cramping of muscles. We had to call an ambulance, and for a moment, we didn't know if he would make it.

The day after this near-death experience, I visited him in the hospital. To my amazement, not only was my brother alive, but he was also remarkably lucid. As he sat up, he immediately began sharing his grandiose plans for the future, detailing his vision for selling his company and mapping out the steps for the next phase of his life. His enthusiasm was palpable. In that moment I realized that his ability to dream big and focus on his future was what had carried him through his excruciating physical challenges. His unwavering belief in his dreams had been his lifeline.

Today, my brother is much healthier. He's working passionately and relentlessly to pursue the very dreams he held on to during his most painful times. His rebound has been nothing short of miraculous, and it's a testament to the power of holding on to your vision, no matter the circumstances.

What's the secret to my brother's resilience? It's his dedication to his dreams. Through all the pain, setbacks, and close calls, he's stayed focused on what he wants to create in his life. His belief in what's possible keeps him moving forward, no matter how many obstacles life throws his way.

So, I ask you: What could you overcome if you had similar dedication to your dreams? How would you approach life's most challenging defeats if you kept your focus on your future goals no matter what? Could you rise above adversity and bounce back stronger, because nothing could extinguish your unwavering belief in your dreams? The power of a tangible, passionate vision for your life is far stronger than any hardship you'll face.

Is my brother still facing challenges? Absolutely. But if you ask him about his future, he'll share his goals and vision with unwavering confidence. Despite all that he's been through, he continues to dream big, work hard, and believe that the best is yet to come. His story serves as a powerful reminder: When life knocks you down, hold on to your dreams. Focus on what's possible, let go of what you can't control, and keep moving forward. The future you're envisioning is within reach.

What dream will keep you going through the hard times? What vision for your future will help you bounce back and keep pushing forward?

Sisterhood's Role in Resilience: How Supportive Friends Can Help You Bounce Back

As we explore the ongoing journey of resilience, it's important to recognize the immense value of sisterhood when it comes to bouncing back from life's challenges. The path to manifesting your dreams is rarely a straight line. There will always be detours, bumps, and obstacles along the way. But it's not the end. It's simply part of the journey, and that's when the strength of sisterhood becomes invaluable.

Resilience—the ability to withstand setbacks, adapt, and rise stronger—is a muscle we all have the power to build. One of the most effective ways to strengthen this muscle is by surrounding ourselves with friends who understand our dreams and struggles. Your Pretty Sisters will be there for you, ready to help you navigate the ups and downs of life.

When life gets tough, a Pretty Sister offers emotional support. Pretty Sisters acknowledge the highs and lows of other women's journeys because they are on their own paths and have highs and lows too. They support their friends and provide them with a safe space where they can share their struggles without being judged and receive empathy. Their encouragement is like a lifeline, reminding you that no setback is permanent, and you're not alone in facing it.

Sometimes, when you're too close to your own dreams or challenges, it's hard to see the bigger picture. This is where sisterhood plays a critical role. Pretty Sisters bring fresh perspectives and insights, helping you find solutions you may have missed. They can offer advice that brings clarity and guide you through tough decisions, helping you stay focused on the journey ahead.

Sisters are also key motivators. When your energy wanes or your enthusiasm fades, they are there to lift you up and keep you on track. Sharing your goals with your Pretty Sisters creates a sense of accountability; and knowing that someone believes in you can reignite your drive. Their support ensures that you keep going even when the path feels hard and uncertain.

If you choose to show up for one another, then you and your Pretty Sisters can learn and grow together. The experiences, wisdom, and lessons shared within your sisterhood can become a powerful environment in which personal development can occur. In such a community, when one succeeds, the whole group celebrates, reinforcing the belief that a woman's dreams are meant to be realized—and that no one has to do it alone.

Unity within a sisterhood builds extraordinary strength. When one Pretty Sister is facing adversity, the others in a unified sisterhood will be there to provide a solid foundation of support. Together, she can weather any storm, knowing that she has the backing of a community of women who genuinely care about her success and well-being.

In addition to providing strength, your Pretty Sisters can bring joy and laughter into your life. They can remind you not to take everything so seriously, helping you find lightness and humor even in the hardest moments. Ideally, laughter helps us stay grounded and reminds us that joy can always be found, no matter what challenges we face.

When your victories come, wouldn't you like to have friends to celebrate with? Whether the victory is a small accomplishment or a major breakthrough, sharing the joy of your success will magnify its significance. Your sisterhood will make each win feel sweeter.

Any time you're struggling and feel like giving up, just remind yourself, *This is not the end yet.* And it's true. Even when things don't go as expected, there's always the opportunity to grow, learn, and persevere until you have what you need to overcome your obstacles and complete the task at hand.

Keep your focus on your dreams and trust that everything you're going through now is preparing you to do either this or something greater.

Keep going, because *it's not the end yet.* Your dream life is still unfolding, and you are right on track.

BELIEF #4: YOU ARE MEANT FOR JOY

PRETTY SISTER PINKY PROMISE

RUN THROUGH THE SPILLING THE TEA TECHNIQUE AFTER reading the three chapters related to Belief #4. The objective now is for you to internalize that *you are meant to live a joyful life* and to believe that everything will work out for you, so you might as well be happy—and if you're not, well, remember it's not the end yet and hang in there.

When I say "I am meant for joy," I THINK: _____

_____

_____

_____

_____

When I think *that*, it makes me FEEL: _____

_____

_____

_____

_____

When I feel *that*, it makes me ACT: _____

_____

_____

_____

Ask yourself, "Is there anything else I am thinking?" Run through this same process as many times as needed until you are thinking from your heart with courage, love, and confidence. Once you feel ready, move on to make the promise.

Find a fellow Pretty Sister (this can be your mom, a sister, a friend, or someone from the online Pretty Sister community) and make the following promise to her. Or speak these words to yourself in the mirror.

"I believe I am meant for joy.
I Pretty Sister pinky promise—
and crosses don't count!"

You are meant to live a joyful life. Believe that everything will work out for you, even when the journey feels tough. Embrace the mindset that happiness is yours to choose, and trust that the challenges you face are part of a bigger plan leading you toward your dreams. If things don't feel perfect right now, remember that *it's not the end yet*. Hang in there, keep believing, and allow yourself the grace to experience joy, knowing that brighter days are ahead. The best is yet to come.

BELIEF #5
LOVE IS THE ANSWER

"Love is the only reality, and it is not a mere emotion. It is the ultimate truth that lies at the heart of all creation."

RABINDRANATH TAGORE

THIRTEEN

ALWAYS LOVE YOUR PEOPLE

Love is what wins. It binds, it heals, it forgives—and in the end,
it conquers everything that would tear us apart.

I WAS PREGNANT WITH BRADEN, MY MIDDLE CHILD, AND getting close to my due date. Life was overwhelming. I was living in a suburb of Boston, far from my sisters, struggling with a challenge that felt personal and difficult, where breathing just seemed hard. On one particular day, I went to the mailbox, hoping for some small distraction, and to my surprise, I found a letter from my sister Martha. It was heartfelt, sincere, and oddly perfect for what I was going through. I had not shared any of my struggles with her, yet here she was, sending me a message that felt like it had come straight from her heart, perfectly in tune with my needs. Despite our distance—both physical and emotional—Martha's words reached me exactly when I needed them most. It felt like a miracle, like love bridging the gap between us, no matter the miles or the circumstances.

Fast forward about fifteen years to when I was living in Utah, once again facing a rough patch. Life was busy with the chaos of raising teenagers, and I was doing much of it alone, because of Dave traveling frequently on business. Once again, I was quietly gritting my teeth as I made my way through this difficult situation when, out of nowhere, a flower arrangement arrived at my door. The card, from my sister Becky, who was living in London at the time, carried the same perfect timing. She had no idea what I was going through, yet she somehow met my need with her gesture of love.

As before, I felt as though I was being lifted up. My sister's love had found its way to me in the exact moment I needed it.

These moments are only a couple of the many times when my pretty sisters have given me a lifeline that has helped me weather a storm in my life. Whether from the receipt of a handwritten letter, a thoughtful gift, or simply a supportive word, I've learned that I am never truly alone. Even when I feel isolated, love from others always reaches me, reminding me that I am seen, cared for, and supported.

But love doesn't just come from others. It emanates from us. I've found that the love I've been blessed to receive is not a passive thing; it's something that requires me giving, choosing, and extending love to those around me. When I do this, love returns to me. That's how we cultivate love in our lives. Whether it's through the unconditional love of my children, the friendship of my Pretty Sisters, or the bond of family, I've realized that the love I have given has profoundly shaped the life I was able to create.

The love we exchange with the people in our lives is what makes relationships our greatest source of happiness. Studies, like the Good Life Study, show that strong relationships are the key to living a fulfilling and joyful life. It's not wealth, fame, or success that brings us lasting happiness, but these connections we build over time. These bonds, forged through shared experiences, time, service, and love, form the foundation of a life well lived.

I remember when Chase, my firstborn and eldest son, was placed in my arms after his birth. The love I immediately felt was overwhelming. He seemed perfect. I had created him with a lot of effort, and he was mine. The responsibility I had for him did seem a bit daunting, but the love was nothing short of miraculous. And thank goodness it was bestowed in such great measure, because the days and years of parenting that followed, while filled with so much love, also required hard work, patience, and some suffering. It's not easy to raise a child.

The nights were often long, the demands were many, and at times I felt like I had given everything I had and had little left to give. But somehow, through all these sleepless nights and emotional rollercoasters, my love for my son kept me going. And what's most incredible is that the love didn't just get me through; it utterly transformed me. It made me a better person, even as it pushed me to my limits.

Raising a child, like loving anyone deeply, is an ongoing process of giving and receiving, of growing and learning.

When I was about to deliver Taylor, my second child and first daughter, I was filled with worry. Could I possibly love her the same way I loved Chase? I was afraid that I wouldn't have enough love to give to both of them. The prospect of parenting two kids felt overwhelming, and I couldn't truly understand how it would work until I experienced it. But when they placed Taylor in my arms, I was flooded with that same love I had felt for Chase. Miraculously, the love I felt for her didn't take away from the love I had for him. The love somehow was multiplied.

The heart has an incredible way of expanding, and I learned that love isn't finite. It grows. And this is a lesson I would experience three more times as I brought the rest of my five children into this world. With each new child, my heart grew larger, and the capacity I have for giving and receiving love has been multiplied.

Now, as I watch my children maturing and think about the day when they will have their own families, I can't help being excited to watch our love multiply even further. When they bear children and I become a grandmother, I know that the love I experience will continue to expand beyond what I ever imagined possible.

That's the true power of love: It multiplies and never ends. It isn't divided when shared, it increases. And this is a gift I will get to experience over and over again in my relationships with my children, with my friends, and with other members of my extended family.

Of course, love isn't always easy. We can all face challenges in our relationships with our spouses, friends, neighbors, or relatives. We all make mistakes. We hurt each other, disappoint one another, and sometimes, it feels like it's easier to walk away than to face the difficult work of reconciliation. But the truth is that real love is not about perfection; it's about showing up for one another, especially when it's hard. Love is about making the choice to stay, to listen, to support, and to forgive.

I've learned that to truly love my people, I must choose love in all its forms, even when it's difficult. It's easy to love when everything is smooth sailing, but the real test comes when life is tough. When I've felt misunderstood, unsupported, or disconnected, I've had to dig deep and ask myself: *How can I love in this moment? How can I be a source of strength, understanding, and compassion, even when I feel drained? How can I offer grace, even when I feel that I've received so little of it in return?*

It's not easy, but the rewards are immense. I've realized that when I extend love, even in the toughest circumstances, I not only heal myself, but I also strengthen the relationships around me. I grow as a person, and I contribute to the happiness of others. By choosing love—every day, in every moment, I create a life that is meaningful, fulfilling, and full of joy.

So, how can we create lives we love? A great life starts with loving our people, especially when they're imperfect. When we open our hearts to others and choose love over resentment, fear, or anger, we lay a foundation upon which to build deep connection and lasting happiness.

I believe that love is the secret to getting everything we desire. It's the foundation of happiness, the key to fulfilling relationships, and the driving force behind our greatest accomplishments. So let's make the conscious decision to love ourselves, to express love to everyone we encounter, and to be a breath of fresh air to the people we hold dear. Because in the end, love is what makes life worth living.

And the good news is, we get to choose it—every single day.

Of course, the range of human emotions includes being mad and upset at times. But when we get mad or upset, we can choose to take responsibility for our feelings rather than acting them out. If you are committed to being a force of love, then you must learn the art of letting go.

The Art of Letting Go

Have you ever found yourself trapped in a cycle of frustration caused by unmet expectations? This is something we've all experienced, especially with the people we love. Whether it's a spouse, a parent, a coworker, or a friend, we naturally expect fairness, respect, and consideration. We expect promises made to be kept, even simple ones like taking out the trash. But life rarely works out exactly as we hope, so we're often left feeling hurt, disappointed, and frustrated. This disappointment can set off a chain reaction, where one frustration turns into another, until, before we know it, it feels like everything is just one big letdown. Fortunately, there's a way to prevent our upset from getting out of control. Instead of letting resentment fester, we can choose to forgive quickly.

Forgiveness is the key to breaking the cycle, which can be done at any point—now or later. It's easy to talk about forgiving, but harder to put into practice, especially when the hurt feels deep. But the intensity of our resentment or sadness doesn't matter. Whether a hurt is deep or shallow, big or small, what matters is that forgiveness will help you feel better. Choosing to forgive allows you to reset your expectations and clear your heart from the weight of frustration.

Holding on to anger or resentment will tether you to the past, keeping your emotions in a state of turmoil. But when you choose to forgive, even when it's hard, you free yourself from the grip of negative emotions. The choice is to perpetuate your own pain or to bring yourself some relief. You feeling bad only hurts you.

Quickly forgiving is a difficult lesson to learn, but it's worth the effort. Forgiving doesn't mean excusing a behavior that upset you or pretending that your hurt didn't happen. It simply means that you are releasing your hold on the issue so it no longer controls you. When you forgive, you become the one in control, instead of the person who wronged you. You take back your power.

The Power of Forgiveness

When we forgive, we often feel as though we're letting another person off the hook. But in reality, we're setting ourselves free. As long as we cling to anger, disappointment, or hurt, we will remain emotionally shackled, and be giving someone else the power to control our emotions.

By contrast, forgiveness does more than free us from resentment. It opens the door to healing, growth, and peace. It allows us to move forward without being burdened by the past.

In the Disney live-action movie *Cinderella,* which I watched with my daughters when they were younger, there's a beautiful moment of forgiveness that encapsulates the nature of this power. After years of mistreatment from her wicked stepmother and stepsisters, Cinderella doesn't retaliate or seek revenge. Instead, she offers them the gift of her forgiveness. When Cinderella stands before her stepmother, she says, "I forgive you," and in that instant, the power that her stepmother exerted over her dissolves. Cinderella reclaims her strength, her agency, and her future. The phrase *I forgive you* is a declaration of personal freedom—freedom from anger, freedom from resentment, and freedom to move forward with grace.

Just like Cinderella, when we forgive, we let go of the effect that others' actions have had on us. We take back control of our emotions and open up space in our hearts and minds for love and healing. In combination, the three little words *I forgive you,* are some of the most powerful words we can say. And in actuality, they not only release us, but they also release the other person. Everyone goes free.

Practical Steps to Forgiveness

If you're ready to forgive, here's a simple exercise: Think of three people or situations that you need to forgive, large or small. One of these could include a situation for which you need to forgive yourself. Many of us hold ourselves to impossibly high standards and carry self-inflicted wounds.

Four points worth mentioning are that:

- None of the people on your forgiveness list needs to know that you've forgiven them; this is a gift you will be giving to yourself.
- If you forgive swiftly and completely, it gives you a chance to step back and watch how your life begins to shift as a result.
- You do not have to express your forgiveness directly to the person who has upset or harmed you. If possible, express your forgiveness directly to the person after you've forgiven them, but if that's not feasible (perhaps because they died), or you just don't want to, then consider writing a letter that you never mail (you can shred it or burn it if you don't want anyone else to see it) or simply saying what's in your heart aloud.
- You do not have to expose yourself to the presence of a malicious or dangerous person in order to forgive them. You can stay safe from an abuser and still get the relief of emotional freedom by relinquishing your need to control them inside you.

Let go of the pain, the resentment, and other emotional baggage you've been carrying with you since the wound occurred.

Forgiveness is not a one-time event, but a continual practice. Just like wiping the kitchen counters, which you need to do every time you cook a meal, or vacuuming the floors once a week, think of forgiveness as the act of tidying up the space you live in—within you. Every time you feel anger or resentment creeping in, choose forgiveness again. Every time you feel burdened by past hurts, choose to forgive. The more you practice forgiveness, the more natural it becomes, and the freer you will feel to lead a life full of joy, love, and possibility. This is a top skill for those who think pretty.

A Final Word on Forgiveness

When we forgive, we let go of our anger and make room for peace. We open ourselves to new relationships, new opportunities, and new growth. We release ourselves from the chains of the past and reclaim our power. It's an essential step in creating a life we love, and therefore critical to living freely and authentically. When you forgive, you are disrupting a cycle of negativity, and initiating a new cycle of happiness.

Forgiveness doesn't mean you'll never feel hurt again. It simply means that you no longer let your past hurts define you. You get to decide how to move forward. You have the power to take control of your emotional health and your future. And just like Cinderella in the moment that she tells her wicked stepmother, "I forgive you," you get to rewrite your story about who you are, free yourself from the pain of the past, and embrace a future full of love, light, and endless possibilities. Pretty Sisters are masters of forgiveness.

Love Requires Good Communication

Good communication is the foundation of thriving relationships. It's the glue that bonds people and makes their interactions seamless. But here's the truth. So many misunderstandings and conflicts in our relationships stem from one simple thing: *not saying what we really mean*. Pretty Sisters work on their communication skills because they want to avoid misunderstandings if they can.

Be honest, how often have you found yourself frustrated because someone didn't "get" what you were thinking or feeling? Let's say you wanted something, but kept this information to yourself, hoping that somehow they would just know or could guess. And then surprise, surprise, they didn't know.

Picture this: You're in the car with your partner, secretly craving ice cream. You drop subtle hints like, "I wonder if there's a good ice cream place around here," and yet, nothing. You end up disappointed and maybe even a little annoyed that he didn't pick up on your clues for how to please you. Here's the reality. *You have to say what you mean.* Dropping hints or assuming people can read your mind only leads to frustration and confusion. It's like playing a game of charades and expecting everyone to guess the right answer without any clues.

Instead, why not try this. *Be direct and clear about your needs and wants.* If you want ice cream, just say it: "Hey, can we stop for ice cream?" Simple, right? No games, no hidden messages—just clear, honest communication. You'll be surprised how much easier things get when everyone knows exactly what you need.

And here's a bonus. If you need to repeat yourself, *it's okay.* People are busy, and sometimes they forget or get distracted. But as long as they're willing to listen and respond to your needs, and do their best to understand what they are, that's what counts. The key is making your intentions known and allowing others the space to show up for you.

For the next week, I challenge you to practice clear communication. Don't be afraid to express your needs and desires in a straightforward way. Set your expectations and speak openly. Also, invite the people in your life to be direct with you about their needs. You might be amazed at how much smoother your relationships can be when everyone is on the same page. No more assumptions, no more frustration—just clear understanding and stronger connections. Give it a try and let me know how it goes!

Daily Acts of Service:
Spreading Kindness and Building Connections

One of the most powerful ways to love your people is through service. Service is how we express our love and strengthen the bonds we share with those around us. It's a reminder that we are all connected, and that our actions can lift and support one another. When we serve others, we are showing them love and also creating an environment where love can grow. This is beneficial both for others and for us.

Have you ever noticed how a simple act of kindness can light up someone's day—and your own? Whether it's holding a door, listening with empathy, or offering a helping hand, the act of service brings both joy and fulfillment. When we focus on the needs of others, we often find that our own struggles fade into the background, even if only for a moment.

Service doesn't need to be grand to be meaningful. It's not about doing huge things all the time; it's about doing the small, thoughtful things. Whether you're helping a friend with a chore, giving someone a compliment, or taking the time to listen, these acts are a powerful way to express love. When you take the time to serve, you're showing others that you care—and that's how relationships grow and deepen.

The beauty of service is that, while it brightens someone else's life, it also fills the "servant" with a sense of purpose and connection. The more you practice being of service, the more your love for those around you grows. It becomes a natural way to nurture your relationships and to show love in a tangible way.

Now, let's focus on making service a habit—because love grows with practice. For the next thirty days, I challenge you to do something kind for someone else every day. It doesn't have to be anything extravagant. Maybe it's sending a text to check in, helping a neighbor, or volunteering your time to a worthy cause. If you miss a day, don't worry—just start over. By the end of one month, looking back on everything you've done and how you feel about it, I believe you'll see how these simple acts of service can deeply impact the people around you, and you'll be amazed at the love you've cultivated.

Pretty Sisters are masters of service. Here are ten guidelines to get you started doing daily acts of service.

Set clear intentions. Be intentional about your service. Think about how you want to show love to the people in your life and set a goal for how you can serve them each day.

Start small. Service doesn't always have to be grand. Small gestures like offering to carry something, sharing a kind word, or lending a hand can make all the difference.

Be consistent. Make service a daily practice. The more you do it, the more natural it will become, and the more love you'll express.

Set reminders. Life can get busy, so set reminders to make sure you don't forget your daily acts of service. Keeping it top of mind will help you make it a habit.

Be open to spontaneous opportunities. Sometimes the best opportunities to serve are the unplanned ones. Stay open to helping in the moment, when it matters most.

Reflect on your impact. Each day, take a moment to reflect on how your service impacted someone else. How did it make you feel? How did it affect them? This reflection helps reinforce the habit.

Share your journey. Let others know about your challenge. Share your experience with your Pretty Sisters, family, or friends. Having support along the way helps keep you motivated.

Celebrate your wins. Celebrate the small victories. As you grow your habit of service, recognize the positive changes it's creating in your life and the lives of those around you.

Adapt and evolve. As you get comfortable with service, challenge yourself to try new things. Find creative ways to show love through your actions.

Practice gratitude. Always take a moment to express gratitude for the opportunity to serve. The more grateful you are, the more love will flow into your life.

Daily acts of service are one of the most beautiful ways to love your people. It's about showing up for those you care about, offering kindness, and strengthening your bonds with them. This is not just a single thing you do; it is a practice. As a Pretty Sister, I encourage you to commit to serving others with love, and watch how it transforms your relationships and creates deeper connections with those you cherish.

Balancing Time, Energy, and Love

As we wrap up this chapter on loving our people, it's important to acknowledge the delicate balance that we often need to strike between our self-care and giving our time, energy, and love to the people who matter most in our lives. It's a juggling act, especially when we're being pulled in many different directions. The truth is, it can be difficult to know where to place our focus, especially when we feel like we should be giving equal attention to everyone and everything at once. Career, exercise, children, partner, elderly parents, friends, and service organizations. But here's the thing: There are times and seasons, and moments where we can—and should—place our energy and love on different people, depending on the circumstances. Throughout our lives, the demands we face will shift and evolve.

As we've discussed, achieving our dreams requires consistent daily actions that lead us to our goals. It's a process of having faith in the journey, trusting our inner wisdom, and putting in the effort, bit by bit. But sometimes, life pulls us in different directions, and we forget that balance doesn't mean everything and everyone gets equal attention all the time. Balance is more about learning to prioritize what matters most in the moment, and sometimes that means focusing on our loved ones and nurturing those relationships first.

Let me share a little personal story that demonstrates the power of this. Balancing the demands of motherhood, work, and personal dreams can feel overwhelming. As a mother, I've been in the thick of it, trying to give my all to my family while still pursuing my career goals. It's a fine line to walk, making sure that everyone feels loved and important while also staying true to my own aspirations. And honestly, it's been tough. But over time, I've discovered one powerful practice that helps: one-on-one trips or dates with my kids and other loved ones.

These trips have had a profound impact on the quality of my relationships. When I'm able to focus on just one child or spend undistracted time with my husband, Dave, it completely shifts the dynamic. It gives me the chance to see them for who they truly are, without the routine distractions of daily life. Whether it's a mother-daughter excursion to New York City or a quick getaway with Dave, these moments allow for deep connection. And the best part is, I often blend business travel with these special trips, so while I'm working during the day, my child is exploring and creating memories of their own. It's the best of both worlds, where everyone benefits.

But we can't be everything to everyone all the time. That's a myth we all try to live by sometimes, and frankly, it's exhausting. There are times when we need to give undivided attention to one person—be it a spouse, a child, or a friend—and that's okay. These one-on-one moments give everyone a chance to grow, and it allows you to build stronger bonds that benefit everyone in the long run. Being alone and giving attention to ourselves is sometimes necessary, too! We matter.

In the hustle and bustle of our lives, it's easy to think that balance is a static, one-size-fits-all concept. But balance is dynamic. It shifts with our needs, priorities, and the seasons of life. Sometimes, you'll need to prioritize one aspect of life over others, and trust that everything else will fall into place. And yes, leaving my kids behind for work can be anxiety inducing.

But every time I return, I find them not merely okay, but actually thriving from having had their own adventures and experiences. I love catching up with them and hearing their news.

So, whether it's with one of your children or another important person in your life, I encourage you to give this individual the gift of your undivided attention. Find a way to make your relationship work, even within your busy schedule. The rewards will be immeasurable. The connection you build will strengthen the love between you and your people. And in turn, the joy and fulfillment that you feel will pour into every area of your life. Trust me on this, as you'll be glad you took the time.

As we've been exploring, the power of love can transform any situation, no matter how difficult it may seem. When we pause, breathe, and choose to love more, we unlock a whole new perspective on life and the people around us. Pretty Sisters understand that love is the most powerful tool we have to improve our relationships, heal wounds, and create meaningful connections.

And here's the beautiful thing: Love is not scarce. It multiplies and never runs out. Like the Grinch in the old cartoon *The Grinch Who Stole Christmas,* whose heart grew three sizes when he celebrated Christmas with the Whos in Whoville, so too does ours when we practice love. The more we give, the more we have to give, and the happiness in our lives grows right along with it.

IN THIS CHAPTER, WE'VE TOUCHED ON ESSENTIAL TOOLS to help love grow, among them forgiveness, communication, service, and balancing the places where we invest time and attention. These practices may take time, but the effort is worth it. As we forgive, communicate openly, serve others, and spend quality time with our loved ones, we cultivate an abundance of love in our lives. It's a journey of patience, practice, and growth. But the rewards—deeper connections, greater joy, and stronger relationships—are immeasurable. By loving our people, we not only enrich their lives, but we also unlock the boundless love we have within ourselves. And in the end, that's what makes life truly meaningful.

FOURTEEN

IT'S OKAY TO LOVE YOUR THINGS

"It is good to love many things, for therein lies the true strength, and whosoever loves much performs much, and can accomplish much, and what is done in love is well done."

VINCENT VAN GOGH

I HAD AN UNUSUAL HONEYMOON. DAVE ARRANGED FOR a horse and carriage to pick us up after our wedding reception and take us to a nearby hotel for the night. It wasn't exactly like a fairytale, but in my heart it felt like the perfect romantic start to my happily ever after. What made it unusual, however, was the wedding gift Dave gave me. At the hotel, he surprised me with a WaveRunner! Not quite the typical honeymoon gift, but Dave knew it was exactly what I wanted.

Growing up, I had fallen in love with boating—not because my family owned a boat, but because I had the chance to waterski with friends who did. I loved the thrill of being on the water, and I dreamed of having my own boat someday. But as newlyweds, purchasing a full boat was out of our financial reach. So, when Dave surprised me with the WaveRunner, I was over the moon. It was the perfect starter watercraft, a two-seater we could ride together, which had enough power to pull a water-skier. My longstanding dream of boating and enjoying watersports began to come true, one small step at a time. Our honeymoon was spent in Park City, Utah, with daytrips to nearby lakes to ride the WaveRunner and waterskiing for the weekend before we had to drive across country to begin our new life in Louisville, Kentucky. It was just the beginning.

Several years later, we fulfilled the next chapter in the dream with the purchase of our very own ski boat. Of course, I loved it even more than the WaveRunner! We got it to celebrate the arrival of our fourth child, Sophie. From then on, the boat became our family's sanctuary during our summers in Massachusetts and later in Maine. I loved the sense of togetherness it created, as no one could wander too far. Whether our children were little or teenagers, the boat was the perfect space for our family to come together and play. It was where we created many memories with friends and family all packed into one beautiful, floating vehicle.

Later, we added a recreational vehicle to our collection. This was another dream of mine that became reality. After taking an RV trip as a teen, I knew I would one day have one for my family. Touring the country in that RV brought us a different kind of joy. The close quarters and family game nights brought us together, and despite the occasional chaos, it was pure joy traveling *en masse* to see the sights across the continent. The RV was more than just a possession; it was an opportunity for us to make priceless memories.

But here's the thing: Possessions are just things. Like money, they are neither good nor bad. The role they play in our lives and what we choose to do with them is where they derive their meaning. A brick can be used to build a beautiful house or it can be thrown through a window as an act of vandalism. It's not the brick, but how it's used that defines how we feel about it. Similarly, money and possessions hold no intrinsic value. What matters is the intention behind how we use them. I didn't desire my WaveRunner and RV for the sake of accumulating more stuff or flaunting wealth. I wanted them to create memories, bring my family joy and deepen our relationships, and so we could experience more of what life has to offer.

Growing up, I was deeply influenced by those who shared their lives and resources with me. I saw how the act of sharing changes lives, and I wanted to pass that same experience forward. Any desire I have for possessions since then has always been rooted in the idea of creating beautiful, meaningful moments with the people I love and the people I can impact.

Abundance is good. It's okay to want things, especially tools that will help you create a meaningful life. The beauty of abundance is that when we share, more comes. Generosity fuels connection, and our hearts grow when we use what we have to bless others. Life is meant to be abundant, and our ability to love and share makes it even more so.

Creating a life we love is a conscious process. We need to set up our environments intentionally. For example, by keeping things clean, organized, and uncluttered. When we curate the space around us, we create a sense of harmony and peace that gives us ease from which to operate. We spend so much of our time in our homes, our cars, and our workplaces that they should be places which inspire us to live with purpose. The way we treat our possessions, the way we love the things we have, reflects how we care for the people and experiences we hold dear that involve those things.

Let's not just love the big dreams and moments, let's love the small things. Let's love our homes, our cars, our gardens, our books, and all the tools and resources that help us move forward in life. Let's be grateful for what we have, use it to serve others, and trust that more will come in its time. The beauty of using what you love for good purposes is that it enables you to build a life full of remarkable memories, joy, and love, and other things that make life worth living.

The Importance of Play: Finding Balance and Joy

As we carefully design our environments, it's important not to forget the power of play. In the midst of all the responsibilities we routinely juggle, such as our work, our obligations to our families, our household chores and everyday errands, and life's pressing demands, it is easy to overlook the importance of play. But playing is important. And it's not just for kids. It's essential for our mental, physical, and emotional health. The truth is that we need to carve out time for fun and recreation—down time—no matter how busy life gets. Otherwise we will get depleted and burn out. Play is one of the best ways to recharge our energy, reduce stress, build relationships, and bring counterbalance to a busy life.

Take a moment to imagine the days when your life has felt a little lighter, when play and joy were at the center of everything. Those moments don't have to be a thing of the past. You can integrate them into your daily routine if you get creative.

When we take the time to engage in activities we enjoy, whether those activities are hobbies, vacations, or board games, we're giving ourselves permission to be happy and carefree when we engage in them. That happiness has a ripple effect which positively influences every part of our lives. It recharges our proverbial batteries.

It's important to recognize that there will be seasons in life where play looks different. There will be times when long vacations or extended breaks aren't possible. But this doesn't mean we can't still find joy in little things we do. I've found that even the busiest of days can include moments of lightness and fun. Music and dancing are a huge part of my life. I've been known to wake up my family on a school day by filling the house with loud, cheerful, up-tempo music. Playing music is the perfect way to start the day on a high note and it sets a positive, energized tone for the day ahead. I also do this on Saturday mornings when I'm waking everyone up to do chores.

The upbeat music makes the tasks feel more enjoyable, and everyone gets into the groove. For us, this is a simple hack that turns mundane moments into something more fun.

Building play into our days can be an effective way to create a sense of reward and motivation as well. While growing up, I learned the power of turning tasks into something more enjoyable, and I made it a practice in my own family. When the kids were younger and it came to chores, I would set a goal and offer a reward for the fastest and most efficient cleaner. This turned the chores into a game where everyone had something to look forward to. Afterward, we'd always celebrate by playing together—whether we played an outdoor game, went on a quick family outing, or just spent some time laughing while we were hanging out together at home. The important lesson I wanted to teach my kids was that hard work pays off, and play is the reward. My children also learned the value of teamwork and perseverance.

Dave and I make sure to dedicate Sundays to family play time. After church, we play games as a family, and this tradition has become one of our favorite events of the week. The value is more than just having fun. The value is connecting with each other, sharpening our social skills, and sharing in laughter and joy. These moments have strengthened our family bond.

The joy and connection we experience through play have had a profound impact on how we interact with one another, and I am enormously pleased to see my kids growing into confident, kind individuals who understand the importance of both work and play. My oldest son, Chase, cofounded a gaming company, Game Afternoon, which develops games designed to strengthen family relationships by fostering fun. Their debut card game, *Kingdoms,* is one of our family favorites, and it's been so fun watching it explode in the gaming world.

Play teaches us that life doesn't have to be all about work and striving. It's about balance. The rewards of play and fun are many, so take a break. Make room for play.

I encourage you to look at your life and ask yourself: *What moments of play can I carve out in the day, week, or month ahead of me?* Perhaps you would enjoy scheduling a game night with friends or going on a spontaneous adventure with your spouse.

Or perhaps you can make a game out of something you do in your job to make it less tedious or physically taxing. Let's say you have a desk job. Try standing up every half hour and doing something physical, like ten wall pushups, or if you're like me, dancing wildly to one song. Play is not just an escape; it's a necessary part of a life well-lived.

And remember, when we invest in fun, laughter, and togetherness, we're not only filling our lives with joy but also creating the kind of happy, balanced lives we all deserve.

Play and Friendships: The Importance of Nurturing Your Girlfriends and Taking Time for Yourself

While family playtime is crucial, it's just as important to make time for play with our Pretty Sisters. Our friendships are vital to our well-being. They give us an opportunity to take time for ourselves outside of the demands of work, motherhood, and family life, which is an essential part of becoming the best versions of ourselves. Our girlfriends are there to provide the support, joy, and emotional recharge that we need, and it's okay to let our kids see us take time for these relationships.

As women and moms, we can sometimes feel like we have to be everything for everyone all the time. But let's face it, that's not sustainable. There's no harm in stepping away for a while to nurture our friendships. It doesn't make us any less of a mother or a partner when we do. In fact, it will make us better ones. When we take the time to recharge, have fun, and connect with women outside our homes, we come back to our families with renewed energy, patience, and joy.

And let's not forget the importance of our partners supporting us in this. Husbands and partners benefit when we take time for ourselves, just as we all benefit from the nurturing of friendships. It allows them to step up in different ways with the kids, and it encourages independence. It's not just about taking a break from the demands of motherhood; it's also about teaching our kids healthy independence and resilience. When our children see us taking care of our own needs, they learn that it's important to have boundaries and to make time for personal growth and relationships. This helps them develop emotional resilience as they understand that healthy relationships and self-care are a vital part of a well-balanced life.

Allowing ourselves to play with our girlfriends, to laugh, to share experiences, and to just be ourselves, is so important. It's in those moments of connection that we are reminded of who we are outside of our roles as wives and mothers. These friendships give us the strength to be our best selves in all the other areas of our lives. And when we take time for these relationships, everyone benefits. Our families are happier, our partners are more supportive, and we are more fulfilled. So, make sure to schedule that time with your pretty sisters—whether it's a girls' night out, a weekend getaway, or a spontaneous lunch date. Everyone will be better for it. And the more we invest in these relationships, the more we bring joy, support, and resilience into our lives.

We all need our families, but we also need our girlfriends. It's time to embrace both and create a balanced life where play, connection, and self-care are just as important as everything else.

Letting Go:
Decluttering to Make Room for Abundance

As we explored the art of forgiveness and letting go of emotional baggage earlier, you began your journey toward creating a lighter, more abundant life. Now I invite you to transition from the emotional world into the physical one. Just as it's important to release emotional clutter, it's equally vital to clear out the physical clutter in your life.

The processes of letting go of past hurts and decluttering your physical space are deeply interconnected. Both practices require you to consciously choose to release what no longer serves you—whether that's emotional weight or physical items. By decluttering your physical environment, you're not just tidying up; you're creating space for new energy, opportunities, and experiences to flow into your life.

Letting go of possessions you no longer need can be just as liberating as releasing old grudges and negative emotions. The act of clearing out old items allows you to release the past and make room for something better. It's as though you're inviting fresh energy into your life, ready to embrace new possibilities.

Here's the truth: Our physical environments impact us more than we often realize. A cluttered home or workspace can mirror a cluttered mind. It can create stress, reduce productivity, and hinder your ability to focus. But when you create a clean, organized space, it helps clear your mental clutter as well. It's a beautiful cycle: Declutter your surroundings, and you'll find it easier to let go of emotional baggage, too.

Think of your home as the physical manifestation of your inner world. If you're holding on to items out of guilt or sentimentality, you might also be holding on to old emotional wounds. Clearing out the physical clutter gives you the opportunity to release aspects of the past that you associate with certain belongings and move forward with clarity and freedom. More than cleaning, it's about making space for new things—ideas, experiences, and people—that are meant to come into your life.

The Power of a Clean, Well-Organized Space

So, how do you begin the process of decluttering? It's simpler than you might think. The first step is acknowledging that you live in a world of abundance. Possessions aren't bad. They're tools, opportunities, and experiences waiting to be appreciated. When you are grateful for what you have and demonstrate that gratitude by taking care of the things you own, you show God that you respect the gifts you've been given. You demonstrate that you understand abundance and you trust that more will come. And you also feel satiated because you are aware of what you have. You won't run off to the store to buy another package of something you already have that's hidden at the back of a closet or in the fridge.

There's a point where too much is too-too much. Overconsumption leads to clutter, and clutter breeds chaos. When you hold on to possessions out of a fear of lack in the future, it becomes hoarding, which is when your possessions begin to overtake your life. Stuff can crowd your mind and your space, and in doing so, interfere with your relationships. The power of a clean-well-organized space is that it supports you in attaining balance. It enables you to be selective in where you place your attention. It promotes peace, clarity, and focus.

One of the first laws of the gospel is order. God is a god of order, and He loves it when we strive to create order in our lives. This doesn't mean everything needs to be perfect, but it does mean we should cultivate environments that are clean and tidy. When we care for our homes and spaces, we are honoring the abundance in our lives and opening the door for even more blessings to flow in.

Six Practical Tips for Decluttering and Creating Space

Now that we understand the importance of keeping a clean, well-organized environment, how do we begin? Here are some simple tips to help you clear out physical clutter and invite new opportunities into your life.

- **Start small.** Begin with one room or area at a time. Start with something manageable, like your closet or kitchen drawers. Break the process down into smaller tasks, and don't overwhelm yourself with the big picture.

- **Use the "one in, one out" rule.** When you acquire something new, get rid of something old. This keeps your space from getting cluttered over time and ensures that you maintain balance in your possessions.
- **Be grateful for what you have.** As you go through your items, take a moment to appreciate them. Dialog with yourself. Ask yourself if they still bring value to your life. If they do, keep them. If not, let them go with gratitude for the purpose they served.
- **Donate or share.** If an item no longer serves you, but could be useful to someone else, donate it. Giving away things you no longer need is a powerful act of kindness and generosity.
- **Create a routine.** Make decluttering part of your regular routine. Set aside time once a month or every few months to go through your belongings and reassess what you have. This ensures your space stays organized and light.
- **Organize with purpose.** As you reorganize, do so with intention. Create spaces that support your goals and desires. Whether it's setting up a creative workspace or making your living room a cozy retreat, design your space to encourage the life you want to live.

Declutter Your Mind and Space to Make Room for the Life You Love

When you release physical and emotional clutter, it is like undamming a river of life force. You allow new energy to flow in. You make space for the things that truly matter, such as relationships, opportunities, creativity, and joy. Letting go of the old gives you the freedom to welcome the new.

This is the foundation of creating a life that reflects your dreams and desires. Whether you're clearing out your closet or letting go of past hurts, you're actively choosing to make room for love, abundance, and growth.

Remember, creating an abundant life isn't about what you accumulate, but what you do with what you have. It's about being grateful for the things in your life, using them with purpose, and sharing them with others. Trust that when you take care of your possessions and cultivate gratitude, more will come to you.

As you move forward in the practice of thinking pretty, remember that love for your things is a natural extension of your love for life. By treating your possessions with care, you create an environment that reflects your abundance mindset, and that energy will return to you tenfold. When you embrace your possessions with love, you make space for the dreams and opportunities that are meant to come your way.

The Power of Gratitude, Abundance, and Sharing

We have seen how our relationship with the things we own can bring meaning, joy, and purpose to our lives when approached with gratitude, care, and a mindset of sharing. Loving our possessions isn't just about acquisition for its own sake, it's about appreciating what we have, using it wisely, and sharing it with others to multiply the happiness we experience.

Just as we imagine the beauty and reverence of God's houses—His temples and sacred spaces—crafted with the finest materials and filled with light and peace, we can reflect that same care in the spaces we inhabit. God has given us everything, and if He has designed His houses with beauty and intention, surely, we can treat our homes and possessions with the same respect. We are His children, and He desires us to have abundance in our lives, to use what we have to create joy, and to honor Him through the way we share and care for the blessings we've been given.

When we choose to share, to give, and to use our possessions for good, we align with a greater purpose. The possessions we have are not just things to hold on to—they are tools for creating joy, bringing people together, and helping others experience love. In doing so, we contribute to the happiness of those around us and multiply the joy in our own lives.

Creating wealth and accumulating possessions can be part of fulfilling our purpose. It's okay to desire wealth, not for selfish gain, but to fulfill a larger mission: to support our families, serve others, and create more opportunities for joy. By pursuing wealth with this mindset, we align with our purpose and begin to use our possessions to make the world a better place. Wealth is not an end in itself. It's a tool for building connections, fostering love, and serving others.

I have experienced this firsthand in the creation of our family cabin known as Moose Lake Ranch. What started as a dream was brought to life through hard work, determination, and the willingness to sacrifice for something we truly loved. The work it took to build that space was immense, but the joy it has brought to our family and the many others who have enjoyed it has been worth every effort. It's more than just a place; it's a legacy of love and connection. The cabin continues to bless us, and by sharing it with others, we've multiplied the joy it provides. Families gather there for reunions and weddings, creating memories in the space Dave and I worked so hard to build. Our joy grows as we see others enjoying what we've worked so hard for.

This spirit of sharing has also shaped the creation of our backyard pool house—a space where our family and friends gather for parties, dance-offs, and unforgettable moments. It's a place that extends beyond us, open to all who wish to experience joy and togetherness. The more we share, the more our hearts are filled with happiness, and the more we see how truly abundant life can be.

We've also learned that the work involved in loving your things is not only necessary—it's worthwhile. The more we love something, the more we're willing to invest in it, whether that's time, money, or care. It's about maintaining and cherishing what we have, so it can continue to serve its higher purpose of bringing joy to our lives and others. Whether we're building a cabin, maintaining a home, or simply taking care of the things we have, it all contributes to a life of love, service, and purpose.

Of course, we must remember that material possessions are not the source of our happiness. While the memories we create in our cabins or with our families are valuable, happiness can also be found in simplicity. Whether a home is a small tent or a grand mansion and its furnishings modest or opulent, the key to bringing love and joy to the people around us is in how we care for what we have, how we share it, and how we use it.

So, as you go forward, remember to love your things with intention. Show gratitude for what you have, take care of it, and share it generously. Your possessions are more than just items—they're opportunities to create joy, to serve others, and to live with abundance. By loving and sharing, you will discover that life is rich, fulfilling, and overflowing with blessings. And in that process, you'll experience the joy and love you are meant to have.

FIFTEEN

FALL IN LOVE WITH YOUR LIFE

"You only live once, but if you do it right, once is enough."
MAE WEST

I HAD LANDED AN OPPORTUNITY TO PRESENT A PROPOSAL for services to Bain Capital, located in the high-rise tower of the Prudential Center in Boston. I was both nervous and excited, having spent countless hours preparing for this crucial meeting. Gaining Bain Capital as a client would have been huge for Providio, my startup company. Providio was a web development company with outsourced development services in India and the Philippines. Both concepts were fairly new at the time and demand for offshore development was growing.

It was 1999, and the dot com boom was alive and well in Boston. Dave was starting his residency at Harvard Dental School (which is affiliated with Brigham and Women's Hospital), my business seemed to be taking off (as I mentioned), and life appeared glamorous for us, a young couple with nothing but ambition and the world to conquer.

If only I could survive this meeting. My nerves were getting the best of me, and I was fighting back the urge to vomit. I excused myself and rushed to the bathroom, and after what felt like an eternity I returned to the meeting trying to maintain my composure. It was clear to me that things weren't going well. Normally, I could charm my way through anything. But not today. I barely kept my lunch down, and I couldn't shake the feeling that I was blowing my chance.

Once the meeting ended, there was no time for pleasantries. I quickly made my way out of the conference room, desperate to escape. But my ordeal was far from over. I still had to navigate the high-end shopping center in the Prudential Mall to reach my car. Halfway through, I knew I wasn't going to make it. I popped into the nearest store, Louis Vuitton, and asked for a bag to vomit in. The snobby sales clerk denied my request—apparently, their bags were only for paying customers. I barely made it out of the store, managing to reach a trashcan just in time. Needless to say, I didn't land the deal that day. To my surprise, a few days later I discovered I was pregnant with our second child.

Life was piling on. I was already struggling to care for our nine-month-old baby while running my startup, with a husband deep in the midst of a demanding residency, and now this—the prospect of a new baby? My previous pregnancy wasn't easy, so I was preparing myself emotionally for months of nausea and exhaustion. How was I going to juggle it all? It seemed almost impossible. Almost.

We lived in an old, three-story home on Cambridge Street, an antique building built in the 1800s that had been converted into condo units. Our place, on the second story, was infested with mice—actually, it seemed like all of Boston had the same problem. I thought we were the only ones dealing with it until we spent a romantic anniversary dinner at Stephanie's Restaurant on Newbury Street. As we dined on the veranda, we watched a rat the size of a small cat scurry by, and no one batted an eye. Apparently, everybody was learning to live with it.

I remember the nights when I would wake up for midnight feedings of my infant son. The trick was to turn on the kitchen light, close my eyes, and count to ten, giving the mice time to scurry away before I saw them. Dave's morning routine included picking up the mouse traps and carefully laying them out again each night. He even had to peel the dead mice off the sticky traps, a chore designed to save money so we could reuse the traps, and a task that meant tossing the mouse out the second story window into a trashcan carefully placed below.

One morning, in his usual rush, Dave discovered a trap that had caught a living mouse—it was alive but stuck to the trap. His solution? He decided to put the entire trap—mouse and all—into a plastic bag and place it in the freezer. When I woke up and opened the freezer to prepare breakfast, I found a bag with something moving inside. I slammed the door shut. After a moment of realization, I understood what had happened. Despite the initial shock, I finally mustered the courage to dispose of the mouse in our makeshift trash chute. Just another quirky morning in Boston.

These were some difficult times. But through all of this, I remembered something I had been told as a young girl: "You can't wait to be happy." I'm so glad that piece of wisdom stuck in my mind. When I was tempted to think, *I'll be happy when Dave finishes school, I'll be happy when the startup is profitable,* or *I'll be happy when the baby sleeps through the night,* I quickly reminded myself that I wasn't going to keep kicking happiness down the road. I wasn't going to let my future steal my present happiness. I knew I had to choose happiness right then.

I made a conscious decision to love every stage of my life, no matter how difficult or messy it seemed. And that mindset wasn't fleeting, it became my way of life. Even with the endless nights of feedings of babies one and two, the financial struggles, and yes, the mice infestation, I chose to find joy in the journey. I began to look at all of it—*mice and all*—as part of a grand adventure, one that I would someday laugh about. Already, I was learning to love it in real time.

Soon I realized I had to get into problem-solving mode. I made some sacrifices, which eventually turned into blessings. I solved one of my business dilemmas by giving up my CEO role in Providio to my older brother, Rob, who made a daring transition from working at Arthur Anderson in Salt Lake City, Utah, to lead our growing tech startup. He moved with his new wife, Dana, to Boston. Taking on a secondary role as the chief operating officer was a difficult decision, but one that was better for needs of both the company and my growing family.

What I hadn't realized when making that tough choice was how having relatives living close to me would turn those years into some of the best few years of our life. Rob and Dana ended up purchasing the condo unit above ours when it came up for sale, and we literally got to live on top of each other. That was genius during those tough years while both Dana and I had babies, and we could juggle the needs of our newborns, work, school, and all the demands upon us. It was sisterhood at its finest as we helped each other through thick and thin and forged bonds of friendship beyond our wildest dreams that continue to this day.

These early years, filled with challenges, weren't always easy to see as "the best." But now, looking back, I realize they were. We made memories with friends like Kemy and Chris, who would join us every Thursday night for a ritual of watching *Friends*. This gave us a momentary escape from our chaotic lives. Our old couch, which had *definitely* been home to more than just us, was passed on to them when we moved. In true Boston fashion, they eventually tossed it out the second-floor window when they realized it had been infested with mice. At the time, it felt frustrating, but now, it's just another funny, endearing story.

Each of these moments has contributed to making me the woman I am today. Life was sometimes tough, but it was also *ours*—our own story to tell. And in that, there is beauty. I get to choose how I view my life, just as you get to choose how you view yours.

No matter the chaos, no matter the challenges, I have chosen to love each stage of my life. In fact, I knew it wasn't just a choice. It was the *best* choice. And as I chose to love each chapter, I found joy in the journey, even when things didn't go according to plan.

Isn't this true for all of us? We all have the choice whether or not to love our lives, no matter what our circumstances may be. Each phase of life can be the next best phase. People often talk about the "glory years" of life. But the best times are different for each of us, depending on where we are. High school might be the best, or maybe it's your newlywed days or the years with young children. The truth is that every phase can be the best. It's all about perspective.

I believe this to be true for both my past and my future. Why? Because I can choose to make it true. I'm the one who gets to decide how I view my life. And no one can challenge that. It's a choice we all get to make—today, tomorrow, and always.

I love teaching my kids this. They often worry about what's coming next—high school, college, and the unknowns ahead. But I tell them, "You're going to love it. Every stage will be the best!"

They argue with me, "But Mom, how can high school be the best? What about college?"

I say, "That's the best too! All of it is the best, because you decide it is. It's all about perspective."

So, I ask you: Are you choosing to love your life today? If there is an aspect of your life that you've been waiting to love, thinking happiness will come later, choose to do something immediately to make it better. The truth is that every stage can be the best and you are not powerless. Every event, no matter how difficult, has something to offer. Life is too short to put happiness on hold. You can love your life right now—mice and all.

But try an attitude adjustment. I truly believe that when you choose to love your life, you will be amazed at how much joy you find in even the hardest of times. You're the producer, the director, the actor, the storyteller of the "movie" of your life. So, make it a movie you can love.

Remember: It's never too late to choose happiness, to love your life in the here and now, and to carry that love forward into every experience.

The Power of Love

After reflecting on the ups and downs of my life in retrospect, it is clear to me that love is a force that shapes our reality. It is more than an emotion. Love is like the secret ingredient in a recipe that transforms it into a delectable meal. Love transforms ordinary moments into extraordinary experiences.

It's easy to think of love sentimentally, as something warm and fuzzy, but it's so much more. It's a dynamic, transformative power that can heal, guide, and propel us forward.

Love is the force that can turn even the most challenging days into opportunities for growth. It lifts us up, motivates us to keep going, and opens doors we didn't even know existed. When you add love to the equation, no matter what situation you find yourself in, you're guaranteed to elevate your experience and make your dreams a reality.

Unlocking Miracles with Love

So, how does this all work? Imagine that love is your personal shortcut to miracles. When you choose to act from a place of love, you open yourself up to receive experiences of joy, peace, and divine guidance. Love is the highest energy vibration we can embody, and by infusing our lives with it, we raise our own energy, creating positive outcomes and attracting good things into our lives.

Even when life presents its challenges, love becomes the key that unlocks new doors and new possibilities. It has the power to turn obstacles into opportunities, disappointments into wisdom, and struggles into success. Love doesn't just make things better; it makes them extraordinary.

Surround Yourself with Love

To begin harnessing this power, start by identifying the things that bring you joy. What do you love? Who do you love? What makes your heart sing? These are the things you need to surround yourself with as often as possible. Whether it's music that makes you dance, time with family that warms your soul, or a hobby that fuels your passion, make room for it in your life.

Incorporate what you love into your daily routine, and soon, you'll notice a shift. The more you focus on the things that bring you joy, the more joy you'll invite into your life. Love, like a magnet, will pull in more of the good stuff. And as you align your life with what you love, you'll start to notice miracles unfolding around you.

Conquering Fear with Love

Here's a truth worth remembering: Fear cannot coexist with love. If fear is holding you back, preventing you from moving forward, remember that love is the antidote. Fear often thrives on doubt and uncertainty, but love wipes that away, leaving you with clarity, confidence, and the courage to take the next step.

When fear creeps in, it's often just an illusion, aka false evidence appearing real. So, what do we do with it? We replace fear with love. Move forward with love as your guide, and watch how it transforms your doubts into trust, your hesitation into action, and your obstacles into opportunities.

Your Shortcut to Success

If you ever find yourself overwhelmed, stuck, or unsure of the next step, remember that love is your shortcut back to a state of clarity. Clarity is necessary to become successful in anything you do.

By embracing love for yourself, your dreams, and your life as it currently is, you create a pathway to the life you've always wanted. It's simple, it's empowering, and it's transformative. Love is the force that will propel you forward, helping you say yes to all the possibilities ahead.

So, as you embark on the journey of saying "yes" to various opportunities in front of you, sprinkle your life with love. Watch as it weaves its magic into every experience, and turns your dreams from possibility into reality.

The Power of Saying Yes: How to Unlock the Life You Want

Have you ever found yourself trapped in a cycle of hesitation, feeling stuck and unsure about your next step? Do you have dreams, desires, or even small things you'd like to do, but fear, doubt, or excuses hold you back? You're not alone.

We often make things more complicated than they need to be. We get stuck in our heads, questioning every possibility and doubting our own worthiness to succeed. But what if the key to unlocking everything you want is actually much simpler than you think?

What if all you need to do is say yes?

Yes, it's really that simple. By saying yes to yourself, to your dreams, and to the opportunities that come your way, you can unlock a life full of possibility. Saying yes is a powerful tool. It's the answer that will set you on the path to your dreams, even when fear or doubt try to convince you otherwise.

I know it's easy to hesitate. We've all been there. We wonder about the logistics: *How will I find the time? How will I afford this? What if it's too hard or I fail?* But here's the secret: The answers will come. The timing will work out. And even if things don't go according to plan, that's okay. Life is a journey, and every step forward is worth it.

I'll share a personal example: I recently spoke to a colleague who was offered a great opportunity to participate in a challenging, yet rewarding program that would help her reach her goals. She had some concerns: the cost, the time commitment, whether she had the right support. All valid worries, true, but they weren't the full picture. I helped her see that she would be able to handle the pressure and that there was support available to her that would alleviate the burden. Also, after talking it through with me, she recognized the program would not last forever. I was happy to lend her a welcoming ear as she made a decision for herself.

Having lived through the regret of saying no to some opportunities in the past, my first instinct when an opportunity presents itself to me these days is to say yes. I don't overthink it. I don't question whether I'm worthy of it or if the timing is perfect. I just say yes if I'm attracted to the idea and I trust that things will work out. I take the first step forward, and I know the answers will unfold along the way. I choose to be an optimist.

Sometimes, we spend so much time weighing the pros and cons, analyzing every detail, and worrying about the roadblocks that we forget the most important thing: *Just take that first step. Say yes.* And even if obstacles arise, you'll work through them and learn along the way. In the process, you'll grow in confidence and start to trust that your dreams are worth pursuing.

Here's what I've learned: The more we say yes to what life brings us, the easier it is to move forward. Saying no or dithering about a decision can be a waste of energy. When you start saying yes, you'll start to see how opportunities lead to growth, and how the challenges along the way shape you into the person you're meant to be. You'll be teaching yourself that you are capable of more than you think.

It's not always easy, and things won't always go perfectly. But when you say yes, you're choosing to take control of your life and your future. And as you do, you'll inspire others to say yes too. Your courage to move forward will be contagious.

So, what can you say yes to today? What dreams or small opportunities are waiting for you? Don't wait for everything to be perfect. Don't let fear or doubt hold you back. Take that first step and see where saying yes will take you.

Create Your Own Opportunities

Because you are the creator of your life experiences and get to decide the direction you want to go, you can say yes to living your dreams today. There's no reason to wait for tomorrow to begin living the way you want to live. Pretty Sisters say yes to themselves.

Many people think that opportunities are limited or scarce, as if there are only a select few chances available to those lucky enough to find them. But the truth is, opportunity is not something that simply falls into our laps, it's something we create. Our approach to the world around us is the key to creating our own opportunities.

Opportunity is born out of our willingness to serve and add value to other people's lives. When we focus on how we can help, uplift, and contribute, we open ourselves up to a new wealth of opportunities that we previously could not see. Therefore, creating an opportunity is about proactively seeking out ways to be of service using resources and skills you already possess. It's not about waiting for a moment of luck or a circumstance to change things for us. By thinking carefully about the kind of services we have and are willing to offer, we pave the way for a deeper alignment with our purpose and unlock opportunities for our own growth and success.

When we consciously seek ways to serve others, it is evident that opportunities are literally everywhere around us. With our eyes open, we can actively discover and create, and we have options. The mindset shift to service naturally leads to more moments where we can say yes to the opportunities that fit our personal combination of abilities, desires, and dreams.

We are allowed to experiment and try things on for size. There's no prohibition against it. As we continue saying yes and having more experience to draw upon, we will find ourselves more aligned with doing what we love. This is how to design a life we can truly embrace. By creating our own opportunities, we effectively shape our lives into something that we find beautiful, fulfilling, and uniquely ours.

A kind of magic happens when we start to actively choose the opportunities that come our way. By saying yes to what matters most to us, that which fills us with passion and aligns with our vision, the things we do will resonate with our heart and soul. Life no longer has to feel like a series of random events or missed chances because we are in the driver's seat, choosing our path with intention and purpose.

The essence of how to create a life you love is to shape your future by saying yes to what brings you joy and fulfillment. The bonus is the rewarding feeling of being of service to somebody or something you value.

Now, let's bring it all together by revisiting a story from my college days, a perfect example of how I designed my life to make it one I loved during what was also a difficult season of life with new challenges and changes. I was enrolled in a freshman honors class in which we learned study habits and techniques that would serve us throughout college. One of the lessons taught was that the first fifteen minutes of any hour are the most productive. Inspired by this insight, I came up with what I thought was a genius plan: to buy a season ski pass. The fifteen-minute ride up the mountain on the ski lift, I reasoned, was the perfect time to study.

I bought a ski jacket with a kangaroo pouch on the front, calculating that this would be the ideal place to stash my study notes. Marnee, my best friend and study partner, was easily persuaded to join me in this venture. So, we made a routine of studying on the way up the lift before skiing down the hill. Sometimes we'd take a break in the "Warming Hut" at the top, enjoying hot chocolate or lunch, and giving ourselves a longer break to study. It didn't take long for us to realize this was the perfect setup for exam prep. While most of our classmates were stuck in the library, we were skiing the slopes and acing our tests.

This became a regular pattern for Marnee and me. On test days, we'd hit the slopes early and, at the end of the day, drive straight to the testing center feeling refreshed, focused, and ready to tackle our exams. It was a game changer for me to see that I could succeed while studying under such conditions, and gave me a glimpse into how I could make even the most challenging tasks more enjoyable. That year, I realized that I could "gamify" life and turn every challenge into an opportunity to create joy.

This insight has helped me design a life I truly love ever since. Whether I am doing business, engaged in my relationships, or following through on my day-to-day tasks, I've learned that by saying yes to the things that excite me and no to the things that don't, and by finding creative solutions for life's dilemmas, I can turn any situation in my favor. Not everything I do is a game, *per se,* but many things I do have a hint of gaming in them—at least from my personal perspective. Challenging myself to improve is a game I play on my own. My life feels fulfilling and vibrant. For me, the key has been to turn every moment, opportunity, and challenge into something I love doing that makes my life more enjoyable and meaningful.

Please remember that, like mine, your life isn't something that is happening to you. It's something you are creating. By saying yes to the opportunities that attract you, seeking out joy, and approaching your challenges in the spirit of love and enthusiasm, I believe you will quickly see that you can design a life that is not only full of purpose and meaning but also full of love, laughter, and joy.

Write your own story, and choose how you want different chapters in it to unfold. Choose to love it all: the highs, the lows, the struggles, and the victories. When you do, you'll find that your life is a masterpiece in the making, one you can't help but love.

Love transforms ordinary moments into extraordinary memories, softens the rough edges of challenges, and reminds us that even in imperfection, there is beauty. By choosing love, you're not just existing; you're thriving in a life that's authentically, beautifully yours.

As Pretty Sisters, we are not just looking for happiness, we are intentionally creating it, with each belief we hold close, each action we take, and each person we love. When we choose to love ourselves, our people, and our lives, we are living the answer and thinking pretty. So go ahead, love your life fully—because this is what you deserve.

BELIEF #5: LOVE IS THE ANSWER

PRETTY SISTER PINKY PROMISE

RUN THROUGH THE SPILLING THE TEA TECHNIQUE AFTER reading the three chapters related to Belief #5. The objective now is for you to internalize that love is always the answer and you can and should love your people, your things, and your life.

When I say "Love is the answer," I THINK: _____
_____
_____
_____
_____

When I think *that*, it makes me FEEL: _____
_____
_____
_____
_____

When I feel *that*, it makes me ACT: _____
_____
_____
_____
_____

Ask yourself, "Is there anything else I am thinking?" Run through this same process as many times as needed until you are thinking from your heart with courage, love, and confidence. Once you feel ready, move on to make the promise.

Find a fellow Pretty Sister (this can be your mom, a sister, a friend, or someone from the online Pretty Sister community) and make the following promise to her. Or speak these words to yourself in the mirror.

> *"I believe love is the answer.*
> *I Pretty Sister pinky promise—*
> *and crosses don't count!"*

At the heart of it all, love is the answer. It's the force that binds us to our people, deepens our gratitude for the things we hold dear, and allows us to embrace the beautiful chaos of our lives. When you lead with love—love for others, for the blessings in your life, and most importantly, for yourself—you create a life filled with meaning and connection.

P.S. I LOVE YOU

"To love and be loved is to feel the sun from both sides."

DAVID VISCOTT

WHEN MY MOM TURNED EIGHTY, MY SIBLINGS AND I threw her a special birthday party to celebrate her life. She had recently been diagnosed with Alzheimer's disease and my sister Martha had a special impression that we should do this while Mom still had memories to share with us. The celebration was beautiful, with a thoughtfully chosen theme. It was a tribute to one of her favorite songs, "P.S. I Love You" by Gordon Jenkins and Johnny Mercer, which was originally recorded in the 1930s by Rudy Vallée, and has since been covered by Billie Holliday, Frank Sinatra, and other musical artists. We decorated the whole venue with the theme and filled it with memorabilia from her life, creating a warm and memorable experience for all who attended.

My mom used to sing that song with her mother, Francis, who could play the piano by ear and was a fantastic entertainer. I remember so many Sunday nights gathered around the piano, listening to them sing "P.S. I Love You." It was a cherished ritual that filled our home with warmth and love. At her special birthday party, we were able to hear Mom sing that song one last time with her sister Julie, creating a forever memory that I hold close to my heart.

Growing up, I always knew my mother loved me deeply because she told me so every chance she got. Over the last decade, my sisters and I became collectors of "P.S. I Love You" signs, and now they adorn our homes as a daily reminder of that love. More than the material signs, though, my mother taught us the importance of always speaking love out loud. The rule is: *If you love someone, you must say it.*

We were given that beautiful gift of being told we were loved, and it has remained with us throughout our lives, especially in our families and friendships. And to us, the P.S. perfectly represents Pretty Sisters.

Pretty Sister . . . P.S. I Love You!

I want you to know that you are loved. That is why I dedicated myself in this book to helping you remember your worth, your lovability, and your absolute right to a happy, joyful life.

WHAT'S NEXT?

THANK YOU FOR READING MY BOOK. I'M BEYOND THRILLED that you've joined me on the incredible journey of being a Pretty Sister, a journey that never ends.

I have something important to share with you: You deserve happiness. You deserve to live a life that's nothing short of miraculous. To take dreams you've held in your heart and turn them into a vibrant reality. Living your dreams isn't just a wish because your life is a powerful declaration of your potential being expressed. A dream is a radiant light that can illuminate not only your life but also the lives of those around you.

Sadly, many people spend their lives feeling disconnected from their true selves and unsure of their immense potential. But I believe you're reading these words at exactly the right moment in your life, because you are ready for change. God has led you here because it's your time to embark on a transformative journey to fulfill your dreams and aspirations. To support you, I've created additional resources you can draw upon.

I invite you to stay connected with your fellow Pretty Sisters and become a part of our growing community at **https://ThePrettySisters.com.** In our vibrant, loving community, we offer programs and opportunities to help you transform your life, and manifest success, health, and happiness. Together, we can dream and create a life full of possibilities, and I can't wait to do it alongside you!

Imagine the incredible joy of not only transforming your own life, but also being a part of a community where everyone supports one another in pursuit of their own miraculous lives. This is a journey that promises love, joy, and endless fulfillment.

Here's to you, dear reader, and the boundless love and success that await you. May you continue to explore, dream, believe, create, and, most importantly, love your life.

ACKNOWLEDGMENTS

THIS BOOK WOULD NOT HAVE BEEN POSSIBLE WITHOUT the incredible support and encouragement of so many wonderful people.

First and foremost, my heartfelt thanks go to my editor, Stephanie Gunning. Your patience, guidance, and steady hand kept me on track through this journey. Your gentle yet insightful feedback brought clarity to my words and brought this book to life in a way I could never have done alone.

To my beautiful sisters, the ones who first called me Pretty and unknowingly gave me a name that would shape my confidence, my outlook, and ultimately, this book. Thank you. Your love, laughter, and unwavering belief in me have been some of the greatest gifts of my life. You taught me the power of sisterhood, the joy of uplifting others, and the magic that happens when women support each other. This book exists because of you, and I am forever grateful for the love and inspiration you've given me.

To my husband, Dave, thank you for your unwavering support and understanding as I poured my heart into this book. Your patience and encouragement mean the world to me.

To my kids, you are my constant inspiration and delight. Thank you for allowing me the space to chase my dreams while raising you—it's a joy and privilege to be your mother.

To my girlfriends—where do I even begin? You are the heartbeat of this book. Your kindness, loyalty, and the true spirit of Pretty Sisters have filled these pages with life. There are too many of you to name, but you know who you are. Thank you for making life richer, funnier, and more meaningful. You have shown me that true prettiness comes from within, and it's a blessing to share life with you.

I want to express my deep gratitude to Sean Covey for writing the foreword to this book, and for offering guidance and insight throughout the process. Your mentorship, thoughtful edits, and belief in the message of *Think Pretty* meant the world tome. Thank you fir using your voice and influence to help shine alight on this work and for encouraging me to share it boldly.

To those who generously offered their endorsements, thank you. Your kind words, support, and belief in this message gave me the encouragement I needed to move forward. I'm honored by your vote of confidence, and I'll be forever grateful for the way you lifted me up and stood behind this project.

Finally, I am grateful to all the readers who pick up this book. My hope is that it inspires and uplifts you, reminding you of the beauty of sisterhood, connection, and kindness. Together, we can make life truly pretty.

NOTES

Introduction

1. *Breakfast at Tiffany's,* screenplay by Truman Capote (1961).

BELIEF #1: YOU ARE PRETTY

Epigraph. French fashion icon Gabrielle Bonheur "Coco" Chanel (1883–1971) is widely quoted as saying this. Source unknown.

Chapter 3: You Were Made for This

[1] James E. Faust. "The Light in Their Eyes," *Ensign* (November 2005).
[2] Robert H. Schuller. *You Can Become the Person You Want to Be* (New York: Hawthorn Books, 1973): p. 11.
[3] Carol Dweck. *Mindset: The New Psychology of Success* (New York: Ballantine Books, 2016): p. 6.

Pinky Promise #1

[1] James Allen. *As a Man Thinketh* (1903).

BELIEF #2: YOU ARE NOT ALONE

Chapter 5 : She's Pretty, Too

[1] "Theodore Roosevelt Quotes," Goodreads.com (accessed December 20, 2024).

BELIEF #3: YOU CAN DO IT

Chapter 7: You Begin with a Dream

Epigraph. Tom Fitzgerald. He was the Imagineer who created the Horizons attraction at the EPCOT theme park of the Walt Disney World Resort in Bayville, Florida.

1. Ibid.
2. Zig Ziglar. *The One Year Daily Insights with Zig Ziglar* (Carol Stream, IL.: Tyndale Momentum, 2009).

Chapter 8: You Must Believe in Yourself

1. Martin Luther King, Jr. The exact wording of this remark may be a paraphrase. It was reported by Marian Wright Edelman, who personally heard him speak this idea, in various interviews and lectures she gave.

Chapter 9: You Create Your Reality

Epigraph. William Hutchison Murray (1913–1996), from his 1951 book *The Scottish Himalayan Expedition.*

1. Phillippa Lally, et al. "How Habits Are Formed: Modelling Habit Formation in the Real World," *European Journal of Social Psychology*, vol. 40, no. 6 (October 2010): pp. 998–1009.

BELIEF #4: YOU ARE MEANT FOR JOY

Chapter 12: It's Not the End Yet

Epigraph. Eleanor Roosevelt. Source unknown. It may have been a radio address or speech during World War II.

1. Friedrich Nietzsche. *Twilight of the Idols* (1888).

BELIEF #5: LOVE IS THE ANSWER

Epigraph. Rabindranath Tagore. "Rabindranath Quotes on Love," BDEBooks.com (September 3, 2023).

Chapter 14: It's OK to Love Your Things

Epigraph. Vincent van Gogh. From his letters to his brother, Theo, which are now housed at the Van Gogh Museum in Amsterdam, the Netherlands.

Chapter 15: You Must Love Your Life

Epigraph. "Mae West," En.Wikiquote.org (accessed November 27, 2024).

P.S. I Love You

Epigraph. David Viscott. *Finding Your Strength in Difficult Times: A Book of Meditations* (New York: McGraw-Hill, 2003): p. 217.

ABOUT THE AUTHOR

CALLIE C. STEUER, M.B.A., IS A PROUD MOTHER, SERIAL entrepreneur, and dedicated advocate for helping others achieve their dreams. With a career spanning over three decades, Callie has cofounded and led numerous successful ventures, including iLUMI, Steuer Management, Oral Surgical Specialists, Dental Specialists of Maine, Level 10 Landworks, and Providio. She is also the founder of Pretty Sisters, a company dedicated to empowering women and celebrating kindness.

A dynamic leader and educator, Callie serves as a dōTERRA Diamond Leader and active speaker, inspiring individuals worldwide to innovate their lives through essential oils, which she fondly refers to as "the magic pixie dust" for transformation. She holds a bachelor's degree in information systems from Brigham Young University and a master's in business administration.

Callie's extensive experience includes serving on advisory boards and mentoring others in both business and personal development. Her mantra, *Dream, Believe, Create*, drives her mission to empower others to unlock their potential and realize their aspirations.

When she's not managing businesses or inspiring others, Callie is an active mother of five thriving children and a devoted grandmother. She loves international travel, dancing, skiing, and wake surfing, and she proudly serves in her faith community as a teacher and temple worker. Callie's life is a testament to the power of faith, family, and perseverance, proving that together, we can rise to achieve extraordinary things.

www.ingramcontent.com/pod-product-compliance
Lightning Source LLC
Chambersburg PA
CBHW050327010526
44119CB00050B/704